PROFESSIONAL IDENTITIES

SOCIAL IDENTITIES

General Editors: Shirley Ardener, Tamara Dragadze and Jonathan Webber

Based on a prominent Oxford University seminar founded over two decades ago by the social anthropologist Edwin Ardener, this series focuses on the ethnic, historical, religious, and other elements of culture that give rise to a social sense of belonging, enabling individuals and groups to find meaning both in their own social identities and in what differentiates them from others. Each volume is based on one specific theme that brings together contemporary material from a variety of cultures.

PROFESSIONAL IDENTITIES

POLICY AND PRACTICE IN BUSINESS AND BUREAUCRACY

Edited by
Shirley Ardener and Fiona Moore

Berghahn Books
New York • Oxford

First published in 2007 by
Berghahn Books
www.berghahnbooks.com

Library of Congress Cataloging-in-Publication Data

Professional identities : policy and practice in business and bureaucracy / edited by Shirley Ardener and Fiona Moore.

    p. cm. -- (Social identities ; v. 3)

Stimulated first by a workshop organised by the Centre for Cross-Cultural Research on Women (now named the International Gender Studies Centre) at Queen Elizabeth House; then mainly by a series of talks on "Corporate Images and Bureaucratic Identities," presented at the ongoing Ethnicity and Identity seminar at the Institute of Social Anthropology at Oxford University.

Includes bibliographical references and index.

ISBN 978-1-84545-054-0 (hardback : alk. paper)

1. Professional employees--Cross-cultural studies--Congresses. 2. Businesspeople--Cross-cultural studies--Congresses. 3. Bureaucrats--Cross-cultural studies--Congresses. 4. Identity (Psychology)--Cross-cultural studies--Congresses. 5. Globalization--Social aspects--Cross-cultural studies--Congresses. I. Ardener, Shirley. II. Moore, Fiona.

HD8038.A1P762 2007
338.501--dc22

                                                                        2007023969

British Library Cataloguing in Publication Data
A catalogue record for this book is available from the British Library
Printed in the United States on acid-free paper

ISBN 978-1-84545-054-0 hardback

CONTENTS

LIST OF FIGURES AND ILLUSTRATIONS

PREFACE

Shirley Ardener

This book deals with the shifting sands and human dilemmas to be found within the overlapping spheres and along the boundaries between businesses and bureaucracies. It considers the identities created by and for working people, professionals and clients – how they are perceived in corporate settings in different parts of the globe, how they see themselves, and how they imagine others see them – and some consequences of these. The identities, and lived experience, according to which the rugby players, immigrants, academics, bankers, politicians, civil servants and aid workers whom we meet here negotiate their ways, often have that 'oscillating' quality to which I referred in an earlier work (*Persons and Powers of Women*, 1992, pp. 6–9). These men and women engage with institutions that are complex social constructions, partly of their own making.

Although writings by social anthropologists take centre stage in this book, it will be of interest to a wider readership: sociologists trying to understand how organisations work, students of identity, others concerned with business and management, good governance, or development studies, not forgetting those whose working lives in a business or bureaucracy rule their own behaviour. They may find here different perspectives, both in the new case studies presented below and in some of the earlier work by anthropologists on the field outlined by Fiona Moore. It should interest those concerned with the privatisation of services and the corporatisation of government (to borrow a phrase from Susan Wright). Through detailed ethnography, the reworking of boundaries between 'public' and 'private', local and national identities, and some of the implications for global issues of analyses of micro institutions, are all addressed in this book.

This is not all that unfamiliar to the academic authors here, who experience for themselves the transformation of boundaries as universities (Oxford no less than others) are led to commercialise their output; where trustees from Big Business are recommended as a check on aims and performance, where managerial-speak is introduced into the vocabulary, creativity is statistically audited and output measured. The university is technically a charity, but the spectre of Oxford Inc. seems to lurk, just as other charities and public bodies similarly are drawn into trade. It has already spawned spin-off companies.[1] As citizens we are also aware of the conflicts that give colour to, for example, the Oxford United football scene, which express the disjuncture between commercial and sportive objectives, as well as between personal egos and passionately defended local identities, as the club owner, the loyal fans, the press and the local council – all feeling themselves to be 'stakeholders' – loudly defend their interests.

The stimulation for this particular volume came from various sources, the first being a workshop organised by the Centre for Cross-Cultural Research on Women (now named the International Gender Studies Centre), which I co-convened with Regine Bendl at Queen Elizabeth House. My colleagues in this group have produced various volumes touching upon personal identities in a worldwide context: see *Persons and Powers of Women* (ed. Ardener), *Transnational Families* (ed. Bryceson and Veroula), *Transnational Business Cultures: Life and Work in a Multinational Corporation* by Fiona Moore; and the forthcoming Routledge volume on globally mobile women (edited by Anne Coles and Meike Fechter) to name but a few. The other main source of inspiration was a series of talks on 'Corporate Images and Bureaucratic Identities' presented at the ongoing Ethnicity and Identity seminar, which I co-convened with Jonathan Webber and Elisabeth Hsu at the Institute of Social Anthropology at Oxford University.

Both editors of the present volume participated in these two events. The material discussed at them raised questions about certain ambiguities, which are usefully dealt with here by Fiona Moore in her Introduction. Not all the papers presented in these arenas could be included in this present volume, but we have selected four – those by Moore, Callan, Abram and Coles – to which we have added papers by Herzog and Whitfield (both presented in Queen Elizabeth House) and Groeneveld (of the Oxford Institute of Social Anthropology). We are grateful to all these contributors, as well as to Tamara Dragadze and Susan Wright for their valuable comments on our draft text, and to our publisher, Marion Berghahn, and her staff.

This volume is the third in this new Berghahn Books series on 'Social Identities', the first being *Changing Sex and Bending Gender* (ed. Shaw and Ardener) and *Medical Identities* (ed. Maynard). Its immediate followers are: *The Discipline of Leisure* (ed. Kohn and Coleman) and *Where Humans and Spirits Meet in Zanzibar: The Politics of Ritual and Gender* (by Kjersti Larsen).[2]

Shirley Ardener,
Oxford, 2007

Notes

1. Increasingly, social anthropologists are turning their attention to their own academic structures, within which they themselves carry out their profession. An early study was on members of the professional body (The Association of Social Anthropologists) to which most working anthropologists in the United Kingdom belong (see E. Ardener and S. Ardener, 'A Directory Study of Social Anthropologists', in the *British Journal of Sociology*, 16 [4], 295–314). More recently David Mills and others have started to look at other professional institutions, including the Royal Anthropology and the International African Institutes, which have provided structures that have determined to some extent the history of anthropological careers and thought (e.g. D. Mills, 'Professionalising or Popularising Anthropology? A Brief History of Anthropology's Scholarly Associations in the U.K.', *Anthropology Today 2003*, 19 [5]). See also E.M. Chilver, 'The Organisation of Social and Economic Research in the British Colonial Territories,' *Journal of the Anthropological Society of Oxford (JASO)*, 29 (3), written 1955 published 1998; Shirley Ardener,' The Funding of Social Anthropological Research: A Preliminary Note to [Chilver 1998]', JASO, ibid., 1998; Marilyn Strathern, '"Improving Ratings": Audit in the British University System', *European Interdisciplinary Journal of Academia Europea,* 5 (3), 1997, and *Audit Cultures*, 2000; and John Davies, "Administering creativity", *Anthropology Today*, 15 (2), 1999.

2. This book is the twelfth book to emerge from an Oxford seminar series entitled 'Ethnicity and Identity'. The first books were issued by Berg (Oxford and New York): *Contesting Art* (ed. J. MacClancy), *Dress and Ethnicity* (ed. J.B. Eicher), *Ethnicity, Identity and Music* (ed. M. Stokes), *Inside European Identities* (S. Macdonald), *Land and Territoriality* (ed. M. Saltman), *Migrants of Identity* (ed. N. Rapport and A. Dawson), *Re-imagining Culture* (S. Macdonald), *Sport, Identity and Ethnicity*, (ed. J. MacClancy), and *Tourists and Tourism* (ed. S. Abram, J. Waldren and D. Macleod). Berghahn Books has currently published: *Changing Sex and Bending Gender* (ed. A. Shaw and S. Ardener), and *Medical Identities: Healing Well-Being and Personhood* (ed. K. Maynard).

Bibliography

Ardener, S. (ed.) 1992, *Persons and Powers of Women in Diverse Cultures*. Oxford and New York: Berg.

Bryceson, D. and U. Vuorela. (2002). *The Transnational Family; New European Frontiers and Global Networks*. Oxford and New York: Berg.

Coles, A. and M. Fechter (forthcoming) *Globally Mobile Professional Families*. London: Routledge.

Moore, F. (2005). *Transnational Business Cultures: Life and Work in a Multinational Corporation*. Aldershot: Ashgate.

INTRODUCTION: BRIDGING BUSINESSES AND BUREAUCRACIES

Fiona Moore

While researchers in the social sciences have studied business and bureaucracy for over a century, comparisons between the two forms of social organisation are still relatively rare, and very few, if any, have explored the relationship between business and bureaucracy. This is particularly problematic in the present era of globalisation, in which business and bureaucracy are transforming and converging as public-sector organisations face privatisation and as private companies take on more and more bureaucratic structures and responsibilities in what is often said to be the era of 'flexible working'. In this introduction, I will take a brief look at the way in which research in both subjects has contributed to our understanding of globalisation, identity and the ways in which studies of bureaucracy and business inform and build upon each other, before outlining the approach and contents of the present volume.

Before we begin, a brief definition of terms is necessary. I will be using fairly inclusive definitions, taking 'business' to mean private-sector organisations, and 'bureaucracy' to mean any public-sector or non-governmental organisation. This definition is, however, not one which can be used unproblematically, and the difficulty of making such a distinction is one to which we will return later. This chapter will first give a brief contextualising overview of the history and current state of play of the study of social and cultural factors in business and bureaucracy, and then conduct an in-depth exploration of the papers in this volume and their innovative perspectives on the study of organisations, and the ways in which they problematise the above-mentioned distinction between the two forms of organisation considered here.

Anthropology, business and bureaucracy: an introductory note

Although it is not a recognised subfield of anthropology in the same vein as, say, gender or kinship, extensive ethnographic research has been carried out in businesses and bureaucracies over the past few decades. In this section, I will set the context for the papers to follow by briefly outlining the history of the study of business and bureaucracy and the present relationship between the two in the context of the present study of globalisation, and describing how this book deals with the exploration of the boundaries and connections which link and divide different types of organisation.

Anthropologists on business and bureaucracy

The traditional focus of anthropologists on small-scale and non-European communities means that although the anthropology of business and bureaucracy has existed since the 1930s, these studies tend to be regarded as esoteric and exotic areas, and not openly recognised as part of mainstream anthropology. Despite this, the study of businesses and bureaucracies has made a strong tacit contribution to the discipline, and has a particularly vibrant connection with the anthropology of globalisation and of migration. This contribution will be explored and considered in its various permutations over the course of this section.

Anthropologists, as well as sociologists and geographers employing methodologies which could be described as 'anthropological' (participant observation, unstructured interviews, life history gathering and so forth), have been explicitly involved in the study of business since at least the 1930s, with Elton Mayo's work in the United States and the later Tavistock school of industrial sociology in Europe, both focusing on how people behave at work (Baba 1998). As numerous excellent histories of the subdiscipline exist (e.g. Baba 1986, Schwartzman 1993), I will not reiterate it extensively here; suffice it to say that virtually every generation of anthropologists sees a brief resurgence of interest in the study of business, with its proponents usually criticising their colleagues for showing little interest in it. Many of those who do undertake such studies, however, find that there are few formal career opportunities for business specialists in anthropology departments (aside from those who studied businesses in the developing world or, the major exception to this rule, Japan). Consequently, they become absorbed into business studies departments or, indeed, into business itself, the latter having the side-effect of ensuring that the study of business remains an esoteric one within anthropology, retaining an air of mystery while at the same time remaining peripheral – 'not *proper* anthropology', in the views of more traditional researchers. Although frequently marginalised, then, the anthropology of business remains a presence within the discipline.

Bureaucracy seems to be even more of a tacit subject in the discipline than business. This is surprising because, if anything, it has an even longer pedigree than the anthropology of business, with the first discernible 'anthropological' work on the subject being Max Weber's 1918 essay *Politics as a Vocation*, and, according to Herzfeld (who regards bureaucracy as a special case of social classification), Durkheim and Mauss's studies of the ways in which societies divide and organise themselves (Durkheim and Mauss 1903; Herzfeld 1992).

Since then, there have been a number of highly-regarded studies in this field by well-respected anthropologists, for instance Mary Douglas' classic *How Organisations Think* (1987) and Michael Herzfeld's *The Social Production of Indifference* (1992), to say nothing of the use which many anthropologists have made of the various works of sociologist Erving Goffman on the subject of bureaucratic institutions (e.g. Burns 1992; Moore 2005). Despite having a similar position to the anthropology of business in status terms, then, bureaucracy has thus been the subject of many prominent studies within anthropology.

The anthropology of bureaucracy, however, does not appear to have established itself as a distinct, let alone 'exotic', subdiscipline in the way that the anthropology of business has; much of the anthropology of bureaucracy has become incorporated into the study of specific areas and cultures, principally into the anthropology of Europe (Gullick 1993) and political anthropology (Martinello 1995). Significantly, three out of five of the studies of bureaucracy in this volume revolve around case studies from Europe or the Nordic area. While this does not mean that one cannot look at bureaucracy from a non-Western or non-elite perspective (see, for instance, Herzog, this volume), it has to be said that much of the interest in bureaucracy has been as a kind of 'anthropology at home'. While there are a number of anthropologists who have become known specifically as 'anthropologists of business' (e.g. Malcolm Chapman, Mary Yoko Brannen, Marietta L. Baba and Thomas P. Rohlen), there are few, if any, who are known specifically as 'anthropologists of bureaucracy'. It is possible that this discrepancy exists because the anthropology of business has a relationship with the disciplines of business and management studies in a way one might regard as analogous to the relationship of more traditional anthropology to external disciplines such as African Studies, Museum Studies and so forth, whereas no such external discipline exists to which one can link the study of bureaucracy.

It is more likely that the reason for the obscurity of the anthropology of bureaucracy lies in the everyday nature of the subject. Every anthropologist has to deal with bureaucracy in their daily lives and fieldwork, for instance when gaining entry to the field (Barley 1983), working for an NGO (Coles, this volume), or simply in day-to-day life in their home institution. The 'mundane' nature of the activities involved, however, means that they tend to be excised from formal ethnographies, taken for granted or dismissed as background activity. While most anthropologists have hilarious stories about dealing with local and/or home-country bureaucracies in the course of their work, these tend not to surface often in their formal, written accounts of fieldwork. The primary exceptions to these are either autobiographies or personal accounts of fieldwork meant for popular consumption rather than strict academic scrutiny, as in the above-mentioned book by Barley (1983). The ironic result of this is, however, that one can find *indirect* studies of bureaucracy salted liberally throughout anthropology. Particularly following the postmodernist movement of the 1980s and early 1990s, accounts of bureaucracy appear in studies of refugees and migrants (Castles and Kosack 1973), life histories (Sweeney 1993) and ethnohistorical studies

(MacDonald 2001). It is perhaps significant that several of the papers on the subject in this volume are not in fact the result of a formally undertaken study of bureaucracy, but are instead accounts of personal experiences as an applied anthropologist, teacher or researcher. The ubiquity of bureaucracy thus means that, while not a formal discipline, it does have a strong presence within anthropological writing, as does the anthropology of business.

Business, bureaucracy and globalisation

One area where the study of business and bureaucracy has made a particularly significant contribution is in the area of the anthropology of globalisation, if not the study of globalisation in general. In this section, I will briefly outline the nature of this contribution and consider how it has affected the study of global social organisations and their movements.

Business-related ethnographic studies have contributed to the study of globalisation, defined as a social process in which changes in communications media, transportation and economics cause an effacement of the perception of geographical distance (see Waters 1995: 3), in four major ways. The first is a development of the earliest form of business ethnography, studies of factories and factory workers. One of the key phenomena which has been of great interest in business studied in recent years is the idea that the processes of globalisation have allowed the development of 'global best practices', that is to say, the worldwide adoption of business practices which have been successful in a particular locale, for instance the 'lean production' system of manufacturing (Womack, Jones and Roos 1990). Factory studies over the years, such as *Japan in the Passing Lane* (Kamata 1984), *Office Ladies, Factory Women* (Lo 1990), *On the Line at Subaru-Isuzu* (Graham 1995), and *Life on the Line in Contemporary Manufacturing* (Delbridge 1998), provide us with key insights into the way in which lean production has spread and developed over the years, as well as into the ways in which the globalisation of practice actually affects people. This debate is indirectly related to studies in this volume, such as Groeneveld's observations of the way in which local businesses are pressurised into adopting global discourses of managerialism, and Whitfield's on the transformations which globalisation has brought about in the aid 'industry.' The study of business thus provides insights into the human interpretation of so-called 'global best practices', contributing to debates on the subject.

The study of businesses and bureaucracies has also contributed to the study of globalisation by providing insights into the transnationalisation of various organisations and social groups, and the cultures of both elite and non-elite economic migrants. This, again, draws out of earlier studies of labour diasporas, particularly the Jewish and Indian diasporas (R. Cohen 1997), but also the studies of labour migration and identity of the 1970s (e.g. Castles and Kosacks 1973). As has been argued elsewhere, in situations in which physical geography is less significant, complex and transitional ways of defining identity emerge (Hannerz 1996, Moore 2005). Anthropologists have engaged in research on diverse transnational groups, from elite businesspeople (Sklair 2001) and journalists (Hannerz 1996) to labour migrants (Portes 1998) and Filipina domestic servants (Anderson 2000), from children in special international educational institutions (Goodman 1993) to multinational corporations (Moore 2005). All of these studies, like the studies of global groups and institutions in this volume, contribute to a greater understanding of the socioeconomics of globalisation, and of the connections between different elite and non-elite migrant groups as they attempt to define and redefine their identities in the context of global economic flows.

Studies of bureaucracy have also contributed to the study of globalisation by examining how local bureaucracies change in the face of the new politicoeconomic situation, and how other bureaucracies globalise. Barbara Czarniawska (1997) has, like Abrams and Callan in this volume, contributed studies of the impact of privatisation on bureaucrats; elsewhere, Martiniello (1995) and McDonald (2005) have both engaged in studies of bureaucracy as a form of identity definition in the European Union. Martinello in particular has contributed to debates on citizenship and identity in the EU, key areas in which public-sector activities and policies have a – sometimes unwelcome – impact on the definition of personal identity (1995). The study of changes within bureaucracies, and the mobilisation of bureaucracy for the definition of identity in the global era, are thus key ways in which the anthropology of bureaucracy has widened our understanding of globalisation.

The ethnographic study of business and bureaucracy has thus contributed to wider discourses on the sort of people who contribute to, support and further globalisation, as well as enabling a greater understanding of what exactly it is as a social phenomenon, and has traced the development of identity under a particular socioeconomic condition. As businesses and bureaucracies are inherently involved with the social and economic processes driving globalisation, it is essential for anthropologists to understand these social formations in analysing the wider phenomenon. The articles in this volume all, directly or indirectly, contribute to our understanding of globalisation, but, in doing so, also call into question the nature of the distinction (if, indeed, one exists) between businesses and bureaucracies, which forms the subject of my next section.

Is bureaucracy business?

In this section, I shall consider what anthropological studies over the years have had to say about the relationship between business and bureaucracy, and the similarities and differences between the two, concluding with a consideration of the status quo at the time of writing, the contributions of papers in this volume on the subject, and speculation upon future developments.

Early studies of business in anthropology tended to maintain that it was totally distinct from bureaucracy, even if there were visible connections. The earliest ethnographies of business (broadly defined) tended, with an eye to the 'etic' concerns of anthropology, to focus on blue-collar organisations, such as Elton Mayo's famous studies of the Hawthorne factory (Baba 1986: 4–5), and/or the developing or peripheral world (as in McFeat's 1974 studies of the traditional basket-weaving industry among the Maliseet). Later on, studies of white-collar organisations also tended to avoid explicit discussion of bureaucracy: June Nash's seminal study of expatriate employees in multinational corporations (1979) was a call for anthropologists to focus on members of the social elite in North America and Europe, but it did not particularly encourage the study of bureaucracy, and did not consider the potential similarities between, say, her informants and the diplomatic corps (see Moore 2005: 66–67). Despite this, however, studies of business have had a strong connection with those of bureaucracy from the outset. Mary Douglas's *How Organisations Think* (1987) is extensively cited in much of the literature on the anthropology of business, and, as noted, Barbara Czarniawska is usually considered a researcher on 'business' rather than 'bureaucracy' (and, indeed, it is hard to say which description fits her work better), and there have been a number of recent 'crossover' works, such as John Law's *Organising Modernity* (1994). Furthermore, as anthropologists explore the experiences of refugees, migrants and other globalising cultures, aspects of business and bureaucracy are taken into account in the same piece (Portes 1998). Sociologist Leslie Sklair, in his studies of 'the transnational capitalist class', includes bureaucrats, diplomats and politicians in his definition of this 'class' as much as he does businesspeople (2001). The division between the two subdisciplines forming the subject of this volume is thus becoming increasingly problematic.

The anthropology of bureaucracy has also been concealed within the anthropology of business. A number of works ostensibly about bureaucracy have gained great credence in the anthropology-of-business field (e.g. Goffman 1961, Douglas 1987) and a number of works on business are cited by the likes of Herzfeld (1992) as inspirations; one frequently cited 'anthropologist of business', Barbara Czarniawska, actually studies public sector organisations, albeit in various stages of privatisation (1997). The designation of a work as the study of an 'organisation' leaves it open as to whether the organisation in question is public or private, suggesting, somewhat problematically, that the two have more in common than not in the minds of anthropologists. The heading of 'organisation studies' thus tacitly contains a problematisation of the idea of distinguishing between public and private sector organisations.

This convergence has been matched by an increasing loss of boundaries between the two forms of organisation in the wider world. As governments in the globalising late-modern world increasingly favour privatisation over social markets, and as businesses are increasingly moving in to fill the gap created by this privatisation process (some more willingly than others), so it is becoming increasingly difficult to tell the difference between business and bureaucracy. Indeed, in a country in which the automobile industry may be nationalised in order to save it, then re-privatised when this fails (Scarbrough and Terry 1996), or another in which the constitution provides for all basic regulation on human resource management, labour regulation and, indeed, diversity management, the resultant company may emerge as a mix of public and private, the bureaucratic and the free-market-oriented. 'Bureaucratic' activities increasingly take place in businesses as they deal with the complex legal and political requirements of doing business in the globalised world, and business is done in bureaucracies, not merely through privatisation, but also through the development and transfer of social capital between organisations and individuals. Labour relations organisations, such as unions or the International Labour Organisation, hover somewhere between business and bureaucracy. Business diasporas, such as German transnational businesspeople, call on images of their local bureaucracies in their processes of self-presentation (Moore 2005: 71); British 'bureaucracy' is different to German 'bureaucracy', and both are invoked when people from these two groups interact within organisations. The anthropology of business and bureaucracy is thus not only causing us to question the distinction between the two, but also chronicling a process of change within organisations.

Particular note must also be made of non-governmental organisations (NGOs) in this context. Although ostensibly public sector, and hence bureaucratic, organisations, they also have particularly complicated relationships with businesses. Researchers such as Held et al. (1997: 163–187) and Harvey (2004) have, for instance, argued that the bureaucratic activities of some NGOs (for instance the promotion of trade over aid as a solution to poverty in the developing world), are serving the interests of large multinational corporations, which stand to benefit from such discourses. It is also questionable how to classify organisations such as 'fair trade' companies, which resemble NGOs in that their activities are charitably oriented, but which are also highly profitable businesses (Low and Davenport 2005). The NGO sector is thus an example of how businesses and bureaucracies combine, and further each other's interests.

Anthropological studies of business and bureaucracy thus, either tacitly or explicitly, challenge and question the distinctions made between them. By considering the nature of each, and the ways in which the two are converging and diverging, we may provide unique insights into the transformations of organisations in late modernity. The papers in this volume deal with the way in which changes in people's everyday lives link to wider processes of political and economic transformation, and consequently explore the impact which greater convergences between types of organisations have on individuals and social groups. We shall now consider how ethnicity and identity are reflected and defined in business and bureaucracy.

Identity and ethnicity in business and bureaucracy: return of the boundary?

The definition of identity, while it may not always be the explicit focus of the study, often forms a key part of the ethnographic study of business and bureaucracy, regardless of whether the practitioner is an anthropologist or not, particularly in the context of globalisation. In this section, I will consider the ways in which such studies investigate, and also contribute to, the construction of identity in business and bureaucracy, and the ways in which businesses and bureaucracies themselves form part of the identities of their members, clients and rivals.

Identity and business

The issue of identity in business is one which formed the core of Susan Wright's seminal article on the subject of the similarities and differences between anthropology and business studies (1994). Essentially, although both disciplines seem more or less to agree on what a company's 'culture' consists of – its values, myths and rituals, collective symbols and so forth (B. Turner 1971: 21; Mead 1994: 155–156) – they disagree on how it is formed. Anthropologists tend to consider culture as a common repertoire of ideas which is reworked in ways that are systematic but not predictable (Wright 1994: 4). Business studies, however, portrays culture as a shared property which is manufactured, and changed at will, by the group collectively or by powerful individuals within it (Anthony 1994: 2; Wright 1994: 2–3). The consequences of this are that where anthropologists traditionally tend to investigate the culture of an organisation as an objective property which should not be actively changed or interfered with – a scientific object of study, as it were – business studies, as a discipline, tends to have a more practical agenda; Kristensen and Zeitlin's monograph on how multinationals look different when seen from global and local perspectives ends with a number of chapters urging the managers of multinationals to take greater advantage of this by focusing more on local aspects of the corporation (2004). While the anthropology of business and business studies both focus on identity in organisations, according to many commentators, they do so from slightly, but significantly, different standpoints.

On another level, however, it is less easy to draw a distinction between the ways in which the two disciplines treat identity in organisations. While the anthropology of business may profess to be a relatively disinterested investigation of the culture of businesses, on another level, it has been involved almost from the outset in the project of defining identities in the wider environment. The anthropological study of Japanese business, for instance, is frequently tied up with the definition of Japanese national identity; see, for instance, Thomas P. Rohlen's (1974) influential discussion of initiation ceremonies in a Japanese business, or Lo's

Office Ladies, Factory Women (1990), both of which explore ideas about national identity in Japan through considering the ways in which Japanese businesspeople define their identities. Even the studies done in the 1950s and 1960s on South African labourers focused on the definition of tribal identity in the workplace, and consequently the identity of the business itself as South African (Meyer 1962). Even studies of American and British factories, which did not particularly focus on national identity, involved the definition of worker and working-class identity as opposed to managerial and white-collar identity, which, as Baba (1986) notes, ultimately led to the development of a particular anthropological agenda towards defining working-class identity through their workplace practices (e.g. Dunk 1991). Furthermore, ethnographies of business become incorporated into the business-studies view of culture; such works as Stewart et al.'s *Managing in Britain and Germany* (1994) are frequently cited, and, when I was studying German businesses in London, I was frequently referred by informants to various books on the 'culture' of German and/or British business which they had found useful. By investigating the 'cultural' characteristics of particular businesses or types of business (Japanese, German, South African etc.), anthropologists are, indirectly, involved in the construction of distinct identities as 'businesspeople' and as businesspeople of particular nationalities.

The anthropology of bureaucracy also exhibits a similarly complicated and tacit relationship to the definition of identity. As Herzfeld argues in *The Social Production of Indifference*, bureaucracy is usually a concept which evokes images of identity loss, the reduction of individuals and groups to particular categories (1992: 1–4); the works of Franz Kafka and George Orwell come to mind. However, Herzfeld argues that bureaucracies are in fact as much agents of the *construction* of identity, if not more so, than its *destruction*. Leaving aside the fact that bureaucracy is an extreme form of social classification (1992: 53), Herzfeld notes that bureaucracy is frequently held up as being part of national and regional identity, for instance in the case of Britain, Germany and, indeed, Europe in general (ibid., 2). A number of key markers of national and social identity – passports, social insurance numbers, birth certificates, work permits – are the products of bureaucracy, meaning that it is this process which ultimately decides who can, and cannot, belong to a particular national and, in some cases, ethnic group (as, for instance, in Canada, where the number of people with the legal status of '[Native] Indian' is fewer than the number of people who self-identify as Native Canadian). The study of bureaucracy, like that of business, is a process of identity definition.

Both business and bureaucracy in and of themselves are frequently employed as markers of national and/or cultural identity. In the case of Germany, for instance, German businesses are frequently taken as a source of national pride and markers of 'German' identity, even if they may be foreign-owned or multinational (Lawrence 1980: 12; also Wollf Olins Research 1995; Bergsten et al. 1978: 47). The British, similarly, use the stereotype of Britons as obsessed with chaotic and illogical bureaucratic practices in such well-known national satires as *Yes Minister*

(Lotterby 1980) or *The Office* (Gervais and Merchant 2001). Long-standing bureaucratic institutions such as the German *Grundgesetz* evoke a similar sense of national belonging as do long-standing private companies such as Barclays Bank. On other levels, both businesses and bureaucracies can relate to other identities, such as ethnic, gender, age or class, depending on the nature of the institution and the use that is made of it. Business and bureaucracy are thus a source of identity, and symbols of identity, for people all over the world.

This process of identification continues despite the above-mentioned problematisation of the distinction between the two forms of organisation. In the U.K., the privatised National Rail system is as much a source of national identity for the British public as its nationalised predecessor British Rail, with the privatisation of the institution frequently coming into play as a reflection on how the way in which the British view themselves has changed in the past thirty years. Similarly, companies are increasingly coming to view their role as involving 'responsibility' to their employees and the people in the communities in which they operate, in a strong blending of corporate and local – or, indeed, multilocal – identity (Blyth 2005). The example of the Nazi war reparations paid out by a number of German and Swiss companies since the 1990s is also an indicator of how national, historic, ethnic and corporate identity can become combined in the same act (*Financial Times* 1999). As business and bureaucracy are both involved in the symbolising of national, local and other forms of identity in similar ways, then, the blending between the two is unproblematic for the people of the nations and groups with which they are affiliated.

In the current phase of globalisation, in which identity becomes if anything even more fluid and flexible, identification with, or through the activities of, businesses and bureaucracies comes even more to the fore. Hannerz writes extensively on how identity under globalisation becomes a form of bricolage, a 'toolkit' not rooted in any connection to a particular geographic location, causing the strengthening of professional, gender, or ethnic identities (1992). Leyshon and Thrift describe how workers in the globalised finance industry create virtual and conceptual geographies through which to orient themselves (1997). Studies done on the 'transnational elite' note that, although they come from a diverse variety of locations, they identify as a common group through attending the same universities, practising the same sort of geographically mobile lifestyle and, more crucially, working for the same companies (Mickelthwait and Wooldridge 2000, chapter 12; Sklair 2001). The question of whether the branches of MNCs draw their cultural traits more from their home or their host country has been a source of debate in business studies for decades (Mueller 1994). The role of businesses and bureaucracies in forming and defining identity is thus even more crucial under globalisation.

The association of business and bureaucracy with identity, the close entanglement between the two in terms of their history within the discipline of anthropology, and the increasing convergence between the two in the twenty-first century, are thus all processes which are linked, and which further the development of each other. Their role in the process of identity formation and maintenance is even more crucial when one considers the impact of the processes of globalisation on social organisation and identity. The ethnographic study of business and bureaucracy thus allows us to problematise not only the artificial boundary between the two forms of organisation, but also the nature of globalisation and its impact on how people define themselves. We shall now take a closer look at the papers in this particular volume, their general themes, and how they relate to processes of identity formation, flexibility and globalisation.

Interpretations and themes within this volume

The papers in this book, as has been noted at various points in this introduction, focus on issues of business, bureaucracy, identity construction and the connections between all three. In the penultimate section, we shall consider the general themes of the volume, focusing on issues of power and knowledge transfer, researcher position, boundary construction and reinterpretation, the socioeconomic transformations brought about by globalisation, and flexibility, as well as the specific aims and agendas of the various papers which compose it.

The structure of the book also follows particular geographical and intellectual themes, clustering broadly around three particular areas. The first two papers, by Groeneveld and myself, focus on business and change in the U.K., with Herzog's paper on Israeli absorption centres serving as a transition to more bureaucratic papers. Abram and Callan's papers follow, both of which focus on the impact of privatisation and managerialist discourse on European public sector institutions. The book is concluded with two solidly bureaucratic papers, by Coles and Whitfield, which consider aid agencies in the developing world from the perspective of employees of aid agencies and recipients of aid respectively. The book thus follows a series of thematic transitions from business to bureaucracy, from the U.K. to the developing world, and from change management in business to the nature of NGO involvement abroad, via privatisation and managerialism.

General themes and ideas

This book does not only deal with issues surrounding identity, globalisation, business and bureaucracy, but incorporates themes of power, knowledge, gender, the fieldworker's relationship to informants, dealing with change, the blending of identities and the blending of business and bureaucracies. In this section, we shall discuss a few of these general themes prior to considering the individual papers in greater detail.

One of the key issues throughout this book is that of power. This is an issue which is crucial to the study of business and bureaucracy in general: as Herzfeld notes, bureaucracy is predicated on the reinforcing of hierarchical relations between different groups in society (1992: 159). Businesses also reinforce and reflect hierarchical relations, whether internal divisions between 'staff' and 'managers', or external divisions relating to access to the means of production (Rohlen 1974). Groeneveld's paper considers how bargaining for players in Rugby Union football is a social act which both reflects and affects the players and the teams they play for; Whitfield looks at the impact of national and international politico-economic discourses about the relationship of donors to government, and of OECD to non-OECD countries, on local and national identity in Ghana; Herzog investigates the ways in which discourses of gender, race and religion are used in an Israeli immigrant 'absorption centre' to reinforce the status of the native bureaucrats over the Ethiopian immigrants, and to define who and what is 'properly' Israeli and/or Jewish, discourses which will no doubt continue to affect the immigrants in their daily lives as Israeli citizens. In other papers, power discourses may be tacit, but are no less present: Coles's description of how her informants distance themselves from the bureaucratic practices of DFID (the Department for International Development) resonates with Herzfeld's remarks on the ways in which bureaucrats disclaim responsibility for their individual actions through blaming 'the system' (1992: 159). The ways in which the definition of identity through business and bureaucracy are used define and reinforce power relations, both in the institution and in the wider society in which it exists.

A related issue is the use of knowledge in business and bureaucracy as a means of defining identity and power relations, both inside and outside of the organisation. Groeneveld's paper, again, considers how inside knowledge of sport is used to build up social capital within the organisation and establish credentials. Callan's paper is a study of an institution, the European Association for International Education, ultimately aimed at defining and regulating the knowledge which is considered 'valuable' in European societies, and how it is transferred between educators and students. My own paper revolves around the ways in which transnational corporations construct themselves through the use, exchange and selection of particular knowledge. In all of the papers, in fact, there is the tacit acknowledgement that these institutions exist solely because they define themselves through their members' possession of information and skills particular to the institution. In business and bureaucracy, which are often detached from traditional geographical and physical boundary markers to define their identities (increasingly so, as the physical costumes, accessories and attributes once seen as the province of these particular institutions are either abandoned or diffused out to other groups – the mobile phone, once the status symbol of top-level businesspeople, is now the affordable accessory of the population at large), identity is of necessity largely defined through symbols relating to knowledge and other intangible forms of social capital.

As a side point, although none of these papers (except, arguably, Herzog's) deals directly with gender, it exists as a tacit subtext to the publication. While gender and business has been a concern of anthropologists for a number of years (cf. Wright 1994; Burrus 1997), this volume is unusual in containing no papers by male researchers (although two did participate in the original seminar series). This fact, on some level, informs the approach the researchers take, particularly as business is traditionally a macho domain; both Groeneveld and I report facing challenges in gaining access due to our gender. Herzog, also, is conducting research in an area where there are strongly gendered power relations between the (female/volunteer) welfare aides (in Hebrew, *somchot*) and the (frequently male/professional) administrators, which means that her access to both worlds is going to colour the relationship she has with each. Although it may not be a definite presence in most papers, then, the gender of the researchers informs the approach and the degree and type of access they had to their organisation.

This brings us to another key theme in this book: that of researcher perspective. It is worth noting that all of the researchers bar Groeneveld and Whitfield were either full members of the organisation which they studied, or else were temporarily affiliated with them in some official capacity or other. One of the particular characteristics of the ethnography of business and bureaucracy is that the researcher is normally able to temporarily integrate with the group as an official part of the group rather than a visible outsider or observer. As Sharma (1986) notes, regarding urban anthropology, in business settings as well as urban ones, the role of 'researcher', or 'researcher'-like roles, exist within the community (which, incidentally, also holds true for the ethnography of blue-collar workers). However, the disadvantage may be that you are expected to integrate into the community; were I not involved in some kind of useful work within the business about which I write in this volume, I would be regarded with sufficient suspicion and distrust that I would find it difficult to conduct any ethnographic research at all. Unsurprisingly, this does not seem to hold true for researchers who engage in less qualitative research activities; for them, presumably because their methodology affords them a formal degree of detachment from the organisation, affiliation with a particular business school seems to be enough in the way of credentials. The problem for ethnographers, however, is that one is frequently expected to fit in with the organisation's particular definition of what a 'researcher' is; ethnographers frequently must distribute questionnaires or gather statistical data in order to justify their identity as 'researchers' to their informants, even if it contradicts their own self-identification as anthropologists (ibid. 32–34). Ethnographers who step outside the boundaries of what is expected of 'researchers' in the organisation, also, may find themselves subject to social sanctions, as Herzog notes regarding her own decisions to step outside her assigned role and actively involve herself in disputes between immigrants and *somchot*. In such situations, as Callan notes at the outset of her paper, the ethnographer's identity comes sharply to the fore, and becomes both a means of understanding the community and a liability.

This approach is also one of the aspects of the ethnography of organisations which distinguishes it from other forms of research on business and bureaucracy.

In business studies, the object of the exercise is often to detach the researcher's personal identity from the context as much as possible, in a similar way to certain sorts of structuralist anthropology. All of the works in this volume, however, not only focus strongly on how the ethnographer's identity affected the research, but also explicitly consider the political and historical context – Abram situating the work in the context of present-day Scandinavia, formerly an area which took its public, socialist-welfare system as a source of identity and which is now having to deal with the impact of privatisation on the system, its employees and its national identity; Coles looking at a Western bureaucratic institution aimed at furthering economic development, at a time when the issue of Western aid to developing countries is a controversial issue, reflecting postcolonial political relations; and Whitfield, by contrast, looking at the way in which politics and identity in Ghana are affected by the very same development process. By using the researcher's identity as a means of investigation, then, issues of wider corporate identity and its links to other identities are able to be explored.

Another common theme among the papers is the construction, and destruction, of boundaries as an act of identity creation. Although early studies on the nature of identity focused strongly on the act of boundary construction (e.g. Wallman 1986), later studies take a more sophisticated approach, arguing that identity is more complex than simply the construction of intergroup boundaries (e.g. Banks 1996). However, the concept of the boundary has featured strongly in all of these articles: a common thread running throughout this book is that the act of constructing boundaries, through metaphors, images and statements about what it is to be 'us' rather than 'them', features strongly in the development of corporate identity among the researchers' informants, whether 'us' are teachers, bureaucrats, *somchot*, Ghanaians, German bankers or working-class English people. At the same time, and in an apparent contradiction to this last, we also see a theme of the blending of ethnic and gender identities into professional ones: not Jewish/female, but Jewish female welfare aide; not German and English, but German and English transnational bankers; not British/male, but British male professional rugby football player. This contradiction highlights one of the distinctive things about the study of organisations: that, on the one hand, they are inextricably linked to the contexts in which they operate; on the other hand, as organisations, their members also must remain distinct. It is possible that members of organisations also have other, possibly stronger, calls on their identity, and as such, have to focus on developing a firmly bounded identity. On the other hand, it may equally be that the competitive nature of business and, indirectly, of bureaucracy, means that organisations develop a strong sense of rivalry against their competitors, and consequently encourage the development of boundaries as a form of identity construction. The papers in this volume thus highlight the way in which people continually define, redefine, question and cross boundaries in their daily working lives.

Another key theme of the book is the process of change. We encounter bureaucratic organisations undergoing privatisation and having to deal increasingly with private companies; football clubs dealing with the impact of controversial legislation; NGOs and governments struggling with transformations in the world order; companies undergoing a change in structure; and new immigrants coming into an established country. This also fits in with the dichotomy regarding the permeability of boundaries, as the members of organisations struggle to define themselves and their identities in a situation in which those identities might change from month to month: like the organisation studied by Scarbrough and Terry (1996), the company which I refer to as 'ZwoBank' in my article in this book no longer exists in the form in which I studied it. In addition, as noted above, the links between business and bureaucracy are becoming more and more complex; Coles's, Abram's and Callan's articles all indicate how bureaucracies are becoming more and more like businesses, and what this is doing to the identities of the people who work in and use the changing institutions. The issue of identity transformation is thus central to this volume.

A related theme is that of flexibility. The papers in this volume were all initially developed between 2000 and 2004, a period of transformation and consolidation within globalisation, at a time when researchers were focusing on the transformations which were being brought about in the workplace, principally with regard to flexibility. This is a broad concept which can include geographical flexibility, or labour migration at all levels; rapid change within organisations as they adapt to new circumstances (Birkinshaw and Hagström 2000); or the loss of the 'job for life' and the advent of a situation in which, as Castells notes, most if not all workers lack benefits and security, which has caused people to rethink their relationship to their organisation and profession (2000: 281–96). This theme is reflected in this volume in the papers on change within banking and Rugby in the U.K., and in the papers on privatisation; however, the geographical sense of the term also comes to the fore in Herzog's paper on labour migrants, as well as my own on transnational elites. Whitfield's paper also deals with how individuals interpret global trends according to local business strategies, engaging in spontaneous transformations as a strategy for economic survival and identity construction. Flexibility is thus also a key theme, related to the discourses of globalisation which these papers explore.

In sum, then, the articles in this book all focus on specific issues relating to the particular problem of constructing an identity in a 'virtual' environment in which the markers of identity may change quite suddenly, of power relations and the existence of outside, sometimes competing, claims on members' identities. To this end, different groups engage in different forms of flexibility with regard to their work and their self-identification in order to express themselves in transforming environments and to employ outside discourses to their own ends. We shall now consider the individual case studies in more detail.

The case studies

As well as having common themes, it is worth noting the specific points and provisions of each of the articles in the book, and how they relate to each other and to key debates in the anthropology of business and bureaucracy. I will thus briefly consider each of the articles in turn, exploring how they reflect the themes of flexibility, power, identity and the relationship between business and bureaucracy under globalisation.

To begin with, Groeneveld's piece on the Rugby League, like most of the papers in this volume, relates to discourses on European identity, in that the European Court of Justice's intervention in the issue of transfers turns it from an issue of local identity into one of labour rights. Groeneveld's players and managers are also affected by transnational business, in that the sport is gradually being restructured by the interests of global media networks, and Groeneveld carefully considers how decisions taken on the global level affect local identities. The ethnographer's identity in the field comes strongly into play, and Groeneveld is very candid about how her relationships with her interviewees affected her data, her areas of access, and so forth. However, the paper distinguishes itself from the others in this volume in being focused on local identity, rather than national, regional, ethnic or gender. Groeneveld also focuses explicitly on class identity, which, while it does have tacit links with the study of bureaucracy, is less to the fore in the bureaucracy-focused articles in this volume.

Groeneveld's paper, interestingly, bears less of a resemblance to the more business-focused studies in this volume, and more to Abram's, Callan's and Coles' investigations of the impact of the privatisation/corporatisation ethos on bureaucracies. Even though Rugby League is technically a business, the introduction of economic discourses into one relating to local identity produced as much distress and dismay among its members as in public institutions that are being privatised: the change, due to the Bosman ruling, of the chairman into 'an employer instead of a somewhat omnipotent controller', reflects similar changes in the nature of bureaucracy in the post-Thatcher era. The way in which club chairmen continually criticise the Super League system, and yet desperately try to get into it, reflects the way, in other papers, all the members of a bureaucracy complain about privatisation, yet they also go along with the new system. Like bureaucracies, also, the Rugby League is strongly focused on hierarchical relations reinforced by the discourse of 'doing things correctly', although the symbolic role of the club chairman as a kind of embodiment of the corporation actually seems to relate more to the corporate discourse of the hero-CEO who is seen as embodying the values of the company. Again, this suggests that there are strong links between business and bureaucracy, and that not all businesses – or, for that matter, bureaucracies – fit the conventional model.

Perhaps the most interesting thing about Groeneveld's paper is, however, how it highlights and questions the definition of business and bureaucracy. Despite the fact that we are surrounded on all sides by UEFA[1]-endorsed clothing, media coverage deals, and corporate sponsorship, many people react with hostility when confronted with the idea that sport is a business. When businessman Malcolm Glazer bought the football club Manchester United, there was a storm of bad publicity and local protest of the sort which would not have happened had he purchased, for instance, Unilever or Wilkinson plc. Groeneveld examines how emotional discourses affect how we view businesses: the chairmen 'love' their clubs, and feel emotional bonds to them, meaning that they will make decisions for reasons other than rational economics, and repeatedly distance these from business calculation, saying, 'You don't make hard-nosed business decisions in sport'. Groeneveld argues that these decisions are not therefore irrational, but possess a different sort of rationality. Groeneveld's paper thus provides the final link between business and bureacracy.

My own study, on the use of symbolism in a German bank, relates to a project which has since been more significantly developed in the monograph *Transnational Business Cultures* (Moore 2005). Although it is one of the more business-focused pieces in the volume, it also straddles the divide between business and bureaucracy, considering the ways in which two cultures meet during a bureaucratic exercise aimed at bringing the two closer together, and how laws, rules and regulations can become symbols of both ethnic and business identity. Like others in this volume, it explicitly takes traditional anthropological concepts (in this case, Anthony Cohen's 1985 study of the Whalsay Islanders) and applies them to a nontraditional setting (in this case, the London branch of a German bank). Like Coles and Callan, it focuses on European identity, but in this case from the business, rather than the bureaucratic, side and, like Herzog's paper, considers the way in which identity is drawn into conflicts and power struggles within organisations.

In terms of anthropology, my piece is in line with studies of globalisation and migration, considering, like Grillo (1985) and Vertovec (1999), how symbols of ethnic identity are used in globalising environments as a means of coping with the multiethnic, fluid nature of the organisation. It looks at the ways in which symbols of ethnic identity take on new significance in situations where people lack the guidance of conventional geography (Siemens, for instance, becomes associated with Germanness at the same time as it becomes associated with global business [Wolff Olins Research 1995]). Some early studies of ethnicity and globalisation questioned whether the focus on ethnic boundaries under globalisation indicated that this was a limited concept, which would soon give way to a renewed nationalism (Smith 1995); however, the bulk of evidence here and elsewhere suggests that this is instead related to an adjustment to the condition of globalisation. Like other chapters in this volume, however, it also relates to a wider discourse in business studies, namely, the literature on how national culture relates to how people do business (e.g. Hofstede 1980) and how this debate is changing with regard to the global nature of business today (e.g. Ferner et al. 2004). This article thus also links in to debates and themes in anthropology and business studies, drawing them together to create new insights into migration, flexibility and change manangement.

Herzog's article considers what is probably the most specifically bureaucratic of the institutions in the volume, an Israeli 'absorption centre' in which immigrants to Israel are 'processed' prior to becoming full members of Israeli society. Consequently, power issues are much to the fore, with the issue of who has the ability to define the 'outsider' and the 'insider' becoming a bone of contention as the symbols of bureaucracy are used to reduce the immigrants to a state of dependency and, in some ways, non-personhood, and to elevate petty officials and volunteers to the status of gatekeepers of Israeli identity. As Herzog notes, 'rules and ideology are formulated in correspondence with concrete and immediate needs of those who seek to attain and preserve power'. Significantly, this study indicates how people react less to an actual physical situation of control than to the symbols of control – the Ethiopian immigrants are not under threat of physical violence, but are being subjected to violent assaults on their identity and emotional well-being (compare Erving Goffman's study of how the inmates of asylums are controlled through being systematically shorn of their trappings of personal identity [1961]). In the process of identity and status-definition described by Herzog, knowledge plays a key role: the people with privileged knowledge of Hebrew, the rules by which the bureaucracy operates, and of what is socially acceptable in Israel, are the ones who control the situation. This concept calls into question the nature of similar processes the world over, and, perhaps, also raises an indirect challenge to the assertions on the part of the British and American forces, regarding the invasion of Iraq and the detention of suspected terrorists, that psychological interrogation techniques, assaults on religious and ethnic identity and humiliation rituals do not constitute 'torture'. Herzog even considers how easy it is for ethnographers to become drawn into the bureaucratic routines and associated power-games when working within an organisation. Herzog's article thus considers the ways in which the defining of identity can become a tool, or weapon, in a situation of bureaucratic inequality.

Subtextually, however, the article also raises the question of what it is to be Jewish. If, according to the ethos of Israeli society, all Jews are equal together within the Jewish state, then the reader must ask how is it that the native Israelis are able to set themselves up as authority figures on Jewishness vis-à-vis their immigrant charges. There is also an undercurrent of racial discourse, with the unspoken idea of 'white/Middle Eastern' Israelis setting themselves up over 'black/African' new immigrants underlying certain aspects of the action. Herzog's article is thus interesting in indicating how bureaucratic processes can tie into more longstanding discourses of identity, even as they seem to relate to more recent global migratory trends.

Herzog's discussion of the role of the *somchot*, or welfare aides, also considers the issue of the merging of gender and political identity. The *somchot* are women, specifically brought in to play a domestic role (one secretary confesses that her criterion for selecting women to be *somchot* is to ask whether or not they have children), but who also use the little power they have as 'professionals' to dominate immigrants, particularly immigrant women, through their supposedly greater knowledge of how to behave in Israeli society, and their official status as role models for the immigrants, through which they are able to define 'proper' gender roles for the immigrants. Herzog's analysis thus considers a variety of ways in which professional and personal identities combine and are used in the exercise of power within bureaucratic institutions.

Abram's article falls deliberately into both the business *and* bureaucracy camps, as it directly examines the way in which, as discussed above, 'pseudo-market' metaphors are creeping into bureaucracy as, in the privatisation era, they are encouraged to think of themselves more and more as businesses. The article covers similar ground to Czarniawska's well-known monograph on the impact of the privatisation of a public institution on its members' identity (1997), but, where Czarniawska uses this process to consider issues relating to the culture of the organisation, Abram is looking at the social impact of privatisation and the use of the business metaphor on the wider culture of Norway. This is particularly significant because, as Abram notes, Norway, with its firmly entrenched welfare state being a point of identity for many citizens, is one place where outsiders would not expect bureaucracy to be in crisis; however, changes are being forced upon the system due to pressures from global, and particularly European, trends and politics. Again, this is an ethnography which is situated within the wider networks affecting the organisation, and addresses issues of flexibility in the face of social change.

Abram focuses primarily on the ways in which, as she puts it, 'a discourse on the separation of administrative and political roles in local government was used in a number of municipalities to legitimise a move towards a market ideology and the creeping privatisation of welfare services', and, as such, on the ways in which the use of business metaphors by council members affects the ways in which they view the organisation. This is in keeping with Lakoff and Johnson's study on how the use of metaphor can have an impact on perception of people, events and groups (1980). However, it is also bolstered by physical activities, such as, for instance, the use of management consultants for guidance on the organisation's identity – something more traditionally associated with business. This process then has a wider impact as, by bringing in the business metaphor, the organisation's accountability to people disappears; it ceases to be about individuals, and starts being about budgets. Abram thus considers how changes in identity relate to changes in organisations, and how the organisations in turn impact on the wider society.

Callan's article also focuses on a bureaucracy, but, like that studied by Abram, one which to some extent relates to business, and to the ways in which the increasing corporatisation and privatisation of public services impacts upon the identity of people in such organisations; in this case, specifically, the industry springing up around 'cross-cultural education'. Like Coles's piece, this is also a work of auto-ethnography, which considers a field (education, in this case) in which many anthropologists will find themselves engaged at one point or another. The role of the ethnographer, as Callan herself notes, is key, with her position in the organisation being a strong influence on her perspective on it. However, Callan here uses her 'insider' status to deconstruct the folk concept (as opposed to the sociological concept) of bureaucracy: although her colleagues are technically bureaucrats, because 'bureaucracy' is a stigmatised term in Europe, used to indicate the frustration and stifling of identity, they prefer not to self-identify as such, focusing instead (like Herzog's *somchot*) on images of 'professionalisation'.

Callan's study ties in with a particular area of anthropology, the study of Europe, which has always had strong links to the study of identity (Tonkin et al. 1991). Since 'Europe' as a social unit in modern times has been strongly tied up with particular political and economic projects, anthropological studies of Europe have often had tacit links with the study of business and bureaucracy (e.g. Herzfeld 1992). Like many anthropological studies of Europe, it also takes a historical approach, looking at how the idea of scholarship has developed in European identity over time (c.f. MacDonald 2001). At the same time, however, there is also an oblique connection to two fields of business studies: the study of development, and the study of cross-cultural management, which has spawned a sub-industry in 'intercultural education', aimed at teaching managers how best to work in, and with, different cultures (Dahlen 1997). Callan's study thus provides a new perspective on various issues in anthropology and in the study of cross-cultural management within Europe.

The paper by Anne Coles, a geographer, is another examination of a bureaucracy by someone who has actually worked inside it; her study of the U.K.'s Department for International Development (DFID) is, as such, another self-reflexive ethnography. Consequently, it raises issues for many anthropologists (and other social scientists) who are, or have been, active in the non-governmental organisation sector: many anthropologists do work, in some capacity or other, with such organisations, and yet the number of researchers who have undertaken analyses of their roles in these organisations is relatively few. Coles thus considers the practical uses of social science, and how anthropology fits into the identity-defining nature of bureaucracy.

A key aspect of Coles's paper, and one which is often overlooked, is the role of national identity in what is ostensibly an international organisation. The question is raised for the reader of whether DFID would be the same sort of institution if it had originated in Kenya, or Germany, or India – and, consequently, of how much other ostensibly 'international' organisations, such as the UN and Red Cross, owe to their national origin and location. This relates to a debate which is more current in international business than in the anthropology of bureaucracy, i.e. the nature and degree of influence which the home country has on the multinational organisation (cf. Whitley 1992). The paper also relates to the business studies literature on 'network theory', that is to say, the way in which the organisation is situated relative to other institutions, political departments and NGOs – an approach still relatively rare in core anthropology, where, due to the nature of ethnographic fieldwork, organisations tend to be studied in relative isolation (see Marcus 1998). The study invites comparison with examinations of the corporate culture of British businesses (for instance, the use of sports metaphors seen in DFID is also notoriously common in the City of London), and also with those aspects of Herzog's article which deal with the development of personal identity (the *somchot* versus the Social Development Advisers). Although power relations are not as directly dealt with in Coles' article as in Herzog's, they arise from the examination of internal divisions and the relationship between the adminstrators and the advisers. Coles's article thus relates to wider discourses in business studies as well as to the study of bureaucracy, particularly as pertains to the role of NGOs in the global discourse of developing versus developed world.

By contrast, Whitfield's paper looks at the same issue from the other side of the coin, as she considers the ways in which development practices affect Ghanaian identities, and further the construction of new discourses of identity among the recipients of development aid. She considers how, in the 1990s, the World Bank, concerned that donor–recipient relationships were overly hierarchical, encouraged a shift in identity whereby donors became 'development partners', thus, in theory, encouraging more partnership and cooperation between donor and recipient. In practice, however, the shift in identity has given donor organisations an even greater say in Ghanaian government policy than before: Ghanaians, Whitfield notes, say that they feel they are ruled by 'two governments', the official one and the donor agencies. Whitfield also calls into question the notion of 'good governance', noting that one must ask who defines and enforces it, and considers how the language used to define and discuss politics and economics affects how individuals see the process of development and aid donation, and define their roles within it. By routinising and institutionalising the relationships between donor agencies and the governments of recipient countries, individuals come to accept the situation as normal, giving the donor agencies the ability to influence not only the policies of the governments of the aid recipients, but even how they see themselves.

The situation is further complicated, however, by the fact that there was also a rise in discourse about 'civil society' and political liberalisation in Ghana at the same time as this process was taking place. While the donor agencies perceive civil society as a way of furthering democracy in recipient countries, it has clearly not escaped their notice that political liberalisation also opens up the way for them to have a greater say in Ghanaian politics than under more authoritarian regimes. There is the same blurring of boundaries between public and private sectors that we see in other papers in this volume. However, their relationship with the Ghanaian people is more subtle than simply one of oppression and manipulation; the idea of civil society as a beneficial thing has filtered into the public consciousness, and the donor agencies also provide Ghanaians with jobs, material and social resources, sites for political activism and opposition, and so forth. This is thus not simply a case of Western organisations imposing their will on helpless developing nations, but a mutual dynamic of collaboration and opposition between agents with a variety of different needs, strengths, abilities and goals.

All of the papers in this volume, therefore, explore in a variety of different ways the question of where business ends and bureaucracy begins. Abram, Coles, Whitfield and Callan all consider how the privatisation of services and the corporatisation of the language of government and NGOs affects the identity of the people involved; the ZwoBank study considers the bureaucratic aspects of business and how they relate to identity; Herzog considers how society-wide issues of gender, power and religion are reflected in the process of integrating refugees into society (with economic discourses, regarding what defines a 'professional' coming very much to the fore); Groeneveld considers the ways in which what appears to be a business can, in fact, go as much against the traditional corporate ethos as a public organisation. Throughout, the interface between them becomes less and less clear: money is made out of bureaucracies, businesses define themselves through rules and procedures, and both relate to national and regional identity while at the same time reacting to changes and developments caused by global movements and discourses. The papers in this book thus all challenge, question and explore the relationship between business and bureaucracy in anthropological parlance in today's 'flexible' world.

Conclusion

This book, therefore, explores connections, similarities and divisions between business and bureaucracy under globalisation, and the ways in which identity and power affect people involved with both. The papers in this volume contribute, not only in-depth studies of how business is done, and how bureaucracy affects this, in Europe, Scandinavia, Africa and the Middle East, but also suggest new ways of looking at organisations in general, considering them less in terms of formal divisions and types, and more in terms of how they relate to issues of identity, power, flexibility and hierarchy in the cultures which produce, host and influence corporations and bureaucracies.

The papers in this volume contribute to the literature on globalisation and flexibility, in that they examine the transformation of identity among groups of people involved with businesses and bureaucracies which are changing under advanced globalisation, and also examine the interpretation of business and bureaucracy in different geographical and employment situations. The papers also question and explore the changing relationships between businesses and bureaucracy, as well as defining and consolidating the anthropological work previously done on this subject.

Through a variety of interdisciplinary papers considering the issues of identity in business and bureaucracy from diverse theoretical, methodological and geographical perspectives, then, we shall consider and explore in this volume the ways in which businesses and bureaucracies relate to and differ from each other under globalisation in the early twenty-first century. As for the transforming nature of professional identities in business and bureaucracy, that must now be left for the reader to explore.

Notes

1. Union of European Football Associations.

Bibliography

Anderson, B. 2000. *Doing the Dirty Work? The Global Politics of Domestic Labour.* London: Zed Books.

Anthony, P.D. 1994. *Managing Culture.* Buckingham: Open University Press.

Augar, P. 2000. *The Death of Gentlemanly Capitalism: The Rise and Fall of London's Investment Banks.* London: Penguin Books.

Baba, M.L. 1986. *Business and Industrial Anthropology: An Overview.* NAPA Bulletin No. 2. Washington: NAPA.

———. 1998. 'Anthropology of Work in the Fortune 1000: A Critical Retrospective'. *Anthropology of Work Review*, 18 (4): 17–28.

Banks, M. 1996. *Ethnicity: Anthropological Constructions.* London: Routledge.

Barley, N. 1983. *The Innocent Anthropologist: Notes from a Mud Hut.* New York: Henry Holt and Co.

Bergsten, C.F. et al. 1978. *American Multinationals and American Interests.* Washington: The Brookings Institution.

Birkinshaw, J. and P. Hagström (ed.). 2000. *The Flexible Firm: Capability Management in Network Organisations.* Oxford: Oxford University Press.

Birkinshaw, J. and N. Hood. 1998. 'Multinational Subsidiary Evolution: Capabilities and Charter Change in Foreign-Owned Companies', *Academy of Management Review* 23 (4): 773–95.

Blyth, A. 2005. 'Business Behaving Responsibly'. *Director*, 59 (1): 30.

Burns, T. 1992. *Erving Goffman.* London: Routledge.

Burrus, K. 1997. 'National Culture and Gender Diversity within One of the Universal Swiss Banks', in A. Sackman (ed.) *Cultural Complexity in Organisations: Inherent Contrasts and Contradictions.* London: Sage, pp. 209–27.

Castells, M. 2000. *The Rise of the Network Society* (*The Information Age* vol. 1), 2nd edn. Oxford: Blackwell.

Castles, S. and G. Kosack. 1973. *Immigrant Workers and Class Struggle in Western Europe.* London: Oxford University Press.

Chapman, M. 1997. 'Preface: Social Anthropology, Business Studies and Cultural Issues'. *International Studies of Management and Organisation* 26 (4), 3–29.

Cody, T. 1990. *Strategy of a Megamerger.* New York: Quorum Books.

Cohen, A.P. 1985. *The Symbolic Construction of Community.* London: Tavistock.

Cohen, R. 1997. *Global Diasporas: An Introduction.* London: UCL.

Czarniawska, B. 1997. *Narrating the Organisation: Dramas of Institutional Identity.* London: University of Chicago Press.

Dahlen, T. 1997. *Among the Interculturalists: An Emergent Profession and Its Packaging of Knowledge.* Stockholm Studies in Social Anthropology 38. Stockholm: Stockholm University.

Delbridge, R. 1998. *Life on the Line in Contemporary Manufacturing: The Workplace Experience of Lean Production and the 'Japanese' Model.* Oxford: Oxford University Press.

Douglas, M. 1987. *How Institutions Think.* London: Routledge and Kegan Paul.

Dunk, T.W. 1991. *It's a Working Man's Town: Male Working-Class Culture in Northwestern Ontario.* Montreal: McGill-Queens University Press.

Durkheim, E. and M. Mauss. 1903 [1963]. *Primitive Classification*, ed. and trans. Rodney Needham. Chicago: University of Chicago Press.

Financial Times. 1999. 'Compensation for Nazi Era Labour to Rise'. 7 October 1999.

Gervais, R. and S. Merchant. 2001. *The Office.* BBC2.

Goodman, R. 1993. *Japan's 'International Youth': The Emergence of a New Class of Schoolchildren.* Oxford: Clarendon Press.

Goffman, E. 1961. *Asylums: Essays on the Social Situation of Mental Patients and Other Inmates.* Garden City: Anchor Books.

Graham, L. 1995. *On the Line at Subaru-Isuzu: The Japanese Model and the American Worker.* Ithaca, NY: ILR.

Grillo, R.D. 1985. *Ideologies and Institutions in Urban France: The Representation of Immigrants.* Cambridge: Cambridge University Press.

Gullick, C.J.M.R. 1993. 'Cultural Values and European Financial Institutions', in T. M. Wilson and M.E. Smith (ed.), *Cultural Change and the New Europe: Perspectives on the European Community.* Oxford: Westview Press, pp. 203–22.

Hannerz, U. 1992. *Cultural Complexity: Studies in the Social Organisation of Meaning.* New York: Columbia University Press.

———. 1996. *Transnational Connections: Culture, People, Places.* London: Routledge.

Harvey, D. 2004. *The New Imperialism.* Oxford: Oxford University Press.

Held, D., A. McGrew, D. Goldblatt and J. Perraton. 1999. *Global Transformations: Politics, Economics and Culture.* Cambridge: Polity Press.

Herzfeld, M. 1992. *The Social Production of Indifference: Exploring the Symbolic Roots of Western Bureaucracy.* London: University of Chicago Press.

Hofstede, G. 1980. *Culture's Consequences: International Differences in Work-Related Values.* London: Sage

d'Iribarne, P. 1997. 'The Usefulness of an Ethnographic Approach to the International Comparison of Organisations'. *International Studies of Management and Organisation,* 26 (4): 30–47.

Kamata, S. 1984. *Japan in the Passing Lane: An Insider's Account of Life in a Japanese Auto Factory.* London: Unwin.

Kristensen, P.H. and D. Zeitlin. 2004. *Local Players in Global Games: The Strategic Constitution of a Multinational Corporation.* Oxford: Oxford University Press.

Lakoff, G. and M. Johnson. 1980. *Metaphors We Live By.* Chicago: University of Chicago Press.

Law, J. 1994. *Organising Modernity.* Oxford: Blackwell.

Lawrence, P. 1980. *Managers and Management in West Germany.* London: Croom Helm.

Lewis, M. 1989. *Liar's Poker: Two Cities, True Greed.* London: Hodder and Stoughton.

Leyshon, A. and N. Thrift. 1997. *Money/Space: Geographies of Monetary Transformation.* London: Routledge.

Lo, J. 1990. *Office Ladies, Factory Women.* London: East Gate.

Lotterby, S. 1980. *Yes Minister.* BBC2.

Low, W. and E. Davenport. 2005. 'Has the Medium (Roast) Become the Message? The Ethics of Marketing Fair Trade in the Mainstream'. *International Marketing Review* 22 (5): 494–511.

MacDonald, S. 2001. 'Trafficking in History: Multitemporal Practices'. *Anthropological Journal on European Cultures,* 11: 93–116.

Marcus, G. 1998. *Ethnography through Thick and Thin.* Princeton: Princeton University Press.

Martiniello, M. 1995. 'Introduction', in M. Martiniello (ed.), *Migration, Citizenship and Ethnonational Identities in the European Union.* Aldershot: Avebury, pp. 1–7.

McDonald, M. 2005. 'EU Policy and Destiny: A Challenge for Anthropology'. *Anthropology Today* 21 (1): 3–5.

McFeat, T. 1974. *Small-Group Cultures*. Toronto: Pergamon Press.

Mead, G. 1994. *International Management*. London: Blackwell.

Meyer, P. 1962. *Townsmen or Tribesmen: Conservatism and the Process of Urbanisation in a South African City*. Oxford: Oxford University Press.

Micklethwait, J. and A. Wooldridge. 2000. *A Future Perfect: The Challenge and Hidden Promise of Globalisation*. London: William Heinemann.

Miller, D. 1997. *Capitalism: An Ethnographic Approach*. Oxford: Berg.

Miller, D. and D. Slater. 2000. *The Internet: An Ethnographic Approach*. Oxford: Berg.

Moore, F. 2005. *Transnational Business Cultures: Life and Work in a Multinational Corporation*. Aldershot: Ashgate.

Morgan, G. 2001. 'Transnational Communities and Business Systems', *Global Networks* 1 (2): 113–30.

Morgan, G. and L. Smircich. 1980. 'The Case for Qualitative Research', *Academy of Management Review* 5 (4): 491–500.

Mueller, F. 1994. 'Societal Effect, Organisational Effect and Globalization', *Organisation Studies*, 15 (3): 407–28.

Nash, J. 1979. 'Anthropology of the Multinational Corporation', in G. Huizer and B. Mannheim (ed.), *The Politics of Anthropology: From Colonialism and Sexism toward a View from Below*. Paris: Mouton Publishers, pp. 421–46.

Portes, A. 1998. *Globalisation from Below: The Rise of Transnational Communities*. Oxford: ESRC Transnational Communities Programme Working Papers.

Rohlen, T.P. 1974. *For Harmony and Strength: Japanese White-Collar Organisation in Anthropological Perspective*. Berkeley: University of California Press.

Sakai, J. 2000. *Japanese Bankers in the City of London: Language, Culture and Identity in the Japanese Diaspora*. London: Routledge.

Scarbrough, H. and M. Terry. 1996. *Industrial Relations and the Reorganisation of Production in the U.K. Motor Vehicle Industry: A Study of the Rover Group*. Warwick Papers in Industrial Relations No. 58. Coventry: University of Warwick.

Schwartzman, H.B. 1993. *Ethnography in Organisations*. Quantitative Research Methods, Vol. 27. London: Sage.

Sharma, U. 1986. *Women's Work, Class and the Urban Household: A Study of Shimla, North India*. London: Tavistock.

Sklair, L. 2001. *The Transnational Capitalist Class*. Oxford: Blackwell.

Smith, A.D. 1995. *Nations and Nationalism in a Global Era*. Cambridge: Polity Press.

Stewart, R. et al.1994. *Managing in Britain and Germany*. New York: St Martin's Press.

Strathern, M. 2005. 'Bullet Proofing'. Paper presented at CMS4 Conference, 4–6 July, Cambridge, U.K..

Sweeney, A.-M. 1993. 'Women Making Cars, Making Trouble, Making History', in T. Hayter and D. Harvey (ed.) *The Factory and the City: the Story of the Cowley Automobile Workers in Oxford*. London: Mansell, pp.116–39.

Tonkin, E. et al. (ed.). 1991. *History and Ethnicity*. London: Routledge.

Truss, C. 2003. 'Strategic HRM: Enablers and Constraints in the NHS', *International Journal of Public Sector Management*, 16 (1): 48–61.

Turner, B. 1971. *Exploring the Industrial Subculture*. London: Macmillan.

Vertovec, S. 1999. 'Conceiving and Researching Transnationalism', *Ethnic and Racial Studies*, 22 (2): 447–62.

Wallman, S. 1986. 'Ethnicity and the Boundary Process in Context', in J. Rex and D. Morgan (eds.), *Theories of Race and Ethnic Relations*. Cambridge: Cambridge University Press, pp. 226–45.

Whitley, R. 1992. 'Societies, Firms and Markets: The Social Structuring of Business Systems', in R. Whitley (ed.), *European Business Systems: Firms and Markets in their National Contexts*. London: Sage, pp. 5–45.

Wolff Olins Identity Research. 1995. *Made in Germany: A Business Survey of the Relevance of the National Badge and Its Image Associations*. London: Wolff Olins.

Womack, J.P., D.T. Jones and D. Roos. 1990. *The Machine that Changed the World: the Story of Lean Production*. London: HarperPerennial.

Wright, S. 1994 '"Culture" in Anthropology and Organisational Studies', in Susan Wright (ed.), *Anthropology of Organisations*. London: Routledge, pp. 1–31.

1

MATTERS OF THE HEART:
THE BUSINESS OF ENGLISH
RUGBY LEAGUE

Margaret Groeneveld

Introduction

Sport has played a very significant role in the construction and maintenance of Northern British identity. In particular, the professional sport of Rugby League has been associated with a working-class, Northern identity since the late 1800s (cf. Collins 1998, Russell 2004). The sport's identification with 'Northernness' at once transcends and complements national, class and county-based identities. The traditionally intense affiliation people feel for their local Rugby League club unites them along lines of village, county and Northern identity.

These spheres of affiliation gained emphasis through a century-long conflict with Rugby Union (a different sport commonly known as 'rugby'), whose participants were characterised by their amateur, middle-class, Southern British nature. Both types of 'rugby' originated from the same schoolboy game played at Rugby School. However, in the late 1800s deep divisions arose amongst the men who ran the game throughout the country as to how they would manage their clubs. In the South, the perception was that middle-class men needn't be paid to play, in an effort to preserve the ideals of the amateur. In the North, however, it was felt by club organisers that they needed to pay their primarily working-class players from the mines and the mills what were called 'broken-time' payments in order to entice them to sacrifice some of their working hours to practise, travel to competitions, and to play the game successfully. In 1895, at the George Hotel in Huddersfield, a group of Northern club organisers decided to break from their Southern counterparts and start their own league with its own rules regarding payments. This was the formation of what is now the Rugby Football League (RFL). In the 100 years that followed, the rules of play changed such that they are now two similar but different games. Yet, the bitter conflicts between North and

South, professional and amateur, and working- and middle-class identities persisted (Moorhouse 1996; Collins 1998).

Rugby League clubs, in villages, towns and cities, clustered mostly along what is now the M62 motorway corridor from Liverpool to Hull, developing their own styles of play, with their own local histories and supporters. Clubs became integral parts of their local communities as employers, sources of entertainment, and symbols of place and identity. Although players typically came from the local community, out of the mills and the mines, a system was developed which enabled clubs to exchange players for money. The premise of this system was that all the players on a club's register could only play for that club. From this concept, the idea developed that ownership of the right to 'play a player' could be bought and sold through what was called the 'retain and transfer' market. If club organisers had money to 'buy' a player with incredible abilities to fill a lack in their own team, then they would pay his club an agreed sum to 'sell' him. The competition, therefore, was not only on the pitch, but also on the books: whoever had the most money at their disposal could essentially buy the best players and win all the competitions.

One of the perennial and central features of Rugby League's history is that of the management and mismanagement of club finances, particularly where transfer market transactions were (and still are) concerned. Annually, the club management would reveal their financial situation to the press, and annually clubs would come and go because of financial ups and downs. At the Rugby Football League's archives in Leeds, there are boxes of old donated scrapbooks containing newspaper cuttings on club finances dating from the early 1900s right through to the last ten years. Not only were the match day results important to those within the wider Rugby League 'community', but club finances also form an important motif in this sport's traditions. The idea that the game is near financial extinction and yet it persists because of its Northern roots is one of Rugby League's most treasured beliefs.

In the 1990s, however, several events occurred which changed Rugby League indelibly. Australian Rupert Murdoch's Sky network paid £87 million for the restructuring of professional Rugby League in England and the creation of a 'Super League', together with the purchase of all corresponding television rights. Super League highlighted the power and money contests between clubs, both on the pitch and in the boardroom, by amplifying the differences between poor and rich (equating to mediocre and successful) clubs. During the same time period, a Belgian football player named Jean-Marc Bosman went to the Belgian courts to protest against a similar transfer system in European football, which culminated in a ruling from the European Court of Justice disallowing the practice as a restriction on the free movement of labour.[1] This ruling (known commonly as 'the Bosman ruling'), which legally categorised professional sport as business, applies to all European sports, and Rugby League had to adjust its practices accordingly. In the same time period, and in a move to promote more professional and business-like practices in club management, a set of best managerial practices, entitled *Framing the Future*, was distributed by the Rugby Football League to all clubs. The document had been commissioned from an outside marketing firm and sparked deep conflict over Rugby League values and practices, considering that, *inter alia*, it outlined a required, organisational architecture and homogenised managerial methodologies which had to be implemented by all clubs. Also during this time, the game of Rugby Union, Rugby League's primary competitor for players and spectators, and century-long foil for the North/South divide, very suddenly became 'professional' by allowing its players to be paid salaries. Put together, these changes, most of which were caused by factors external to the Rugby League community, deeply affected its cultural fabric, which perhaps explains why the set of changes is often referred to as the 'Big Bang'. Interestingly, the changes all occurred around 1995, the 100th anniversary of the creation of Rugby League as an independent sport.

The role of the chairman

As much as Rugby League identifies itself with its working-class heritage, this applies to the players much more than to those who run the clubs. Throughout Rugby League's history, most clubs have been run by local businessmen in their spare time. Until *Framing the Future* was implemented, few of the nearly thirty clubs had formed private liability companies; most were being run as associations. Local people sat on the Boards of Directors and played their part in the Northern activity of running a Rugby League club, The Chairman was traditionally the one who took the final financial decisions, and, importantly, was the person who negotiated player transfer market transactions.[2]

My fieldwork, from 2001 to 2003, focused on the economic anthropology of the player transfer market, which included learning to understand the role of the chairman. Interviews with them were normally held in their offices, which set things in a professional, business-like context. Those from wealthier clubs tended to have an aura of secure, measured calm, while others seemed increasingly unsettled the lower they (or their clubs) were down the ranks. At the beginning of each interview, I would review my research objectives, and then begin asking my questions. This was when I was normally interrupted and the tone of the meeting became more intense. My identity was 'unpicked': I was asked to go over the points of who I was, where I came from, who I knew within the community and the basic nature of my research. Sidney Mintz described this process in the ethnographic interview as mutual interrogation (1996: 301). Only once this was over would the interview continue.

This introductory sequence had become so routine that, when looked at objectively, it became apparent how vital it was for facilitating conversation. The chairmen wanted to know my cultural background. They needed to know how I knew about Rugby League. They wanted to know my main research questions. They wanted to know to whom I had already spoken. They wanted a sense of why I had chosen to talk to them. I discovered while looking at the transcripts that I had begun to volunteer all this information myself at the beginning of the meeting as a social convention.

To understand the role of chairman, it is important to understand why they were critiquing my role as researcher. Being from Canada automatically defines me as an outsider to the Rugby League community. Discovering how I had come to know about Rugby League was a way of discovering how I had entered into the community, which the chairmen perceive as bounded, closed and relatively unnoticed by the wider world. Being open about my research questions gave them an idea of why I had entered their world (although I had always included the questions in my pre-interview contact emails and letters). Learning who I had talked to previously gave them an idea of what I knew (although I had to be a bit circumspect in my responses to protect interviewees' privacy). They each know the others' biases and opinions, and, therefore, if I had spoken to Chairman A it was assumed that I would have thereby been educated in that person's beliefs and practices as well as having first-hand knowledge of his or her character. Rather than being considered as a complete unknowing novice to Rugby League culture, I was viewed as being layered with knowledge, and it was important to each chairman to know whom I had spoken to and, therefore, what I knew. Lastly, I had to answer why I was now talking to this interviewee, which had curious consequences. My answers were typically along the lines of desiring to learn of their experiences and their insights into the transfer system's inner workings. This was true, of course, but it had an interesting result: they switched, visibly, from their official, public chairman persona to their more private selves. They would then begin to talk openly, express and release thoughts and opinions they seemed to feel no one had previously wanted to listen to. It was a bit like embarking on a philosophical journey with them. This was about filtering: before they knew what to include or exclude from what they told me, they needed to categorise me. As each interview progressed, it was as if they themselves were exploring their ideas with me as a neutral person. These were punctuated with educational moments, along the lines of, 'Okay, Margaret, I am now going to give you a lesson about what transfers are about.' Yet, much of what they talked about was far more personal than I would ever have expected.

The challenge of (financial) survival

The role of chairman is somewhat elusive. People perceive chairmen as figures of seniority and authority. They take on a public persona, particularly in the media. What one reads in the media about a particular chairman is not necessarily an accurate reflection of his real character, nor of his personal methods of doing business. Chairmen describe distinct boundaries between their public and private identities, as well as between their emotional and rational business choices when faced with the responsibility for the continued survival of their clubs. Survival, first and foremost, means balancing the finances. It features at the top of the list of chairmen's concerns. Financial survival requires very finely tuned financial management, doing everything possible to bring fans through the turnstiles, and getting the most sponsorship possible for the club. Ultimately, each of these must be done in order to ensure that the books balance and salaries can be paid out, as described by these chairmen:

> ... as things got more commercial and competitive financially a lot of that's gone [helping out the other teams] and that's very sad. I think clubs should realise that there's no good being so successful that you put most of the other clubs out of business 'cos you can't keep playing two or three, four teams all the time. You need a healthy Rugby League ... and if the clubs at the top don't do what they can to help the clubs scraping [by] then we'll lose them ... it does mean taking a wider view than being purely selfish.

> Well, some clubs were spending over 100% of turnover [on salaries].

> ... at the end of the day they've got to find a way to balance their debts, um, and it's not rocket science ... you've got to cut your overheads, cut your outgoings and increase your incomings.

These themes have existed throughout Rugby League's history, as proven by the scrapbook clippings and in general Rugby League lore. Still, not every club can manage to balance the books and stay in business. During the 1990–2002 period, a handful of clubs came and went or were resurrected by banks and benefactors, all as the result of financial problems. However, as the first quote indicates, financial survival is not only club-focused: there is a general understanding that the health of each club contributes to the health of Rugby League in general. Thus the local is situated as part of a larger whole.

During my research, I discovered that discussions with chairmen on transfers illuminated the importance of how they identify themselves within the community, the club, and the sport on local and broader levels. They revealed conflict and competition between chairmen, conflict within themselves, and conflict in their construction of the player, as person and as object. The transfer market from the chairman's perspective is an arena for social interaction with his counterparts, a means to enact power hierarchies. As such, transfers can be a sensitive topic because they often involve very personal contests of power between the chairmen conducting the negotiations.

Today, the financial negotiation of a player transfer still transpires through interaction between chairmen. These are the buyers and sellers in the transfer market, no one else. They set prices and make offers for players. Communication takes place over phone lines, in letters and in faxes, and culminates in the signing of forms and contracts. The market has no fixed location. The final sale or purchase is decided on the basis of their interactions, and this role has been well defined since Rugby League's inception. They are involved in a daily process of developing what MacClancy described as 'an embodied practice in which meanings are generated, and whose representation and interpretation are open to negotiation and contest' (1996: 4). He used that description for sporting activity on the pitch, but it suits the organisational aspects equally well: engaging in transfer market exchange means engaging in the generation of meaning, representations and interpretations which may be culturally understood but which are also potentially contentious. How chairmen communicate with each other and enact their power hierarchies through transfer negotiations are essential facets of the continuation of this social practice. Additionally, how they make these financial decisions is deeply rooted in how they identify with their role at the club, versus their role outside it.

Transfers, however, are not chairmen's sole activity. They also have responsibilities within their club to ensure its general success, both on and off the pitch. The exercise of this authority role, although internal to the club in nature, is also competitive when compared to other clubs. The practices they condone and conduct within their administration – for example, in contract negotiations with players or accounting within salary cap regulations – are considered by themselves and those within the community to be reflections of their off-pitch success or failure. The connections between internal, boundary-defining practices, inter-club competition, and how the role of chairman is defined are common, traditional features across this sport with which everyone is familiar.

The Bosman ruling

The Bosman ruling, referred to earlier, changed all European transfer systems dramatically. Chairmen argue that the income derived from selling players in the old transfer system was used to sustain a redistributive cycle of funds and has no potential replacement. The stresses of having to restructure their financial practices accordingly have affected some of them quite deeply. Since a Rugby League player can conceivably play professionally up to the age of forty (Jeff Grayshon is one example), and begin a career at eighteen, the post-Bosman limitations mean that the number of years in which a club can make money by selling a player in the transfer market has been significantly curtailed. However, despite erroneous reports (often from chairmen themselves) that the transfer market in Rugby League is dead, these negotiations and contests of value between chairmen remain a common, competitive form of social interaction.

Chairmen's reactions to the Bosman ruling are thoughtful and reticent, as if it were something they had expected. Some even went so far as to say they had predicted it. The contents of Bosman itself are not mentioned, but the story of Jean-Marc Bosman, the mythologised 'one man against the establishment,' is spoken of sympathetically. They do not speak of him or his actions in critical terms. That he was in the right is quietly acknowledged. They talk about their surprise that it took so many years for the system to be challenged in the first place. To them, the effect of the ruling extending as far as Rugby League is just another major challenge and change brought about during the 1990s, part of the package of changes and seemingly no more or less severe than the rest of the Big Bang elements.

However, the changes brought about as a result of the Bosman ruling in fact deeply affected how the chairmen go about their club business. They openly tell of how it has changed the way they make and spend money, and that they have had to adopt new methods in response. It has also changed the way they relate to their players, although they describe this aspect of change indirectly, not as an overt reality. Being an employer instead of a somewhat omnipotent controller is, for some of them, a major social role change, away from the traditional roles of master and servant. Still, the changes are viewed as just part of this new, post-Big Bang reality in Rugby League. Comments are typically those of defeat, along the lines of, 'Oh well, it was good while it lasted', coupled with a sigh and a shoulder shrug, indicating that these challenges are making their roles more complex than ever. They are quick, though, to then place the changes in the context of the Big Bang, considering them all as a whole. The chairmen are change-weary, but also change-ready (as opposed to change-averse) since major change is an anticipated, traditional part of running a Rugby League club. Adaptability is also seen to increase the survival chances of one's club. It is perhaps due to this resilience that they openly discuss their expectation that the whole transfer market is going to be eradicated and that this could happen any time now. Some even believe that it is already over. When (or if) it does actually end, they are prepared to make changes in order to survive.

Bargaining

The practice of bargaining is a key aspect of transfers. The process was most often likened to the property market, and more than once to the art market. This equating of processes was intended to give me an example that I would relate to and thereby understand their activities. After more clarification, it became clear that the bargaining process is a critical social aspect of the transfer market. Through this process, chairmen shape their roles in the transfer market hierarchy (cf. Bourdieu et al 1992, Nader 1997, Gledhill 2000). Setting a price too high looks greedy or needy. Setting the price too low signifies they want a quick sale or that they are trying to get rid of a bad player whilst making a bit of money in the process. The price-setting process adds a social dimension upon which hierarchies of power and competition are built.

The opposite side of pricing a player is that there has to be an offering price. There is a general rule of thumb between chairmen that the halfway point between asking price and offer will end up being the sale price. By making an offer, a chairman signals how much money his club has, how much they would like to spend, how much they want to give away, or a combination of the above. It can also be a way of insulting another club, by offering something very low. The bargaining process is a game, adding to the multi-layered nature of Rugby League competition. John Davis's description is apt:

Exchanges are important to us as individuals. They are the way we acquire goods and services; they are expected of us, and we gain reputation for doing the right kinds well and in the right proportion. And they are exciting – it is often fun, amusing, to exchange: people get a buzz from exchange. (1996: 215)

Besides the buzz, the question that remains, though, is why they persist with this practice. One answer lies in the fact that their contextualisation of players, as well as their handling of financial transactions, forms part of an organisational culture which they share across Rugby League. The fundamental practices are common to each of them, engendering a shared understanding of each other's role within their clubs. The chairmen are united in the ritual of having to administer contracts within the RFL By-laws, English law, and the EU legal and regulatory environment, to bring in fans, to manage their facilities, and to promote the game itself. These practices (with the exception of the EU regulations) began in the 1800s. What has changed within the last twenty years is the nature of player movement between clubs, which is experiencing a shift from club control (and ownership) to increased player freedom and self-ownership. The result of this has been major change in the culture of club administration.

Doing things properly

Each chairman separates his club's business practices from those of other clubs. This usually takes the form of a differentiating statement such as, 'I don't know what they do at other clubs, but here we do [XYZ].' On the one hand, this is about marking the club's boundaries of knowledge and practice, and, on the other, it is about the community and how it measures acceptable practices. Doing things 'correctly' serves to mark the boundaries, the differences between the clubs, while also denoting that they are all part of the same larger community.

For example, Chairman A asked how I had got along with Chairman B. I said that he had seemed concerned that I was asking questions about transfers. The curious chairman's reply was that if you '[have] principles, do things honestly, then you don't mind if people write about the things you do'. Although this is a generally acceptable statement of ethics and morality, the subtext to this statement is that he believes that Chairman B is not quite as principled as he ought to be. It was not the first time I had heard this point being made by one chairman about another; not only is the good/bad argument presented in club-to-club terms, it is also a reflection on the character of the other club's chairman. The two are intrinsically linked by the intense competition between them. Each is the 'leader' of his (or her) club in terms of power and authority. Transfer market transactions in particular give them the opportunity to challenge these attributes in others.

Framing the Future enters the picture alongside mentions of doing things properly. In many organisations, the aim of best practice documents is for them to be followed precisely, particularly when they come with sanctions for not being obeyed. Compliance with *Framing the Future* is, however, patchy. Because each club identifies with its own traditional business practices, *Framing the Future* threatens boundaries by requiring clubs to be alike in many respects. It also gives the RFL rights to monitor their compliance, and thus their internal practices. With this comes the threat of chairmen being publicly penalised for doing things badly, and, when each club considers their actions correct, this is humiliating.

None of the exact contraventions is stated openly by the chairmen. What is evident is that *Framing the Future* is an uncomfortable topic for those with moderate compliance, and a non-issue for those with relatively complete compliance. This latter group is quick to claim that they made the requisite changes prior to being told to do so. The former group is openly critical about the programme and the unfair and unrealistic expectations it contains. That this best practices document was supposedly created to improve and/or update business practices to a marketable professional standard is never mentioned, nor acknowledged. That it is something to be resented on principle is representative of the hierarchies of power and control within the community.

Another aspect of this is that when a club does encounter major financial problems, it is incredibly public about them. Clubs pass in and out of financial administration, as they have done throughout Rugby League's history, despite measures being put into place to protect against financial failures, such as a salary cap on total salary expenditures. It is a badge of pride not to have gone through 'administration' (a precursor to bankruptcy), but it is also a badge of pride to have been there and returned. Some of the chairmen who belong in the former category get angry when they speak of clubs who have received handouts from the RFL to keep themselves afloat. There is an element of measuring fairness: clubs who receive handouts are seen as unfairly supported by clubs who do not receive the extra support. No one disagrees that it is a struggle to run a Rugby League club, but those who have done so without handouts truly resent the system that supports those who haven't been responsible for their own actions.

Super League: the constant battle

The onset of Super League, of course, was a major change to the way Rugby League conducted itself. Primarily, it heightened existing divisions between clubs. The dividing process into Super League and non-Super League clubs was itself fraught with interpersonal conflict. There is a longstanding belief that the initial twelve Super League clubs were personal favourites of those in charge of the process. Those in charge have become vilified in the stories told by non-Super League club chairmen today. The story they tell of Super League's inception describes feeling defeated, shut out, left out of the in-crowd, tinged with sadness and a bit of despair that everything turned out so unfairly.

There also seems to be a division between the past and the present. Super League is modern, business-oriented and fully professional. The atmosphere at lower division clubs, particularly at the lowest level, is similar to traditional sports clubs, and not that different from some of the amateur clubs. Lower division clubs exist in a local space, and are very local in outlook, although they are sometimes depicted as small-town and small-minded. This sentiment is typical of some Super League chairmen, who feel that the lower division clubs bring down their professionalised image and should revert to the amateur game. Chairmen of lower division clubs expressed the most suspicion of administration practices at the top levels. This evokes an interesting mix of themes: superiority/inferiority, corruption/purity and professional/amateur.

From a detached economic sense, the hierarchies off the pitch make the on-pitch competition interesting. Leagues seek competitive equilibrium but were they ever to reach it with all teams being equal on the pitch, they would lose the fundamental 'unknown outcome' factor which makes games interesting to observe. Except perhaps for the very top Super League clubs, the unknown outcome factor is ever present. Add to this the competitive factor of buying and selling players – or team components, as one might think of them – and the unknown outcome factor takes on a new dimension. Thus, there are very successful clubs and there are underdogs. There is a wide range of sentiment between chairmen at the top and those at the bottom, which is expressed either in critical, derogatory terms (top to bottom) or in bitter yet admiring terms (bottom to top). For example, lower-level chairmen refer to the *big clubs* and thereby define themselves as small. Small to them means less important, less wealthy, less likely to succeed.

One Super League club chairman described the situation thus:

> In the old days the smaller clubs … the smaller clubs in the lower division who were lucky enough to sign a brilliant schoolboy for 500 quid and then develop him into a much sought-after athlete, they were able to sell players for 50, 60 thousand pounds and that sustained them both in a trading capacity and in a cash flow capacity.

The bigger clubs also define the lower division clubs as small. I asked what the small clubs will do now the transfer market is limited and one reply was, 'They'll have to play at a lower level [move to the amateur ranks]. They'll have to. They'll have to amend their budgets, lower their ambitions.'

This is in contrast to the views of a lower division club chairman:

> It's amazing how we exist really … [our club] would like to get into Super League but I can't, I mean – a lot of people would probably hang, draw, and quarter me if they heard me saying this – I can't see [our club] ever being able to do that because all their sources of income really … all we get now is what we get through the gates and the gates aren't very good [at this level] … when we were playing the Wigans and the Leeds of this world we could have 8 and 10 thousand in gates. Of course we don't play them anymore.

These statements, when written on the page, cannot do justice to the intonation and body language of their speakers. The tone of loss and nostalgia is unmistakable. The Super League chairman was emphatic and forceful, whereas the lower division chairman was slouched and visibly saddened. The former is the victor and the latter the defeated. It was striking, as an observer coming from outside the community, to see how deeply the hierarchy is felt.

However, the focus of many lower division chairmen remains to get into Super League. This lends a certain excitement and attraction to following their clubs' competition standings. As much as they may criticise the Super League 'clique', they long to be part of it. This longing has financial roots in the panacea of Super League payouts and in the desire for personal accolades. Chairmen often conflate club success and personal success.

Another curious aspect is that most chairmen believe that the Super League clubs are wealthier than lower division clubs. Solely on the basis of annual turnover and as far as company reports are available, this is true, although it doesn't necessarily match up with the final placings at the end of the season within the divisions. What is interesting is that the story of Super League clubs being wealthiest is told and retold everywhere as fact, although none of the chairmen had actually consulted Companies House records to verify what is effectively rumour. So, fuelled by this rumour that Super League clubs are immensely wealthy, the resentment of having been cut off from Super League gets compounded with elements of jealousy and envy. Yet, because of the competitive nature of the chairman's role, none of them would think to consult with others to share experiences or management techniques. To do that borders on the unthinkable.

Contracts and salary caps – conceptual conflation

Chairmen are responsible for their club's contractual agreements with players and also for upholding salary cap regulations at their club. It is the responsibility of club chairmen to determine how much money they have to 'play' with in the player market. They have to balance the money spent on transfers and the money to be spent on players' salaries against the expected prize money and income from gate receipts. They might also include the potential income from the sale of other players in their calculations. However, it is a traditional tale in English Rugby League that club finances are run badly and that the inability of a chairman to handle the financial specifics of transfers and salaries can, in a worst case scenario, lead to bankruptcy. All too often, they do in fact take financial risks which lead to financial administration, if not bankruptcy. This is a very delicate balance and is high on their list of concerns. Players on expensive contracts are seen as financial burdens. To some chairmen, the financial burden of the contract is more serious to club welfare than how good the player is on the pitch.

Chairmen considered the salary cap almost as a punishment for the bad policies at other clubs. Because others decided to spend 120 per cent of turnover on contracted salaries (it is rumoured), they all have to suffer. No one will admit to having been guilty of overspending themselves, nor will they name names of the guilty chairmen. The point they present is that others did this, not them. Still, they all agree that something had to be done to control the problem of overspending leading to CVAs.[3]

When asked about the fairness of a turnover percentage salary cap versus a flat rate salary cap, their responses are mixed, again, along the lines of Super League versus the lower divisions. The percentage is favoured by the wealthier clubs, because it means they have the most money to offer. However, the small, poorer clubs struggle with either system; a percentage of their turnover is tiny compared to the largest clubs, and the flat rate is often much higher than they can reasonably afford. In both cases, the poorer clubs are disadvantaged.

So why offer unaffordable contracts in the first place? Hope. Hope that by paying a good salary one gets a good player who will increase the success of the club and either win them more money or bring in more sponsorship money. Players will sign the contracts believing the club's finances are in place; after all, this is a contract with conditions to be fulfilled by both parties. However, players are also aware that clubs which cannot afford to maintain their side of the contractual bargain will release them in one form or another. It is an awkward cycle in the eyes of the law, but it is an understood facet of employment in Rugby League, albeit mostly in the lower levels. What it signifies, however, is the perspective, common to each chairman, that although finances and players are inextricably linked, finances are always going to be more important.

> ... I mean, well, I think there's two sides to it: the players' point of view – they tend to want to develop their careers and they often feel the need to move on like the rest of us in any sort of job – and, from the club's point of view, the structure of the teams changes, they, uh, don't achieve their aspirations therefore they need to make changes ...

> ... there were some people who seemed to go on ego trips I guess, I mean I think they believed that if they actually bought in good players, won matches, crowds would flock in and that the club would be successful and they'd get into Super League but financially it didn't stack up. Now whether some of them didn't do their sums properly or whether they thought it would all come good when they got into Super League and they didn't get in Super League and it all went wrong ... one of the problems we had in the early days [at this club] because we were trying to run things on a commercial basis and we weren't prepared to spend money on players that we couldn't afford and therefore the results were suffering um as a consequence of that because we were playing against other clubs who outbid us for players that we wouldn't pay what was necessary, and when I say outbid I mean in terms of the player's contract ...

The role of emotions

The common depiction of chairmen, particularly those involved in the initial Super League, is as cold, inconsiderate, money-loving, controlling people. Yet this is not the true picture, and it is certainly not how they see themselves. This is critical for understanding why and how the transfer market works. The main themes discussed above defined the bounds of how chairmen perceive their club versus others, and also how they locate their club within the bounds of the Rugby League community. Their concerns each have a competitive element. Although their competitive environment has undergone considerable, externally driven change in the past ten years, most of the themes are traditional in the sense that they are not significantly different from those of club directors from the past century. Besides the obvious financial element, there is a very personal undertone to their comments; chairmen take the results of their efforts and the reactions of others to heart. There is a sensitivity about them which is expressed in the way they present their concerns. Perhaps Rugby League is not the environment in which one would expect to find it, but it is a key aspect of the chairman's game.

A very important lesson learned from fieldwork lies in the significance chairmen place on their definitions of emotional decision making versus rational business decision making. The two are not often the same in Rugby League. Despite its being seen as a game for tough guys, it has an emotional side. This does not mean to say that the chairmen lack masculine forcefulness; in fact, what is meant is that they consciously make business decisions which they identify as 'emotional' – for example, the taking of financial risks in order to avoid a winding-up order on a club that has been in existence since the 1890s.

Early on in my research, I discovered the work of economists who had been making an attempt to explain player trading between clubs in North America (Neale 1964; Bougheas and Downward 2000; Barros, Ibrahimo and Szymanski 2002). The style of their discussion is based in neoclassical ('modern') economics: a firm with scarce resources seeks to maximise revenues (and hopefully profits) by making rational spending choices in markets where the price for a good or a service is determined as a function of supply and demand. When there is more than one item on offer in the market, individuals are faced with making choices as to the amount of each item they can purchase, limited by the price of the item and the 'scarcity' of their purchasing resources (which typically means money). The key concepts of economics as applied here is that scarce resources are to be maximised and that there are rational decision-making processes regulating this maximisation. Economic models are based in the belief that one can create an algebraic formula which represents the logic of a market, and that one can model this equation through graphs, typically with intersecting lines for supply and demand. The point of intersection is often coincident with an equilibrium, the point which economists and management gurus believe describes, in mathematical terms, the choices most rational market actors will make.

What Rugby League chairmen categorise as emotional decisions are those which defy the economic and business 'logic' of the market. Faced with an unsuccessful club on the pitch, most chairmen will traditionally decide to 'do what it takes' to turn the club around, regardless of long-term effects on the club's financial situation. Closing the books of an unsuccessful club is practically unthinkable; one must keep it going no matter what. The maximisation of revenues (and the balancing of the budget) is set aside in lieu of the preservation of tradition. Therein lies the role of 'emotions' as they describe them.

I presented a paper on the role of emotions to the British Society of Sports History conference in 2003, with some hesitation. The audience was mostly middle-aged British male academics, with vast knowledge of the history of sport in Britain. I was concerned about what their reaction would be to a discussion of emotions in the Rugby League boardroom. I discovered that this was in fact something they all felt or knew existed, but had never discussed in an open scholarly forum. The emotional/rational distinction is so commonplace as to be taken as a given, beneath the radar of their academic attention. I had expected a taboo on the topic but there was none; this is social fact. Whereas in an economic or management setting this might have been viewed as a weakness which the audience would have found discomfiting, here, amongst scholars of British sport, it was taken as an accepted given. As it was, the fact that I am a foreigner and also female meant that I was able to express this social fact with a level of objectivity and, to some extent, impunity.

Therefore, to an outsider, it is somewhat surprising that the distinction is made so openly by Rugby League chairmen. Outside the bounds of the club, in their other professional lives,[4] they take pride in the fact that they make sensible, rational, successful business decisions. Within the bounds of their role as Rugby League chairmen, they more often than not make what they call emotional business decisions. This wording is theirs, not mine. I did initiate discussions on the distinction, usually posed as a question about other clubs' business practices: there are pervasive rumours that directors take wild gambles with money at their clubs that they would never dream of doing in their 'other' businesses. The degree of awareness of this emotional decision making was remarkable:

Well, people don't make hard-nosed business decisions in sport, at least not in Rugby League …

… that wasn't a business decision but a decision from the heart.

[another chairman] loves the history of the sport and the spirit of the game but you have to do hard-nosed business at the [same] time. You have to blend both. You need the heart of a fan and the head of a manager.

… there've been lots of barmy decisions like that done by businessmen who, if it was their own business, they wouldn't do it.

... sports clubs don't have a good history of decision-making. Sports clubs in the U.K. were traditionally run by very well-meaning people who had specific interests in or hobby which is sport and they have made money in other industries and they are fulfilling their passion by developing, investing and developing a sports club. Therefore, they are fans of the club and their decision-making is very different from business. They ... made decisions in the evenings and at weekends that they wouldn't have made 9 to 5, Monday to Friday. Now it's very different. Sport is run by a better tier of professionals'.

Each of these statements was made by a different chairman. In each of these examples the context was buying and selling activities on the player transfer market. One former insider, commenting on chairmen's financial decisions, said that:

All they see is the player out on the field on a Sunday afternoon. Is he performing? Yes. Okay, he's a good investment. If he's not performing, you get rid of him and play someone else. They don't, they have no understanding of what it is, what it takes to make that player, and what his needs are on an ongoing continuous basis. As far as they're concerned he represents their team, their club, their standing within the community and he's got to deliver on their behalf. If he can't deliver they're not particularly interested in why, they just want somebody who can.

In this description, we see the player-as-object clearly presented. The chairman's emotional decision making is described as completely disconnected from the player as a whole person. The chairman's identity is derived from the performance of 'his' players on the pitch. His feelings and his actions on those feelings are justified because he is acting as a Rugby League club chairman. That is what he is expected and allowed to do. They recognise the actions in each other, thereby reinforcing their own behaviour. Some may lean towards more actions based on emotion (associated with old times and traditional ways) whilst others may take a more hard-nosed approach (associated with the future and professionalism), but they all openly accept that both approaches exist and that they themselves have done both. Ultimately, though, their discussions on transfers contextualise the player as an object. Regardless of 'emotions', their construction of players in a transfer market is as objects of possession and trade, and not as persons.

Risks, rationality and rewards

The role of emotions and emotional decision making separates club chairmen's Rugby League activities from their other business activities. Within their Rugby League role, they describe emotions ranging from love for and pride in their club and the game, to anger, disappointment and belligerence when involved in transfer practices. The boundaries chairmen describe when they speak of emotional versus rational decision making signify both their personal identity as 'chairman' and also the broader identification of Rugby League business practices as being somehow different from those of other businesses. These practices and their 'otherness' are known and understood within the Rugby League community, which serves an identifying process. In addition to the sport's Northern working-class identity, the practices of Rugby League chairmen highlight the ways in which people connect with its 'corporate' identity through the logic of emotion.

Kahane and Reitter (2002) present an interesting discussion on what they call 'narraction' (narrative + action), or the ways stories are told within corporations which engender shared corporate identity. In anthropological terms, they are describing the very essence of enculturation and cultural transmission through narrative. What they also point out is that corporate narratives have shades of reality and fiction designed to depict an ideal corporate identity: 'Identity relies on the effective creation of collective narraction'. (2002: 127). Everyone within the corporate culture lives and believes in the same story, which has strategic benefits. Through the Rugby League chairmen, we are able to see the bounded nature of their different spheres of (corporate) identity as they cross from inside to outside practices. Their narratives, particularly within the research interview context, were 'narractions' intended to engender understanding of their personal identity as 'chairman', the corporate identity of their particular club, and the general cultural identity of Rugby League, both on and off the pitch.

This boundary between internal, traditional practice and external expectations of practice standards is not unique to English Rugby League by any means. The wider application of (or expectation of the existence of) modern, cutting-edge managerial practice is increasingly prevalent in many previously 'othered' sectors, with higher education being one example. These are the sectors in which balancing the books and exhibiting a high level of financial acumen are relatively recent measurements of their success. As outsiders, we may be surprised (or not) to find the absence or presence of common business 'best practices' in these organisations. However, pressures to change and update occasionally create conflict when they challenge boundaries, particularly when they lack sensitivity to the connections between traditional practices and traditional organisational culture. When the prescribed changes are attached to a metric which determines future funding, this can be especially problematic. What this paper seeks to expound is that traditional, in this case 'emotional', practices and up-to-date ones may not be congruent. The whole set of existing practices needs to be understood as part of the organisational culture in which they are practised. Without a thorough analysis of the internal culture, the effective implementation of change and appropriate assessment of change is problematic, both for those who assign the 'best practices' and for those who are expected to adhere to them.

That said, the dichotomy of emotional versus rational decisions this paper discusses also remains underpinned by a deeper dilemma about the 'othered' nature of professional sport. Dyck reasons that:

> The capacity of sport to absorb the attention of players and fans so utterly and intensively, the carnal pleasures of play that may visibly be shared by spectators as well

as athletes, the excitement that is formulaically stoked up by the unscripted outcomes of games and athletic contests, the degree to which fate and chance may enter into distinguishing winners from losers, the ostensibly irrational faith and loyalty that some fans invest in particular teams and athletes – these and other properties of sport have been implicitly interpreted as legitimating the systematic segregation of sport from central social, cultural and political concerns. (2000: 31)

People identify professional sport as somehow 'other'. For instance, player transfer markets, of which Rugby League's is a revealing example, are undeniably different from what one might define as 'normal' employee–employer relations. The answer as to why this difference exists lies in the fact that professional sports have been 'othered' because many people still relate 'sport' to play and games and not to business. Chairmen themselves often make these category shifts. They define the categories and then contradict themselves or cross their own categorical boundaries. This is not an individual practice; they share the same understandings of the categories, and they make the same categorical shifts. It begins with their identification with the chairman role versus their outside world businessman role. For example, their position assigns them with power and control over transfer market exchanges. The fact of the matter, which the Bosman case tried to emphasise, is that these are businesses and their players are employees.

The 'othering' of sport, however, gave, and in some cases still gives, legitimacy to player exchange and control mechanisms, particularly in the eyes of the law. This legitimacy allows for capitalistic marketplace gains to be made from the exchange of players, gains upon which the financial health of many clubs relies, and over which many chairmen seek to maintain control, despite making statements that the market no longer exists. Chairmen seem to be in conflict between the role of employer to players, and the role of buyer and seller of players. The latter conflict is emotionally challenging. Transferring a player exercises sociabilities which give chairmen a buzz. Post-Bosman, they have had to refocus on their now officially, legally defined role as employer, which bears an increased financial burden and also an awkward new social role. Chairmen who present the exchange of players as a good thing try to reconcile this conflict, yet by doing so they effectively outline the core paradox of the category of professional sport being 'other' to the category of business.

Shifting this around slightly, if people identify with Rugby League business as 'emotional' as opposed to rational, does it mean that these business practices are irrational? The answer lies in the fact that professional sport is by its very nature characterised by a different scale of risks than other businesses. Brunsson's discussion on irrational organisations (2000) discusses the subjective nature of uncertainty and risk as leading to what outsiders to an organisation could interpret as irrational practices. Decision rationality can be divided into rationalistic and impressionistic modes, neither of which is, in fact, irrational. What his discussion highlights is that 'rational' decision making is very much a matter of perspective. The decisions chairmen make fit within the particular organisational culture of their club locally and of Rugby League more broadly. The emotional/rational distinction implies a continual, active awareness and comparison between Rugby League and non-Rugby League business practices. Returning to the idea of othering, this responds to a debate as to whether sport should be categorised as business. Fundamentally, the debate is fuelled by the fact that people identify so differently with the business practices of sport from how they do with most other business practices. Many perceive this difference in corporate identity creation, or narration, as implying a separate category of activity, when, in fact, it is actually a case study from which much can be learned.

The engendering of people's identification with and through sport, particularly people in the North of England and their relationship to Rugby League, is a powerful example of 'narraction' at work. It enables us to interpret chairmen's statements such as, 'that wasn't a business decision but a decision from the heart'. Quite simply, the identification of these very decisions as being from the heart is what defines the corporate identity at the heart of the business of Rugby League.

Notes

1. Cf. Case C-415/93 Union Royale Belge de Sociétés de Football v. Jean-Marc Bosman [1995] ECR I-4921; Blanpain and Inston (1996).
2. Because the word 'chairman' is typically used to describe this role, it will be the term used here to represent the person in charge of running the club. Rugby League has had only one chairwoman in its history. The term chairperson, although gender neutral, is not appropriately applied here since the generic term used within this community is *chairman*.
3. A Company Voluntary Arrangement ('CVA') enables an insolvent company to make an agreement with its creditors to delay or renegotiate the payment of its outstanding debts.
4. Since most have their own successful businesses or are employed at senior levels 'outside' the game.

Bibliography

Barros, C.P., M. Ibrahimo, and S. Szymanski (eds). 2002. *Transatlantic Sport: The Comparative Economics of North American and European Sports*. Cheltenham, U.K. and Northampton, MA, USA: Edward Elgar.

Blanpain, R. and R. Inston. 1996. *The Bosman Case: The End of the Transfer System?* London: Peeters, Sweet and Maxwell.

Bougheas, S and P. Downward. 2000. *The Economics of Professional Sports Leagues: A Bargaining Approach*. Nottingham: University of Nottingham.

Bourdieu, P., et al. 1992. *Language and Symbolic Power*. Oxford: Polity Press.

Brunsson, N. 2000. *The Irrational Organisation: Irrationality as a Basis for Organisational Action and Change* (2nd edn). Bergen, Norway: Fagbokforlaget.

Collins, T. 1998. *Rugby's Great Split: Class, Culture and the Origins of Rugby League Football*. London: Frank Cass.

Davis, J. 1996. 'An Anthropologist's View of Exchange'. *Social Anthropology*, 4 (3): 213–26.

Dyck, N. 2000. *Games, Sports and Cultures*. Oxford: Berg.

Gledhill, J. 2000. *Power and Its Disguises: Anthropological Perspectives on Politics*. London: Pluto.

Kahane, B. and R. Reitter. 2002. 'Narrative Identity: Navigating between "Reality" and "Fiction"', in B. Moingeon and G. Soenen (eds.), *Corporate and Organisational Identities: Integrating Strategies, Marketing, Communication and Organisational Perspectives*. London: Routledge, pp. 115–29.

MacClancy, J. 1996. 'Sport, Identity and Ethnicity', in *Sport, Identity and Ethnicity*, J. MacClancy (ed.). Oxford: Berg, pp. 1–20.

Mintz, S. 1996. 'The Anthropological Interview and the Life History', in D.K. Dunaway and W. K. Baum (eds.), *Oral History: An Interdisciplinary Anthology*. Walnut Creek, California: Altamira, pp. 298–305.

Moorhouse, G. 1996. *A People's Game: The Centenary History of Rugby League Football, 1895–1995*. London: Hodder and Stoughton.

Nader, L. 1997. 'Controlling Processes: Tracing the Dynamic Components of Power', *Current Anthropology* 38 (5): 711–38.

Neale, W. 1964. 'The Peculiar Economics of Professional Sport', *Quarterly Journal of Economics* 78 (1): 1–14.

Russell, D. 2004. *Looking North: Northern England and the National Imagination*. Manchester: Manchester University Press.

2

WHEN WORLDS COLLIDE: BRITISH BUREAUCRACY MEETS GERMAN BUREAUCRACY IN THE GLOBAL FINANCESCAPE

Fiona Moore

Introduction

In globalised environments such as financial multinational corporations, recent anthropological theory suggests that identity does not consist of, as earlier studies would have it, the maintenance of symbolic boundaries between groups. Rather, it is a process of selecting from repertoires of symbols to construct a flexible self-image which is changed and altered by actors to fit the social context. However, while this seemed normally to be the case in the London branch of a German bank which I studied, I observed that, when adjusting to a restructuring programme instigated by its Head Office in Frankfurt, the staff switched to a rigid, boundary-based, ethnicised model. An examination of the wider context, however, suggests that this inflexibility is less inconsistent with the normal uses of identity in global environments than it may at first seem.

This paper is intended to contribute both to the anthropological literature on the nature of identity and ethnicity (e.g. Banks 1996), particularly as it relates to transnational economic migration, and to the various calls to 'study-up' over the years (see Nash 1979), that is, to apply traditional anthropological methodologies to nontraditional settings: in this case, a European transnational business. Finally, it will add to the growing literature on the anthropology of business (see Chapman 1997), and on the viability of doing ethnographic fieldwork in organisational settings.

Methodology

This project is based on an ethnographic study which was carried out at a German multinational bank, which I will here call 'ZwoBank', between January and June 2000, with follow-up work done between July 2000 and January 2001, as part of an eighteen-month study involving fieldwork in the London and Frankfurt branches of this bank and others (the final results of which can be read in Moore 2005). The material on which this paper is based consists of, firstly, six months' worth of observation of and participation in the office environment, which involved coming in to the bank most working days and having access to a desk in a shared office, the canteen and other basic staff resources, and meeting rooms in which to conduct interviews. The location of the desk changed three times over the six-month period, allowing me to see different parts of the organisation in action.

Formal interviews were conducted on a periodic basis over the course of the six-month participant observation period and the six months following it, with sixteen individuals at the London branch. Of these, six were expatriate Germans, five were Germans living permanently in the U.K., two were English who had lived in Germany, and three were English with no German connection. The people interviewed were mainly junior and middle managers, with three members of top management and two nonmanagerial staff members also participating. In addition, formal interviews of this type were conducted at the bank's Head Office with six managers in the personnel department and one in a front office division; these were conducted during three trips to Frankfurt, in April, September and October of 2000, with follow-up work done via telephone and email. Each participant was interviewed between one and four times, with interviews lasting approximately an hour apiece. Although a standard questionnaire was used to start the interview, it was normally abandoned early on, with the interests of the interview subject being allowed to shape the proceedings. Bilingual interviewees were given the option of being interviewed in English or German; although most at the London branch chose English, and most at the Head Office chose German, no interview was conducted exclusively in one or the other language, as participants would occasionally drop into the other language for expressions that they felt unable to translate, or if they found giving an explanation in a language which was not their mother tongue too difficult.

These interviews were also complemented by informal interviews and conversations with about twenty other members of the branch's staff. These followed no set pattern, although I made certain to ask whether or not I could use the relevant part of the conversation in my study, and were usually conducted over lunch or after work. Informal interviews of this sort were held with all but four of the formal-interview participants; of the other people with whom I regularly had conversations of this sort, five were Germans living permanently in the U.K., six were non-Germans who had lived in Germany, and nine were non-German employees with no connection to Germany.

My position with regard to the bank was as an outside consultant to the London branch, brought in to advise, based on my interview results, on the impact of the above-mentioned matrix integration programme on Anglo-German relations in the branch. I was expected to submit a report at the end of the first six months detailing the issues in this area which had arisen from the matrix integration and suggesting solutions. Interviewees were thus aware that the results of their interviews might find their way – albeit anonymously – into the final report; I have tried to compensate for this by evaluating each interviewee's answers in the context of their political agenda with regard to the bank and the matrix integration programme, and thus to factor their individual biases into the report.

This project was, therefore, conducted using ethnographic research methods while the researcher acted as consultant on Anglo-German cultural issues to the bank in question. This approach was judged to provide a solid basis from which to examine the lived experience of culture in the London branch of a German financial corporation.

Think globally, act locally? Identity under globalisation

In this section, I shall consider the debates surrounding ethnicity and identity, and consider how they might be applied in globalised settings. In particular, I shall focus on Cohen's model of the 'symbolic boundary' (1985), and its strengths and weaknesses as a tool for examining social behaviour among transnational businesspeople.

Identity, most researchers seem to agree, is generally expressed through the use of symbols. Anthony Cohen (1985), following Sperber (1974), sums it up by proposing that symbols are used to express identity because they are capable of compressing complex ideas and stimulating powerful emotions; furthermore, although the meanings of these symbols do vary from individual to individual, key aspects of their interpretation are shared by all group members. This view has been adopted unproblematically by later writers such as Strecker (1988) and Hannerz (1992). However, the form which this symbolic expression takes has been open to more debate; while earlier researchers such as Cohen and Barth (1969) treat identity as a single object or, at best, a system of knowledge, which everyone in a given group 'has' and of which they only 'have' one, Banks (1996) argues that one cannot consider a single identity, such as ethnicity, without considering related identities such as 'race' and gender. It is not enough, that is to say, to consider someone's identity as, for instance, Pakistani or a fisherman without considering them also as a man or a Muslim. Jenkins, similarly, prefers to define social identity as an ongoing dialectic between 'our understanding of who we are and of who other people are, and ... other people's understanding of themselves and others' (1996: 5). We shall thus consider identity to be a continuous process of defining a group or individual through the selection of different symbols.

What form this process takes, however, is open to debate. The classic, and still most widely held, view of the operation of identity was outlined, if not initially at least most comprehensively, by Anthony Cohen. Cohen, in *The Symbolic Construction of Community* (1985), argues that identity consists of the construction and maintenance of a symbolic boundary between one group and other groups, which define themselves using different symbols, or, alternatively, through different interpretations of the same symbols; this boundary can be more or less permeable depending on the group and the circumstances, but is always present in some form. This can be seen in Cohen's studies of the Whalsay Islanders (1982a, 1892b; 1986), who define themselves in opposition to mainlanders, other islanders and visiting sojourners, using symbols relating to Whalsay's history, geographical position and traditional economic activities. Cohen's model of identity as boundary construction would thus seem to explain the ways in which groups define themselves in relation to others.

Although it is applicable to many groups, however, Cohen's theory runs into difficulties when one considers groups that are much more closely engaged with globalisation than were the Whalsay Islanders. The key issue here seems to be the problematic nature of boundaries under global conditions. Waters defines globalisation as 'a process in which the constraints of geography on social ... arrangements recede' (1995: 3), and the key traits of this process are generally agreed to be, firstly, advances in electronic communications and transportation acting to compress time and space (Schein 1998); secondly, the 'freeing' of capital, leading to a 24-hour global financial market in which the state plays a minimal role in regulation (Leyshon and Thrift 1997: 46–47), and finally, the rise of a 'flexible' workforce, for whom part-time and temporary jobs are more the norm than are long-term careers (Castells 2000). All of these forces thus act on concepts which are frequently employed as social boundary markers.

Additionally, globalisation is said to lead to the weakening of national boundaries in favour of 'transnational' groups, that is to say, groups with 'multiple ties ... linking people or institutions across the borders of nation states' (Vertovec 1999: 447). These differ from earlier groups of migrants in that these cross-border ties form a conduit along which people, goods and information are constantly flowing, and which enables simultaneous communication between localities (see also Portes 1998). As a result of this, Manuel Castells argues, social boundaries, and particularly national ones, are becoming less important than are decentralised social networks. While it seems to be generally agreed that globalisation is far from universal, it appears that, for such groups as Portes' Dominican migrants (1998) or Sklair's transnational managers (2001), its effects are to cause boundaries, if not to weaken, at least to take on a different form than that found in Cohen's account.

It may thus be that, for such groups, a boundary-focused model of identity is less useful than one focusing on multiple identities. Hannerz postulates that identity is not so much a wall or boundary as it is fluid and flexible. Hannerz suggests that different cultures nest within each other and yet form part of each other, as tile and matrix form more and less visible portions of the same mosaic, although Hannerz also notes that which elements are tile, and which are matrix, vary with the situation. Identity is similarly fluid: A Catholic German woman, for instance, may see herself and/or be seen as Catholic, German and female, or female, German and Catholic, or German, Catholic and female, depending on the context in which she finds herself; to further complicate things, she may view herself as German, Catholic and female, but be viewed as female, Catholic and German. Hannerz also suggests, although he does not develop it further (1983), that actors may select from a repertoire or 'toolkit' of symbols in order to present themselves to the best advantage in the given context, echoing Erving Goffman's theory that individuals tailor their self-presentation to fit the situation in which they find themselves (1961). Hannerz thus views identity as a complex, continuously shifting idea, involving an element of selection and self-presentation, and which, as such, crosses and questions rather than affirms boundaries, much as the globally engaged individuals who comprise his informants do.

However, it must be said that other social scientists have called the extent and scope of the boundary-effacing effects of globalisation into question, some even suggesting that these do not exist at all. McDowell, for instance, feels that the recessions of the 1990s have led to a renewed focus on social boundaries in the City of London, implying that the effects of globalisation can be easily reversed (1997). Hirst and Thompson (1996), similarly, argue that the rhetoric of globalisation employed by such writers as Kenichi Ohmae (1990) obscures the fact that social inequalities still exist, and thus hint that, behind the hype, the old boundaries are still rigid. While none of these writers discuss identity as such, the implication is clear that the flexibility of identity under globalisation is open to question.

While it seems undeniable, then, that social identity for transnational migrant groups is less like the traditional, boundary-focused model employed by anthropologists such as Anthony Cohen, and more like the mosaic, strategically inclined model proposed by Hannerz, it is debatable whether or not this is a permanent condition, or even whether or not it is all an illusion. Although globalisation is very much a reality for some groups, then – for instance the employees of financial multinational corporations – it is debatable whether or not this means that the boundary-focused model of identity no longer applies.

Corporate identity: the City, ZwoBank London and globalisation

In this section, I will describe the setting of the study, and consider how the identities of the employees of ZwoBank's London branch were expressed and negotiated in a globalised environment, in which concepts such as identity and ethnicity are inherently flexible.

The City of London (referred to by most of the people who work there simply as 'the City') is a financial district of approximately one square mile which forms the core of London, U.K., one of the three largest of what Sassen refers to as 'global cities' (1991). Global cities are, according to Sassen's definition, those which have as many ties to countries around the world as to their host countries, if not more so (ibid.). The financial and legal professionals who work in the City are inherently engaged with the process of globalisation. The nature of their work links them, directly or indirectly, with the 24-hour global financial market; most, if not all, employ the new communications and transportation technologies in their business and personal lives to such a degree that national borders become largely academic; and, as a group, they form an inherently flexible workforce. I was repeatedly told, and indeed observed for myself, that in the City it is detrimental to a person's career to stay in the same job for longer than ten years, and younger staff were expected to change jobs about once every twelve to twenty-four months. Several human resource specialists told me that the main advantage for a company to have a branch in the City (as opposed to, say, Frankfurt or Paris) was London's unusually large pool of relatively short-term jobs and well-educated jobseekers. The City's professionals thus show all the characteristics of a group engaged with globalisation.

Unsurprisingly, expressions of identity in the City environment tend more towards Hannerz's than Cohen's model. Throughout the City, people tend to define themselves in terms of more than one identity simultaneously, using such terms as 'European' or 'cosmopolitan', which allow them to incorporate multiple identities and place different aspects of these to the fore in different situations (see Moore 2004 for further details). Sklair (2001) speaks of top businessmen, such as Rupert Murdoch, changing passports to suit their business circumstances. The symbols used to define particular identities, also, were those that referred to multiple identities which varied in importance; the German CEOs with whom I talked over the course of the study spoke of emphasising the image of the 'efficient German' in advertising and client meetings in order to obtain business, and, at times when the mood in other countries was tending towards the anti-German, to use the same symbols of efficiency and diligence to refer to an individual corporate identity. For instance, a Wolff Olins survey of German companies conducted in 1995 noted that many German multinationals, most notably Siemens, were replacing their 'Made in Germany' product labels with ones reading 'Made by [company name]'; however, given that Siemens, at least, can be identified as a company of German origin, its identity as German can be emphasised under other circumstances using the same symbols currently used to identify it as an electronics multinational. For City multinational corporations and their employees, then, identity is less about the maintenance of boundaries than about the selection of the symbols which best express the desired identity under specific circumstances.

The German bank which was the setting for my study in many ways exemplifies this globally engaged, flexible profile. ZwoBank's London branch was one of three overseas branches of a medium-sized German bank, with a branch staff of about 160, about one-third of which are German. ZwoBank was fairly small and localised as multinationals go, being strongly focused on Germany and lacking the sheer volume of branches and international vision of, say, HSBC or Citibank. However, as Stopford (1998/1999) notes, it is the degree of cross-border interaction, not the size, of a corporation, which determines its transnationality, and ZwoBank's German focus – which is more or less typical of German banks other than the so-called 'Big Four' private banks – makes for a large degree of transnational interaction. There existed, for instance, three entire departments which did business exclusively with domestic German clients, and yet, for administrative reasons, their activities could not be located anywhere other than London. These departments thus existed simultaneously in both the U.K. and Germany. Furthermore, the large percentage of Germans, and the fact that these were until recently distributed fairly evenly throughout the bank, made for an atypical degree of cross-border engagement; the more typical pattern for a branch this size is for Germans to form about 10 per cent of the branch staff and to be concentrated in managerial positions. At ZwoBank London, then, the bank's structure and staff composition combined to produce an environment of weak social boundaries, 'virtual' interactions, and transnational business practices.

The work and lifestyles of its staff were similarly flexible. The work done at banks is premised on the exploitation of the continuous fluctuation and flow of rates of exchange, interest and prices around the globe. Furthermore, a sense of flexibility pervaded non-business aspects of life at ZwoBank London, even the bank's material culture: not a month went by without the layout of an office being changed or a whole department being physically relocated. At ZwoBank there were some staff members who effectively 'commuted' between Frankfurt and London on a weekly, biweekly or monthly basis, either as part of their jobs or because they are maintaining a job in one country and a family in the other; most employees think nothing of spontaneously spending a weekend in Italy or France. Cosmopolitanism, in Vertovec's sense of an individual who is both interested in cultural diversity, and able to be at ease in many cultures (1996), is an ideal at all levels, from maintenance staff through to General Management. ZwoBank London staff members thus inhabit a shifting, impermanent world in which even seemingly fixed objects continuously move and in which boundaries are routinely crossed and altered.

Despite this, however, the potential exists for a less flexible, more bounded social system. Individual departments displayed a striking degree of solidarity, socialising together, sitting together in the canteen, fielding sports teams and having their own sets of collectively held symbols: dealers, for instance, are seen as macho, rugged gamblers, as explicitly opposed to more conservative groups such as auditors. Furthermore, an unspoken but often-acknowledged division was present between English and German staff, with those who fitted neither category being assimilated into one or the other. German staff frequently ate together in the canteen and often spoke German together, which, as well as a symbol of common identity could be, as one German noted, a means of excluding the largely monolingual English. In practice, these categories often cross-cut each other– one often could not say, for instance, whether a group was eating together because it was German or because it was composed of trainees– and were flexible, with Germanophile English staff being, under some circumstances, assimilated to the 'German' social category. However, the possibility of division was continuously present. While the bank's structure was predominantly flexible and globalised, then, the potential existed for more bounded systems to emerge.

Like most, if not all, multinational branches in the 'global City' of London, then, ZwoBank London Branch was a transnational institution strongly engaged with globalisation. As with other examples of transnational cultures in the literature, its social structure was characterised by flexibility, networks and fluctuation. However, other, more rigid, discourses underlie ZwoBank's structure, which are more like the nontransnational groupings than the setting in which it finds itself might suggest. It thus remains to be seen whether this structure is in fact compatible with extant theory on globally engaged groups, or whether it suggests that globalisation does not herald as much flexibility as was once thought.

'Welcome to the real world, Neo': the impact of the Matrix

Given the shifting, globally engaged nature of the transnational business world, it is inevitable that corporations will go through changes and transformations as they adjust to the environment. An examination of the way in which ZwoBank London dealt with one such major change, and the impact on its employees' identities, should give us some idea of how the process of defining individual and group identities reacts to such a fluctuating social environment.

From its establishment in 1980 until July 1999, ZwoBank London had effectively operated autonomously from its head office in Frankfurt. The heads of individual departments reported to the general manager, who mediated between the branch and the Head Office, and who was therefore the only London staff member in regular contact with Head Office superiors. At the time at which I was there, however, the branch was being restructured under what my interviewees termed a 'matrix integration' programme, such that individual department heads reported directly to individual departmental superiors in Frankfurt, turning the branch's structure from a pyramid, with workers on the bottom, the general manager at the top, and the head office as a nebulous external force with whom the latter communicated, to a series of straight hierarchical lines radiating out from Frankfurt and including all members of particular departments in all branches around the world. The rationale behind the change was usually explained in terms of 'keeping up with the competition' (i.e. competitor banks): at the time the decision was taken, the laws in Germany regarding mergers and acquisitions had recently been modified to make them less restrictive, and German companies in general were strongly focused on the idea of becoming 'more global,' with a more flexible structure which allowed for greater international expansion while not relinquishing the centralized control which is one of the central features of the German business system (Binney 1993). ZwoBank's top management, in anticipation of possibly conducting an international joint venture with another financial company, consequently wanted to implement a structure which gave greater control over the branches' activities to the Head Office, while at the same time furthering employees' sense of belonging to a single, global organisation rather than a disparate collection of branches. Furthermore, the system was deemed more "flexible" in that workers in the different departments would be able to respond directly to orders from Frankfurt, rather than having them being filtered through the branch hierarchy, meaning that the bank would, in theory, be able to respond to global developments more rapidly. The matrix integration programme was thus driven by a perceived need to restructure in accordance with the activities of competitors and possible partners.

This change was regarded with mixed feelings by most of the affected staff. While all more or less accepted it as inevitable, the disruption to an existing system which they felt was sufficiently effective caused resentment. Most employees who spoke to me on the subject expressed nostalgia for the days when London was effectively independent, and resented what they saw as unwanted and unnecessary interference from Head Office in the systems which they had developed over the years for managing local affairs; the loss of their autonomy not only caused resentment, but occasionally lack of understanding of local ways of doing business in the U.K. on the part of Frankfurt managers caused difficulties. There was also disagreement over how the concept of 'globalisation' was constructed, with Head Office viewing it as the need to develop overseas virtual networks, and London staff generally defining it more in terms of the German concept of *Weltoffenheit* (Vertovec 1996), literally 'openness to the world', but more specifically meaning the cultivation of cosmopolitan and culturally aware attitudes among businesspeople. Furthermore, friction between branch and Head Office staff was generated by the fact that the changes inherently had negative effects on two important symbols of the London branch's identity: first, its autonomy from Head Office and second, its general manager, who was a charismatic figure well liked by most of the staff. The feelings of ambivalence about the situation were symbolised in the staff's half-humourous use of the phrase 'The Matrix' to refer to the programme, an abbreviation which recalled the title of a popular film of the preceding summer, *The Matrix* (Wachowski and Wachowski 1999), in which the hero discovers that his world is in fact a construct controlled by outside forces (the hero being tacitly equated with London branch, and the outside forces were normally equated with Head Office). The matrix integration thus brought the bank into greater transnational engagement, but in a manner which called staff identities into question, particularly London's sense of itself as a distinct institution.

While it is effectively impossible, given the pervasive nature of the changes and the fact that the matrix integration was already well-advanced when I arrived, to determine exactly how the ZwoBank employees' identities had changed as a result of the programme's implementation, it did seem that, outside of situations in which the matrix integration was directly at issue, the expression of identity fitted best with Hannerz's model. When identity was expressed, the symbols used were not employed so much to delineate as to cross over the boundaries of groups, and to express multiple identities consecutively and simultaneously. English staff, for instance, frequently greeted each other with short phrases of German, employing a symbol more commonly indicative of Germanness to express ZwoBank's corporate identity. A fondness for football could be used within the same interaction to express identity as a man, a dealer, a bank employee and an Englishman. Bureaucratic procedures pertaining to one or the other country were frequently used both as ethnic and as corporate identity markers: certain German laws pertaining to banking regulation to which the branch had to adhere could be taken as indicative of its identity as German, a multinational, or as a bank, in any combination. Similarly, U.K. procedure, particularly its short-term focus, was a symbol of English identity within the context of the wider banking group, but a symbol of banking culture within the City. Symbols were thus not used so much to create and maintain boundaries as to cross boundaries and develop mixed and flexible categories.

Furthermore, these properties of symbols were also used in strategic fashion by individuals and groups within the bank. English people working in the above-mentioned German-focused departments frequently made a point of speaking German and emphasising their links to particular areas of Germany – in a sort of parallel to the German practice of identifying with a specific *Heimat* ('home place'; see Applegate 1990 for more on the concept) – in order to integrate successfully with their German co-workers. Germans in predominantly English environments often used their identification as 'cosmopolitan' or 'European' to seem, as one put it, 'more at home' in a non-German setting. Similarly, staff moving from one department to the next could do so by deemphasising their departmental identity in favour of a more general one. A manager from the Credits department, for instance, could transfer more easily to Media Financing if she emphasised her identity as a manager over her identity as a member of Credits. In ZwoBank London, then, the process of defining identity seems to be normally flexible, and to involve the selection of different symbols of identity to adapt the individual's self-presentation to the social context.

Within the context of the matrix integration, however, the situation was quite different. The problems arising from the programme were expressed by the people interviewed almost entirely in ethnic terms, and specifically in terms of a boundary between English and German identities. The very fact that I was brought in to assist with the adjustment to the new structure is itself significant in this regard, as it was on the basis of my past work with another German bank on the adaptation of expatriate staff to English culture that I was invited to study ZwoBank. In interviews with English managers, even those who were strongly Germanophile couched their account of the matrix integration in terms of ethnicity. New bosses who had transferred in from Head Office were described as 'typical Germans, always keen on procedure'. One English interviewee specifically asked me, before discussing the handling of the matrix integration, whether or not I had any German blood – suggesting that, had I said 'yes', he would have described the programme in different terms than the ones which he used, and also suggesting an explicitly ethnic dimension, as he did not ask about my familiarity with the culture but rather my 'genetic' connection to the ethnic group.

Similar patterns were seen with Germans. One German brought in from Head Office to help with the transition to the new structure was quite stilted and formal with me until he found out that I spoke German, and from then on, even though we still mainly communicated in English, he seemed more inclined to view me as 'one of ours'. Discussions in interviews of changes in procedure inevitably were brought back to German versus English practices in accounting, auditing and dealing; Head Office contacts' lack of English skills were sometimes said to be German linguistic chauvinism. All but one interviewee, when explicitly asked, said that they felt that there was a German–English divide in ZwoBank London. Interviews with managers involved with the matrix integration thus showed an explicit discourse of bounded ethnic identities, which contrasted sharply with the more flexible concept of identity used under other circumstances.

This was borne out by casual discussions among staff on the subject of the matrix integration. The case was often compared with the then-recent, and notoriously problem-fraught, BMW takeover of the Rover group, which was explicitly, and more than a little inaccurately, described by staff as a case in which a German company's attempt to impose German procedures upon an English workforce caused the latter to revolt. Although the group of expatriates brought over from Frankfurt to help with the ZwoBank transition were all Anglophiles, in practice they mainly associated with each other and spoke German more often than not. Similarly, German managers and staff who had nothing to do with the matrix were assumed to be sympathetic to Head Office's position. Indeed, many would begin criticisms of the matrix integration with a phrase along the lines of 'Although I'm German, I disapprove ...' implying that they believed that Germans should normally approve of a plan instigated by Head Office. Others cited the fact that there had been a large number of English people in senior management as evidence that the bank had been 'English', and the presence of the expats in the managerial corps had now made the branch 'more German', even though the branch's ethnic makeup had not changed appreciably. Outside of formal interviews as well, then, the ethnic boundary is maintained in situations involving the matrix integration.

Even more interestingly, evidence existed that there were other discourses which could have been adopted to describe the matrix integration, which were largely ignored in favour of the ethnic one. Within interviews, for instance, the programme was often likened to a takeover or a merger, or to an internal restructuring, activities which are seen as a normal part of a bank's life cycle.

Additionally, some referred to it in terms which implied that the problems in the integration were a case of cosmopolitanism versus noncosmopolitanism: one interviewee described his new boss as less used to other cultures than the general manager, and Head Office personnel's lack of English skills were also sometimes said, given the status of English as the 'global language' of business (Ohmae 1990), to be a marker of parochiality rather than of ethnicity, particularly as many Germans view English skills as the mark of a good businessperson. While it is not surprising that other models exist, what is surprising is that none were adopted as an alternative discourse, as there is, on the face of it, no reason why ethnicity should be more important than any other identity in the integrated organisation. Furthermore, given ZwoBank London staff's usual behaviour and given the complexity of the situation, one might have expected a combination of diverse discourses without one dominating, as opposed to a single discourse focused on ethnicity overwhelming all others. The reaction to the matrix integration is thus interesting not only in that it demonstrates a return to bounded identities, but in that one set of symbols of identity takes precedence over other potentially utilisable sets.

The case of the matrix integration thus raises interesting issues for anthropologists of globalised groups. First of all, it suggests that even under globalisation, boundaries are not always fluid and identity not always flexible. More importantly, it may be able to shed some light on the question, raised in popular as well as academic literature, of why increased globalisation has seemingly been matched by increased fundamentalism, including that of an ethnic nature. It thus remains to be seen whether the reaction to the matrix integration in ZwoBank is an indicator of the limits of globalisation or a reaction to particular aspects of transnational operation.

Strategic withdrawals: boundaries under global conditions

The most obvious explanation for ZwoBank London's sudden adoption of a boundary-focused model is that it was an early indicator of the end of a period of globalisation and a return to bounded national and/or ethnic identities. Many writers see the rise in so-called 'ethnic nationalism' which has accompanied the weakening of national boundaries in Europe as indicative of the formation of new boundaries, a suggestion which has intensified in some quarters due to the adoption of nationalist discourses in the U.S.A. following September 11, 2001. Anthony D. Smith (1995), maintains that the 'globe' is too broad a concept to inspire the feelings of solidarity that are inspired by one's ethnic group; people's strong feelings for their ethnic groups will, he feels, ultimately wear through the fashionable cosmopolitan veneer and bring a return to nationalism. Hirst and Thompson (1996) take this even further, suggesting that the presence of ethnic nationalism is evidence that globalisation is in fact a myth. Under this scenario, then, the rise of ethnic boundaries in ZwoBank London indicates that globalisation will reach its limits in any organisation, and the matrix integration is simply the final straw which shatters the bank's cosmopolitan facade.

However, this does not explain a number of key aspects of the process. Leaving aside the fact that, in the years since the study was conducted, globalisation has, if anything, become stronger as a social force, the fact that Hannerz's 'globalised' model of identity (1996) appeared to be the norm, not the exception, even after the matrix was implemented; the same informants who couched every issue to do with the matrix integration in ethnic terms were more flexible when it came to other situations in the bank, and maintained a folk model of identity which bore striking similarities to Hannerz's. Additionally, staff continued to do business across borders and employ the technologies of globalisation without showing any signs of a desire to return to boundarised models; only in the matrix integration context did boundaries take this rigid form. The delineation of boundaries thus does not indicate the limits, let alone the end, of globalisation at ZwoBank London.

It is also possible that the sudden adoption of a bounded model by ZwoBank employees is a psychological reaction to the stresses of an abrupt increase in global engagement. Zygmunt Baumann, in his paper 'Europe of Strangers' (1998), discusses the rise of ethnic fundamentalism in Europe as stemming from anxiety caused by the sudden alteration of borders due to the integration of Europe. The implication is that people have a psychological need for boundaries and, when extant ones are removed or weakened, cleave to new ones in extremist fashion. This is also supported by traditional ethnography: Larsen's earlier study of a Northern Irish town tells of how neighbours who had lived together in relative harmony suddenly retreated behind religious boundaries as the anniversary of the Battle of the Boyne neared (1982: 287). Given that the staff of ZwoBank London affirmed that the restructuring had given rise to stress – one expatriate, explaining the state of morale in his department, said that his staff 'used to be a unit under the old system and now they are all cut to pieces' – a reaffirmation of a bounded model of ethnic identity seems not to be an atypical reaction to the sudden increase in transnational engagement which it brought. However, this raises the question of why staff seemed to find no difficulty in dealing with increased globalisation in other spheres of their lives. Furthermore, it does not explain why the boundaries chosen were specifically ethnic; following the matrix integration, ZwoBank entered into talks with a non-German bank regarding a joint venture, in which staff anxieties about the outcome were expressed in terms of the size and function of the partners rather than of their respective ethnicities. The psychological explanation is thus similarly unsatisfactory.

The best explanation may lie in Erving Goffman's theory of strategic self-presentation (1956, 1961). Although Goffman was writing long before the present period of globalisation, and avoided specific discussion of the business world, he suggested that actors select from different aspects and elements of their identities in order to present themselves in the most efficacious way possible. While such theories have been attacked as verging on Rational Action Theory, evidence exists that this does not always take place on a conscious level, and one might also add that to act strategically is not always to act rationally, or even consciously (Burns, 1992: 119; Jenkins, 1996: 70–71; 1992: 78–79). Consequently, the use of a discourse of ethnic boundaries to express the issues arising from the matrix integration may be a strategic move on the part of the staff of ZwoBank London to maximise their social benefits in a difficult situation. An example of how such actions might take place can be seen in the case of Thomas Cody's memoir *Strategy of a Megamerger*, an account of the merging of two American medical-supply companies with a history of cooperation, but in which the decision to merge was treated with dismay by staff (1990). While Cody, a businessman, is not writing explicitly about symbolic expressions of identity, the partners in the merger can be seen to use symbolic expressions of identity in strategic fashions; one partner, for instance, picking up on the other's use of marriage metaphors to describe the mergers, defined itself during a crisis point as a violated and betrayed party, forcing the other to make concessions or be defined as a rapist. More interestingly, however, is the fact that in the early stages of integrating the two companies, former employees of both maintained rigid boundaries between their corporate cultures, but later on, as the new corporate culture emerged, these boundaries quietly faded and became a non-issue. Strategic expressions of identity were thus used in what Cody calls a 'culture war' between merger partners, to further their own aims and interests.

In the case of the matrix integration at ZwoBank, the situation called for a degree of diplomacy. It cannot be denied that the restructuring had caused friction within the branch and between branch and Head Office; however, the fact remains that the change was inevitable and was to be accepted in the end. Consequently, staff are faced with the problem of integrating the matrix structure into the branch's culture while coping with the problems which such restructuring inevitably brings. As mentioned above, an ethnic division was already present within the branch, and was regarded for the most part as unproblematic; indeed, it was in some ways a symbol of the branch's identity relative to other banks in the City, as many staff members seemed to take the large ratio of German to English employees as a point of pride. The complaints about the imposition of 'German' bureaucratic procedure might thus be a development, if one accompanied by a rise in tension, of the everyday interethnic banter which was part of daily socialisation at the branch; additionally, it could cause the integration to be seen as similar to the German focus of the departments which dealt with German clients, which tended to describe their identity in ethnicised terms. Again, one might also note that the use of a bounded model was more or less confined to the matrix situation, not generalised in all cases of structural change. The use of a discourse of ethnic boundaries might thus not be the reappearance of the true, normal form of identity expression, but a short-term strategy for coping with and incorporating the new structure within the branch.

The reason why other discourses do not feature as strongly might also be explained by the fact that other sets of symbols are all more divisive than the ethnic one. The alternative discourses open to staff to express the matrix integration would, if used, generate more division between branch and Head Office; to see the matrix integration as a merger would imply no connection between the two companies, and indeed that Head Office is a hostile outsider imposing its will on a smaller company. Similarly, given the value placed on cosmopolitan skills in banking, to view it as a case of cosmopolitanism versus noncosmopolitanism would be a grave insult to Head Office, not to mention the expatriate staff, all of whom were from Head Office, more or less cosmopolitan, and in positions of power. Finally, to liken the integration to an internal restructuring would be difficult to do, given the importance of the image of the London Branch as an independent unit to staff members. Again, the focus on a single set of symbols which fit into an extant discourse can be seen as a strategic move for the internalisation of the changes.

The use of an explicitly ethnicised and bounded discourse to describe identity within the matrix integration of ZwoBank London is thus not the breaking-out of long-smouldering nationalism within a cosmopolitan bank branch, nor is it a panicked flight from the uncertainties of increased degrees of globalisation. Rather, the best explanation for the rise of ethnic boundaries in ZwoBank London seems to be that it is a semi- or nonconscious strategic move, of varying degrees of rationality, on the part of staff to integrate the changes within their daily working lives while simultaneously acknowledging the problems which the new structure has inevitably brought.

Boundaries in the wider context

The case of the reaction to the matrix integration of ZwoBank thus raises questions about earlier studies of identity under globalisation, and as such is relevant to more cases than simply that of one group of transnational businesspeople. While a number of writers, including Baumann (1998) and Smith (1995), consider cases in which globalisation is accompanied by a sharp delineation of ethnic boundaries, they often do not consider the possibility that this behaviour may be part of a wider strategy on the part of their informants to present themselves in the most effective way in a given situation, and that the bounded situation may in fact be a relatively temporary phase of an ongoing discourse. Furthermore, it suggests that the seeming strength of discourses of ethnic fundamentalism in Europe may be an 'artefact of media focus and historical concerns; apart from in studies of European Muslims (e.g. Amiraux 1997), cases of other forms of fundamentalism largely go ignored, and in the case of the Muslims religious identities are often given second billing to ethnic ones. The ZwoBank London case thus suggests that it might be worth looking at the classic cases of 'ethnic nationalism' in Europe over the longer term and considering other aspects of participants' identities.

Furthermore, the ZwoBank London case suggests that the division which I made at the beginning of the paper between Cohen's and Hannerz's models of identity may be a fallacious one, and that it may be closer to the truth to suggest that both models are part of a larger system of expressing identity, which tends more or less towards the maintenance of boundaries between groups depending on the actors involved and the circumstances under which the expression of identity takes place. Taking it further, one might also suggest that the construction and expression of identity is not simply a matter of selecting the symbols most appropriate to the occasion, but also of selecting the very system through which these symbols are expressed according to a strategic process. While it remains to be seen whether these implications hold true for other groups, then, the study of the matrix integration suggests that the very theories used to describe the process of identity expression are, paradoxically, part of the process itself.

Conclusion

The case of the matrix integration of ZwoBank's London branch, then, is more than simply a case of two bureaucracies meeting in a global space, or even a refutation of received ideas about the limitations of flexibility in a supposedly 'flexible' firm at a time when the flexibility of globalisation is emphasised. Rather, the fact that the branch's employees maintained a system of identity which could be either boundary-focused or flexible, and indeed could be both at the same time, suggests, firstly, that no single theory can explain the expression of identity among globalised groups, and secondly, that not only the expression of identity but the system through which this identity is expressed are part of a wider strategy of shifting self-presentation.

Bibliography

Amiraux, V. 1997. 'Turkish Islamic Associations in Germany and the Issue of European Citizenship'. In S. Vertovec and C. Peach (eds.), *Islam in Europe: The Politics of Religion and Community*. London: Macmillan, 245–59.

Applegate, C. 1990. *A Nation of Provincials: The German Idea of Heimat*. Berkeley: University of California Press.

Banks, M. 1996. *Ethnicity: Anthropological Constructions*. London: Routledge.

Barth, F. 1969. 'Introduction'. In F. Barth (ed.), *Ethnic Groups and Boundaries: The Social Organisation of Culture Difference*. Oslo: Universitetsforlaget, 9–38.

Baumann, Z. 1998. *Europe of Strangers*. Oxford: ESRC Transnational Communities Programme Working Papers.

Binney, George (1993) 'The British Company and the German Company Compared'. In *Debunking the Myths about the German Company*, G. Binney (ed.). London: Chameleon Press, 15–18.

Burns, T. 1992. *Erving Goffman.* London: Routledge.

Castells, M. 2000. *The Rise of the Network Society.* (*The Information Age*, vol. 1) 2nd edn. Oxford: Blackwell.

Chapman, M. 1997. 'Preface: Social Anthropology, Business Studies and Cultural Issues', *International Studies of Management and Organisation*, 26 (4), 3–29.

Cody, T. 1990. *Strategy of a Megamerger.* New York: Quorum Books.

Cohen, A.P. 1982a. 'Belonging: The Experience of Culture'. In A.P. Cohen (ed.), *Belonging: Identity and Social Organisation in Rural British Cultures.* Manchester: Manchester University Press, pp. 1–17.

——. 1982b. 'Blockade: A Case Study of Local Consciousness in an Extra-Local Event'. In A.P. Cohen (ed.), *Belonging: Identity and Social Organisation in Rural British Cultures.* Manchester: Manchester University Press, pp. 292–321.

——. 1985. *The Symbolic Construction of Community.* London: Tavistock.

——. 1986. 'Of Symbols and Boundaries, or, Does Ertie's Greatcoat Hold the Key? In *Symbolising Boundaries: Identity and Diversity in British Cultures*, A.P. Cohen (ed.). Manchester: Manchester University Press, 1–22.

Goffman, E. 1956. *The Presentation of Self in Everyday Life.* Edinburgh: University of Edinburgh.

——. 1961. *Encounters: Two Studies in the Sociology of Interaction.* Indianapolis: Bobbs-Merrill Ltd.

Hannerz, U. 1983. 'Tools of Identity and Imagination'. In A. Jacobson-Widding (ed.), *Identity: Personal and Socio-Cultural, a Symposium.* Uppsala: Almqvist and Wiksell International, pp. 347–60.

——. 1992. *Cultural Complexity: Studies in the Social Organisation of Meaning.* New York: Columbia University Press.

——. 1996. *Transnational Connections: Culture, People, Places.* London: Routledge.

Hirst, P. Q. and G. Thompson, 1996. *Globalisation in Question: The International Economy and the Possibilities of Governance.* Cambridge: Polity Press.

Jenkins, R. 1992. *Pierre Bourdieu.* London: Routledge.

——. 1996. *Social Identity.* London: Routledge.

Larsen, S.S. 1982. 'The Glorious Twelfth: A Ritual Expression of Collective Identity'. In A.P. Cohen (ed.), *Belonging: Identity and Social Organisation in Rural British Cultures.* Manchester: Manchester University Press, pp. 278–91.

Leyshon, A. and N. Thrift. 1997. *Money/Space: Geographies of Monetary Transformation.* London: Routledge.

McDowell, L.M. 1997. 'A Tale of Two Cities? Embedded Organisations and Embodied Workers in the City of London'. In R. Lee and J. Willis (eds.), *Geographies of Economies.* London: Arnold, 118–29.

Moore, F. 2004. 'Symbols of Organisation: informal Ways of Negotiating the Global and the Local in MNCs'. *Global Networks* 4 (2): 181–98.

——. 2005. *Transnational Business Cultures: Life and Work in a Multinational Corporation.* Aldershot: Ashgate.

Nash, J. 1979. 'Anthropology of the Multinational Corporation'. In G. Huizer and B. Mannheim (eds.), *The Politics of Anthropology: From Colonialism and Sexism toward a View from Below.* Paris: Mouton Publishers, pp. 421–46.

Ohmae, K. 1990. *The Borderless World: Power and Strategy in the Interlinked Economy.* London: HarperCollins.

Portes, A. 1998. *Globalisation from Below: The Rise of Transnational Communities.* Oxford: ESRC Transnational Communities Programme Working Papers.

Sassen, S. 1991. *The Global City: New York, London, Tokyo.* Princeton: Princeton University Press.

Schein, L. 1998. 'Forged Transnationality and Oppositional Cosmopolitanism', in M.P. Smith and L. E. Guarnizo (eds.), *Transnationalism from Below.* London: Transaction Publishers, pp. 291–313.

Sklair, L. 2001. *The Transnational Capitalist Class.* Oxford: Blackwell.

Smith, A.D. 1995. *Nations and Nationalism in a Global Era.* Cambridge: Polity Press.

Sperber, D. 1974. *Rethinking Symbolism.* Cambridge: Cambridge University Press.

Stopford, J. 1998/1999. 'Think Again: Multinational Corporations', *Foreign Policy* 113: 12–24.

Strecker, I. 1988. *The Social Practice of Symbolisation: An Anthropological Analysis.* London: Athlone Press.

Vertovec, S. 1996. 'Berlin Multikulti: Germany, "Foreigners" and "World-Openness"', *New Community* 22 (3): 381–99.

——. 1999. 'Conceiving and Researching Transnationalism', *Ethnic and Racial Studies* 22 (2): 447–62.

Wachowski, A. and L. Wachowski. 1999. *The Matrix.* Warner Bros.

Waters, M. 1995. *Globalisation.* London: Routledge.

Wolff Olins Identity Research. 1995. *Made in Germany: A Business Survey of the Relevance of the National Badge and Its Image Associations.* London: Wolff Olins.

3

IMAGE AND REALITY IN AN ISRAELI 'ABSORPTION CENTRE' FOR ETHIOPIAN IMMIGRANTS

Esther Herzog

Introduction

In this article, I will discuss the continuous negotiations concerning bureaucratic identities, roles and power, between three groups of people interacting in an Israeli Absorption Centre. The first two are the *insiders*, who can be divided into *staff* and *immigrants*, the latter being Ethiopians living in caravans at the Centre. In structural opposition to these two groups are the *outsiders*: visitors and bureaucrats who, from time to time, impinge upon the insiders. I describe the efforts and various means in this bureaucratic context which staff employ to give an appearance of formal power in order to achieve recognition of their roles, and to their professional attributes and authority – which are relatively weak in reality. These critical relations between theory and reality were played out through micro-performances in the theatre of everyday life at the Centre.

The staff include three officials (the Director, the Secretary and the Matron) who are supported by, among other workers, a number of welfare aides (of whom more later). The staff assert a supposedly self-evident control over the resident immigrants from Ethiopia, which appears to be accepted by the residents who, at the same time, subvert that power. I suggest that this behaviour by the staff serves to establish mediation roles, as well as positions of control over access to the Centre and its inhabitants. Thus, they assume the role of 'gatekeepers', and a self-proclaimed indispensability as mediators between insiders and outsiders, through a continuous process of negotiation.

I concluded from my observations that the officials in the Absorption Centre had only limited formal power and professional skills, and were in fact often performing needless tasks. Yet they constantly had to convince both themselves and the immigrants inside the Centre, and their superiors outside the Centre, that their skills and roles were genuinely needed. I suggest that the bureaucratic setting and performance therein encouraged the emergence of social distance, since it was based on images of essential differences between people seen as belonging to different social worlds. During my fieldwork, for instance, I was perceived by the residents of the Centre, and perhaps even by myself, as a kind of official. Reflecting on my own behaviour, I realised that once a structured binary opposition of collective identities – 'immigrants' and staff in this case – was established, the people involved needed to identify themselves, and indeed were identified, with one of either of these two categories. This allocation became more significant than any personal, formal or professional affiliations and skills.

The chapter also examines the immigrants' responses to this bureaucratic control, as well as those of the people outside the Centre. It appears that the immigrant residents did not see themselves as 'powerless people' who were extremely dependent on patrons: that is, on the staff, especially the officials. Rather, they saw themselves as temporary residents who only had to humble themselves when staff were present. Moreover, the immigrants employed diverse means of resistance to authority, thus indicating their awareness of the officials' actual vulnerability and limited powers.

Images of bureaucratic control in a reality of evasive power

The Absorption Centre in Or-Akiva (Figure 3.1), in which I carried out eighteen months of fieldwork,[1] was one of more than 60 centres owned by the Jewish Agency between 1984 and 1985. Some 15,000 immigrants from Ethiopia were concentrated in these social frameworks at the time. The Absorption agencies, mainly the Jewish Agency, the Ministry of Absorption and the Ministry of Labour and Welfare, defined the immigrants from Ethiopia as a social category with special problems which necessitated their organised intervention. All three presented themselves as suitably equipped for the professional care of people with special problems in need of care. The Jewish Agency funded most of the centre's expenses, among which were: maintenance of the offices and of the immigrants' caravans, the administrative and welfare workers' wages, the kindergarten expenses, vocational training, gardening, guarding etc. The Hebrew classes were funded by the Ministry of Education. One year of health insurance was paid for by the government. The care which the Centre provided implied large budgets and control over the immigrants. Thus, the Jewish Agency, drew on the Absorption Centres, which were in their control, to demand the overall caring for the immigrants in 'their' Centres.

The Absorption Centres were described as the Agency's main device for 'helping' immigrants to integrate into Israeli society. Despite extensive ideological rhetoric concerning the immigrants' successful integration, as implied in the name 'Absorption Centre',[2] and despite the various services provided to the immigrants (e.g. language studies, vocational training, childcare services etc.), in reality the opposite usually happened. The immigrants' concentration in the centres actually *delayed* the immigrants' integration, fostered dependency, vulnerability and future social and economic marginalisation (Herzog 1999). The whole centre/project thus served the various bureaucratic organisations involved in 'absorbing' the Ethiopian immigrants, rather than serving the immigrants themselves, meaning that most of the 'work' done in the Centre was 'make-work', semi-useless activities designed to give the illusion of progress rather than generate any actual activity. The workers admitted sometimes in private that they were not really needed by the immigrants, but this was not something which was openly discussed. On the declarative level the immigrants (especially the men) were supposed to use their vocational training, offered by the Ministry of Absorption, for integration in semi-professional jobs. Nevertheless, in practice the training was too basic and did not contribute significantly to their chance of getting jobs with good or high salaries or occupational status. In fact there was no 'real' plan for the immigrants' integration in the labour market. There were a few projects that were financed by the Jewish Joint Distribution Committee (JDC) (an international Jewish organisation) to support young Ethiopians in getting higher education and technological training, but these did not take place in the centre that I studied, but rather in a few boarding schools for young immigrants.

This context – which restricted the immigrant residents' free mingling in the labour market, in social networks and educational systems – enabled the bureaucrats to gain control that was based on compliance. Nevertheless, control was neither taken for granted nor was it one-sided. Both the concept and the practice of control were constantly negotiated. My data regarding Or-Akiva

Figure 3.1. The Or-Akiva Absorption Centre

Absorption Centre reveals the various means (including physical, ideological, verbal and coercive) that were used in daily encounters in the pursuit of recognition of bureaucratic control.

Yet although the Or-Akiva Absorption Centre *appeared* closed and autonomous, it was in fact open and dependent on its social surroundings. The image of the Centre as an autonomous territory was a significant aspect of the staff's claim for control over the place and its inhabitants. Different forms of separation (the fence and the guarded entrance in particular) lent a closed form to the place and also generated images of ownership, indicating the officials' responsibility for the place and the people in it. These images of *closure* and *ownership* influenced everyone's behaviour and generated the need to negotiate over the rights to enter the place. Thus, the access to the immigrants that resided there was negotiated between 'outsiders' and 'insiders', by those who claimed authority. Generally, outsiders, that is, people who did not belong to the Centre's population, complied with the officials' manifestations of ownership of the place and of access to the immigrants. Nevertheless, the officials often found it difficult to demonstrate that their control and authority was self-evident. 'Problematic' situations often occurred when outsiders who did not belong to the Centre attended encounters, and had to be convinced of the officials' ownership.

The following examples will illustrate this argument. The first case relates to a private visit from a nurse who worked in the absorption centre in Safed. Odeda, a white woman, was the girlfriend of Amos, an Ethiopian immigrant from Safed. At their invitation, she stayed overnight with Shlomo, Amos's brother, and his wife Zehava. On learning of this, Jacob, then the Centre's Director, who knew about my friendship with Zehava and Shlomo, said to me: 'I told her that if anything happened to her it would be our responsibility. She shouldn't have slept here without our knowing about it.'

Another example is a conversation I had with Jacob, following an argument he had had with Tova, the director of the Hebrew classes (*Ulpan*). Jacob was very annoyed that Tova had refused to allow in some visitors who had already been vetted by him. He said: 'I was very angry with her, and said to her, "You are a wicked woman".' He then told me that he had criticised her in very strong terms, telling her that he had reported her to the appropriate authorities. He said to me:

> I'll show her this is unthinkable. I could understand it if a committee of inquiry had turned up, but these were two guests having a general look around the Centre, walking through the rows of caravans, looking at the gardens and meeting the Director. Tova decides that the Hebrew classes, the *Ulpan*, are out of bounds! I almost said to her: 'Tova, I will count to three and if you continue to defy me I will enter the *Ulpan* by force.' If the Director cannot make decisions, what am I here for? We have enough dolls in the kindergarten.

Jacob's anger with Tova, like his attack on Odeda, reveals his vulnerability and his difficulties in gaining the recognition of others (including mine, in this case) of his authority and in facing their assumed expectations from him as having such an authority. His attack may have been both a defence against a threat to his control, and an effort to make others believe that he really had it. Jacob saw himself, and assumed that others perceived him, as responsible for the Centre and for what happened there, but he was not consistent in using his power. He reacted strongly, even aggressively, when Odeda stayed overnight at the Centre, but did nothing when other guests (Ethiopian friends and family members from other absorption centres) stayed.

Thus, in the first case it seems that it was the obvious difference between the hosts' and guest's skin colour that influenced his reaction. In other words, a visitor who was perceived as a 'stranger', and therefore as not belonging, elicited a different reaction to the norm, quite probably because others at the Centre (the other officials in particular) would also recognise the person as a stranger and expect Jacob to exercise his authority. In Jacob's own words, 'She shouldn't have done this without our knowledge.' He was disturbed because Odeda took permission to enter the Centre as self-evident. She had ignored his position of responsibility and control.

In the second case, the debacle involving Tova and Jacob underlined the weakness and vagueness of authority at the Centre. Jacob felt threatened by Tova's attitudes. She, for her part, defied his authority and demonstrated her own power over at least one part of the territory, the *Ulpan* area. In showing her ability to control this area, she cast doubt on the concept of overall authority at the Centre to which, presumably, Jacob was referring. His statement that 'the Director makes the decisions' may be seen as emblematic of his thinking. In other words, if the Director cannot decide, he is no more than a figurehead: he lacks any authority worthy of the name.

The threat to Jacob's image of authority was so strong that he admitted considering the use of force to impose his will and decisions upon Tova. He stated that he had already taken action by sending letters of complaint to his superiors. Thus he was, by his own admission, unable to impose his authority. What appeared to be a loss of authority was, in fact, so critical in Jacob's own eyes that he felt it necessary to appeal to an outside authority to assist him in the reinstatement of it. He would, so he declared, 'show her [Tova] who is in control'.

Tova, however, seemed to be reacting in a manner similar to Jacob. She, too, demanded control over 'her' territory, the Hebrew classes, and the privilege of deciding who may and who may not enter 'her' territory. She, too, distinguished between those visitors who were welcome and those who were not. Where Jacob said that he would 'understand' avoiding entrance from a 'committee of inquiry' (as anything associated with potential criticism was perceived as dangerous and had to be kept at bay), Tova's objection to the visitors was for much the same reason. This objection (which was only actually declared on the day in question) most likely emerged because on that day only a very few students attended the classes. The two visitors whom Jacob wanted to visit the Hebrew classes would have found out that Tova had only a few students in 'her' classes. This, from her point of view, had to be concealed from 'outsiders', much as Jacob wished to head off potential criticism from other quarters.

It follows, therefore, that the efforts to present to 'outsiders', and to each other, images of control over the Centre and of its being well run played a significant part in the officials' daily interactions. They seemed to be struggling continuously for recognition of their authority and to prevent any threat to the image of their control over the Centre as a whole, and over its parts.

The participants in encounters with officials often challenged their authority, as they would sometimes ignore the manifestations of bureaucratic control. Thus, for example, the image of the officials' control over entrance to the Centre has played a major role in making clear to 'outsiders' the self-evident necessity to approach them to attain permission to enter the Centre and have access to its inhabitants. It follows that permission to enter the Centre has become a major symbol of the bureaucratic control. This image of control could be and, in fact, was, challenged quite easily. Coming when the officials were away and were unable to stop outsiders from entering, as Odeda did, was one way of challenging the officials' assumed control and authority, which exposes the absence of any actual control on the part of the officials over the place.

A similar conclusion may be derived from the incident in which a young Ethiopian man came from another centre to visit his father in Or-Akiva, when I was making my first visit to the Centre along with Israel, a photographer who was writing a report about the immigrants from Ethiopia. The two of us were invited to the Director's room after being questioned about the reasons for our visit to the Centre. Lussy, who succeeded Jacob as the Centre's Director, as well as Chana, the Matron, and Yardena, the secretary, did not want the young Ethiopian to enter the Centre, because he was, so they explained to us, a 'troublemaker'. At this point an unpleasant discussion took place right in front of us when the young immigrant entered Lussy's office and demanded to be allowed to enter the Centre and his father's caravan. The encounter became gradually louder, and almost verbally violent, as Lussy raised her voice and eventually threatened to call the police. It was only when the secretary started to dial the police telephone number that the immigrant gave up and left the room. However, he turned up later on, in the afternoon, when the officials had left the place, and went to see his father regardless of what had happened.

It seems, therefore, that as long as the man believed that his entrance to the Centre and the access to his father's caravan depended on the officials' permission, his entry could be prevented. But once he realised that they could not prevent him from entering the Centre when they were away, he entered it freely. Moreover, forcing his way into the Centre's office despite the officials' objection suggests that the young immigrant had challenged their claim for recognition of their supposedly self-evident control over the place. It follows that the officials' control over entrance to the Centre was not always automatically accepted by outsiders. The fact that Lussy went as far as thinking of calling the police to help her out in this situation reveals her distress and her weakness. Through his actions, the young immigrant succeeded in negating the performance of the Director.

The fact that we, the outsiders, were present might also have affected Lussy's behaviour, making her feel more threatened and therefore aggressive. She, probably, had to prove to us, the passive audience, that she was in control of the situation. She had to call the police to help her to establish her control over the place and people, when it was clearly doubted and seriously jeopardised. Given this incident, the Director's formal control seems more a theoretical concept than a stable, self-evident organisational construct.

This line of argumentation is supported by Strauss. He suggests that social order is constructed by continuous negotiations. He argues that, in the hospital he studied, 'many administrative arrangements do not rest firmly upon either administrative rulings or relatively established procedures ... some administrative arrangements must be continually renegotiated' (1981: 302). Also, he suggests that 'it is necessary continually to reconstitute the bases of concerted action, of social order'. (ibid., 312). Moreover, Strauss says that even rules, which are perceived as 'a tiny island of structured stability', are negotiable. The data presented here indicate that in the Absorption Centre there is neither structured stability nor firmly established arrangements. All arrangements were negotiable, and formal control was constantly challenged.

In many of my encounters with the immigrants, I became an outlet for various complaints and criticism about the officials. Usually I was sympathetic and thus, probably, encouraged the immigrants to confide in me and to protest against the officials' behaviour. They might have hoped to transmit through me their complaints and expectations to the officials, or to express their resentment at the officials' manners, which they considered as domineering and demeaning. I suggest that this antagonistic attitude of the immigrants towards the staff indicates that they perceived them as having authority and power, whereas, in truth, they did not have real professional or bureaucratic authority.

It is important to note that, in fact, the staff could not help the immigrants, but rather had to be on their guard constantly, to protect their own positions. An example will serve to illustrate this argument further. Zehava, an immigrant to whom I got very close, expressed her reservations about the educational standards of the kindergarten teachers in the Centre. She told me once, 'this kindergarten here is no good. It exists only for the sake of the Hebrew classes. They don't know anything'. She meant that the only purpose of the kindergarten teachers was enabling the immigrant women to participate in the Hebrew classes, rather than to provide a good education for the children. I agreed with her criticism, saying: 'That's correct. The kindergarten teachers are there only to provide babysitting services, they do not really give any proper training.' Zehava responded: 'I keep my son Eitan at home.'

It appears, therefore, that, when talking about the officials, the immigrants revealed an ambivalent attitude. On the one hand, they rejected the officials' claim that their bureaucratic position and professional expertise should be taken for granted. They raised doubts and expressed clear reservations concerning the officials' skills, their functioning and their authority. At the same time, however, the immigrants seemed to perceive themselves as *depending* on the officials to get various resources. Thus they acknowledged the officials' power to control the access to resources they needed.

The degree of dependence and compliance was not the same for every immigrant. Their reactions to the officials' interference in their lives and to the pressure[3] put on them to make them change depended, to some extent, on resources and choices they had. This can be demonstrated by comparing several circumcision ceremonies held at the Centre (Herzog 1999: 119–39). These events were essentially bureaucratic in character. They were conducted by the staff according to their own considerations and needs. The immigrants seemed to have no choice other than to accept official control over each family event of this kind. However, immigrants who did not rely completely on the staff – if they had some financial and social resources to organise the circumcision ceremony – could have more control over it. Thus, Shlomo, who worked outside the Centre (as a translator in another centre), had organised his son's circumcision ceremony by himself, while ignoring the cultural coordinator's demands to accept his responsibility over the event (this entailed organising the club and the refreshments, coordinating with the circumsciser, inviting the 'guests', meaning the staff, and running the whole show). Nevertheless, as a result of the overall contol exercised by the officials in the bureaucratic context of the Absorption Centre, a traditional cerermony such as circumcision lost its character and its religious value as well as its function in nurturing new and existing social relationships.

The immigrants could behave aggressively in their attempts to protest against the officials' decisions. That happened, for instance, when the immigrants' maintenance allowances were reduced considerably because they had missed the required Hebrew classes. The immigrants became extremely angry with the officials, whom they perceived as responsible for their deteriorating situation. One day, when I entered the office, Yardena, the secretary, and Chana, the matron, were chatting cheerfully. Yardena said: 'You wouldn't guess what you've missed yesterday. I was beaten up. I was just about to be taken to the emergency unit in the hospital … Rachel [an immigrant] hit me … She came to me yesterday and screamed at me "you have a belly full of bread; all the time you sit there writing", and she pushed me aside to get into Eliahu's [the Director at the time] room. I would have pushed her back, if Eliahu were not there, and it made me uncomfortable to want to do that.'

Supporting each other when the immigrants threatened their position was essential for the officials to keep an appearance of control. Thus, the officials used to laugh together, and to ridicule and mock the manifestations of the immigrants' opposition and resentment. They co-operated in substantiating their position in the face of any threat to the legitimacy of their control. Significantly, these instances of collectively acting out often used to take place in the office. These situations served, to borrow Kunda's expression, as 'presentational rituals'. Kunda defines such events as 'occasions for enacting, enforcing, and reinforcing the display of the managerially sanctioned member role and are thus a mechanism for mediating normative demands and normative responses' (1992: 159). The instances of collectively acting-out encouraged the emergence of staff solidarity in handling 'problematic' immigrants.

This was not only the case among the office workers. Rachamim, the maintenance worker, who was despised by the immigrants, one day complained to us, his colleagues in the office, about one of them. This particular immigrant used to leave items such as old beds and pieces of furniture outside his family caravan. Rachamim told us that the immigrant had told him, 'you're dirty'. Rachamim then began cursing in a very vulgar way and continued, 'I told him "Who's dirty, you bastard?" I'll show him, I'll take his head off. I almost put my finger, like that, into his eye, but someone held me back.' Rachamin went on with his story while Chana and Yardena encouraged him to go into more detail. Thus, gathering in the office and condemning the immigrants worked together as a kind of ritual, creating a collective solidarity and collegial conformity among all of the staff.

However, the immigrants were not the only ones to cast doubts over the officials' professionalism and essentialism. When among themselves, staff would ridicule their own colleagues for their inefficiency, and criticise their idleness. Once the staff did not have to bother about presenting a unified front against the immigrants, they could engage in harsh criticism and cynicism towards each other. In one of many discussions in the office about Rachamim, for instance, Yardena criticised the welfare aides. She told me that Avner, another maintenance worker, saw the welfare aides sitting in the office, and he had teased them about wasting time, drinking coffee, and doing nothing. The welfare aides had reacted by claiming that Rachamim often cooked *shakshuk.a* (a Moroccan dish) for himself. Yardena said to me, 'What did they need this for? Rachamim said nothing about them, and he can open his big mouth and talk.' It follows that everybody was aware of the fact that both the welfare aides and Rachamim did not do much in the Centre, but that it was in the mutual interest of all staff members that this fact should not be spelled out clearly. It was also the case that the senior staff, Yardena and Chana, felt responsible for keeping the peace in the office. Because the Centre's directors were replaced every few months, they seemed to act as if they were the ones in charge of the organisation; as they were assuming managerial responsibility, they had to be more careful about incurring Rachamim's ire than about insulting the weaker welfare aides.

In sum, 'doing nothing' may be seen as an apt description of the activities of the staff, both in the residents' opinions and in their own. In an intimate social context such as the Centre, where people were perceived as being either residents or staff, everyone was aware of the fact that there was 'nothing to do' to achieve the Centre's formal goals. The workers could not 'help' the immigrants, and the latter knew it. However, both the residents and the workers cooperated in maintaining these images of the staff's ownership of the Centre, professionalism, and control of the bureaucratic order, in a way that took place through continuous negotiations over the image of control.

The *somchot* – between images of professionalism, female identity and formal control

The temporary nature of the Absorption Centre played a significant, if tacit, role in determining the Centre's social life. As noted, the Directors changed frequently. Immigrants were expected to leave it after a short period of time (officially, up to six months after their arrival) and there was never any definite information about subsequent inflows of immigrants to the Centre. Most of the staff were hired on a temporary basis. Only a few – among whom were the Director, the Secretary, the Matron and the head of the maintenance staff – were permanent employees. Thus, the possibility of losing their jobs at a day's notice was at the back of most workers' minds. In response, they employed various techniques to keep their places for as long as possible. More than anything, these temporary workers had constantly to remind their superiors that the 'clients' (that is, the immigrants) needed them, and to assert that they themselves were an asset rather than a burden to the organisation. Presenting themselves as skilled workers was the main technique which the temporary workers used to strengthen their hold over their jobs. The temporary workers also searched for continuous approval of their affiliation by the officials in the Centre, a pursuit which involved distancing themselves from the immigrants. Meanwhile, in order for their colleagues to conceive of them as authentic and useful performers, the temporary workers needed the immigrants to act as an audience in the dramas of daily life, thereby validating their role. Having such an audience enabled the Centre's workers to present their assumed skills, to distinguish themselves categorically from the immigrants, their clients, and to gain the desired recognition of value from their peers.

Discussing the social context of violent behaviour, Emanuel Marx suggests using the term 'appealing violence' to emphasise the crucial part played by the audience in violent encounters. He argues: 'The assailant's aim is to appeal to other persons for a way out of his impasse' (1976: 63). In a similar vein, I suggest that workers needed and used the immigrants as an audience: through them they conveyed to their peers their claim to be perceived and treated as professionals, just like the officials in control of the Centre. A conspicuous example of this social phenomenon (which, following Marx's expression, might be described as 'appealing professionalism') can be found in the seemingly aggressive conduct by one specific group of women workers, the 'welfare aides' (*somchot*, sing. *somechet*), towards the immigrants.

The role of *somechet* was adopted by the Israeli social services in the mid-1970s, taking the formal category from the United States, where it had been introduced in the 1960s (Figure 3.2). The co-optation of para-professional indigenous workers served, in practice, to reduce social tensions. The job has been developed as a female occupation, being based on homemaking and childcare (see, for example, Etgar 1977). Most of the *somchot* were recruited locally; they possessed limited professional skills and were supervised by social workers. Very often women social workers that authorised them to intervene in 'families with social functioning disabilities'. The Welfare Department in the Jewish Agency adopted the role of the welfare-aide as a means for 'guiding Ethiopian families' in maintaining their family life. The Agency planning team defined the welfare-aide as 'a guide for implementing trained skills ... a tutor, an educator and an instructor for the Ethiopian family ... a learning family in an integration process ... for implementing learned skills needed for integration in Israeli society' (Horowitz and Frenkel 1984: 9). In constructing the content of the welfare aide's role the Agency officials drew upon notions of women's 'role in the family' and 'role at work', combining formal and informal elements. Through these welfare assistants, who acted as representatives of the social order at large (Herzog 1999), the female Ethiopian immigrants were, to a large extent, placed in the category of 'housewives' and 'mothers'.

This was illustrated on one occasion when the Secretary in the Centre, Yardena, drew my attention to the way in which she chose *somchot*: 'Do you know how I chose them? I didn't know a thing about what a welfare aide is and what is expected from her, so I asked each of them if she had children.' Yardena's confession reveals the fact that she did not refer to the formal written job prescription, but rather to some vague image that she had of what a welfare aide should be. In fact, she was not even familiar with the Agency's formal description of a welfare aide's role. Thus, it appears that this was identified, in practice, with having children and raising families. It follows that the formal role description has only an indirect relation to the secretary's decision to hire the welfare aides. She referred, quite probably, to the perceived image of the role, associated with her own female identity. Thus, there was no direct connection between the formal role prescription adopted and disseminated by the Jewish Agency, and the implementation of the welfare aides' role in the centres. It appears, therefore, that the heads of the Agency needed the ideological phrasing to develop what Kunda (1992) and others (Ouchi and Wilkins 1985, for example) define as organisational culture.

The Agency presented itself as controlling professional services, and as committed to the ideology of helping the needy newcomers from Ethiopia. This image served to establish the claim for monopoly over treating the immigrants, in the competition between absorbing organisations, and over budgets and donations. Thus, the detailed role prescription of the welfare aides was directed at the latter rather than at fieldworkers. Neither was it meant to be used as guidance for hiring employees. Organisational ideology was developed by the heads of the Jewish Agency, by both internal ideologists and external experts who, following Kunda's argumentation, 'create a systematic and full-blown theory' (1992: 218) of the organisation's culture. However, in our case, ideology serves financial and political needs rather than being a means of gaining normative control, as happens in the high-tech corporation Kunda studied.

This argument contradicts Strauss's hypothesis that 'the tendency to emphasise rules as part of structure is derived both from the rise of bureaucratic phenomena and from an inherited language of law and politics' (1981: 314). Inferring from my ethnography, rules and ideology are formulated in correspondence with the concrete and immediate needs of those who seek to attain and preserve power, rather than by inherent characteristics of the organisation.

There were six *somchot* in the absorption centre I studied. Each of them was attached to approximately ten families, or rather, in practice, to ten women. In their encounters with the immigrant women in the Centre the welfare aides functioned as representatives of the social environment of which they formed a part. The women immigrants in the Centre were perceived and encouraged by the welfare aides to fulfil the conventional 'normal' Israeli woman's role. The immigrant women were expected to accept, without question, responsibility for child and home care, like any 'ordinary' Israeli woman is supposed to. Thus, the unique role and the professional identity of the welfare aides in the social reality of the Centre was their *personal embodiment* as a live role-model for women as 'mothers' and 'housewives' according to so-called Israeli standards.

The following interaction between a welfare-aide and a woman immigrant, in the presence of the Centre's cultural coordinator and myself, demonstrates the need for the welfare aide to prove her expertise as an instructor of conventional 'women's roles', Israeli style. She had to work hard to make clear, to all participants in the encounter, her advantage as a nominated supervisor in matters of female duties, responsibilities and identity. The encounter demonstrates the daily need of the welfare aides to be recognised as professional members on the Centre's team and to gain recognition for their contribution in treating the immigrants.

> One day, in the cultural coordinator's office, while I was chatting with a welfare-aide and the cultural coordinator, an Ethiopian woman came in. The welfare-aide turned to her and told her aggressively, 'Enough with the coffee. You sit for two hours with one woman, then she sits for two hours at your place.' Then she turned to me and to the cultural coordinator, and added, 'Instead of drinking coffee all day long, she should wash her child's head. What do I do? Every day I comb my daughter's head and check it. Even the child says, 'Ma, look and see if I have lice.' I asked her what was wrong with drinking coffee with your friends, commenting that I do the same. She answered, 'Well, we too have this problem [where she lived], but I'm not like that. With me the house has to be clean before I do anything else.' Then she turned to the woman, saying, 'enough coffee', and pushed her slightly in her back toward the door.

The officials (including myself) controlled this encounter. We outnumbered the immigrant woman and enjoyed the advantage of the bureaucratic context of the office. Thus, the immigrant was made to feel an outsider intruding in the bureaucratic domain. She could be told to go away and clean her child's head, instead of wasting her time in socialising with friends. She could even be reproached, as if she were a child who had disappointed those in charge of her proper behaviour. Nevertheless, the point to be made here is that the welfare-aide used this situation to emphasise her role, in front of her colleagues who became her audience, as an expert on homemaking and childcare. Yet the content of the discourse exposes the fact that no 'real' expertise was involved in her work. Rather,

Figure 3.2. *Somechet* and Immigrant Woman with Children

the welfare aide used trivial instructions, such as the need to wash children's hair every day and check their heads regularly at times when there was a possibility of catching lice.

My question about what was wrong in drinking coffee with friends, however, opened up the welfare aide's efforts to look professional to ridicule. In questioning her statement about what the immigrant woman should not do, while presenting her own behaviour as a self-evident professional instructor as a model, I had discredited her expertise. I did not mean to offend her. My reaction was the result of feeling bad about the way the immigrant woman was being treated. This anti-collegial reaction means that I sympathised with the immigrant woman while putting aside my expected bureaucratic solidarity with the other officials, preferring to identify myself more with the underdog participant than with the more powerful participants in this bureaucratic encounter. The fact that the immigrant woman did not utter a word implies her social weakness, which derived in this white-controlled scene both from the structured bureaucratic power gaps and from her black skin.

This event also illustrates the efforts of the welfare aide to be perceived as a role model for the immigrant women. Her reproach to the immigrant was derived from her personal life experience. She referred to her duties as a housewife and a mother. Her excellence in performing these tasks justified, from her point of view, her condescending assumption of authority over the immigrant woman. Moreover, it appears that the welfare aide had to struggle for recognition by her colleagues of her professional expertise in a situation in which this was not self-evident. When one considers the act of physically pushing the immigrant woman, it appears that the welfare aide urgently needed to be perceived as vital, in a situation where she was neither needed nor essentially respected. She pushed the woman as a way of proving her own physical presence. Encounters in which welfare aides would enter immigrants' caravans without knocking on the door, criticise the women about dirt, cooking, childcare, and the like, were an everyday occurrence in the Centre. Criticising the women was one of the ways to claim control, due to their homemaking expertise, over the women immigrants. Thus, presenting themselves as 'role models' to be imitated, the welfare aides, as apparent from the above example, may use harsh criticism in trying to gain respect from the other officials.

The expression 'drinking coffee' was used by the welfare aide to denote 'a problem' which called for her interference. Playing the role of expert while prying daily into women's lives by inspecting for tidiness, the welfare aides strove to legitimate their presence and work in the Centre. Blaming the women for failing to clean their homes profoundly stigmatised them, while it restricted them to care of the home and children. In his study of a developed town, Shachak (1985) indicates the connection between negative stigmatisation, 'dirt' being one of its more conspicuous expressions, and bureaucratic control. Stigma, he argues, results from social distance put between those who supply services and those who receive them. Following Shachak's argument, it was clear that when the women's cleanliness was criticised, social distance was created. The welfare aide needed this distance to strengthen her claim for authority and for an uncontested professional position. The welfare aide taught the woman very little in this encounter that she did not already know.

My conversation with Zehava, my Ethiopian friend, about the Matron's demand that I evacuate my caravan for four days, illustrates the welfare aides' difficulties. Trying to sympathise with me, Zehava told me how she and other women immigrants were treated by the welfare aides: 'Nava [Zehava's welfare-aide] is not good. All the time she says, "Why don't you clean up?" I tell her that I am pregnant, my back hurts and I can't stand, but nothing changes her attitude.' Zehava went on to tell about the other welfare aides. 'They come to women who have had many guests and say, "Why is it dirty? Why don't you clean up?" The woman answers, "I am tired now. I shall clean in the evening".'

Zehava complained about the unkind and inconsiderate attitude regarding special circumstances, such as being pregnant or having guests. She did not, however, reject the principle of interference in her private life. Neither did she complain about being treated as responsible for cleanliness, while her husband's share of the responsibility was ignored. This example illustrates how daily prying by the *somchot* into the women's lives was given legitimacy by the immigrants themselves. The welfare aides behaved as if they had the self-evident authority to enter the caravans whenever it suited them and to instruct and criticise the Ethiopian women. The latter, however, did not seem to object to this intrusion but rather seemed to passively accept these manifestations of control.

Nevertheless, the immigrant women were not completely passive and vulnerable, but often used tactics of indirect resistance. They discussed and criticised the welfare aides' behaviour among themselves when the latter were not present. When talking with me, Zehava and other young Ethiopian women characterised the welfare aides as stupid and insensitive. All the immigrants mocked them. Moreover, the immigrant women ignored their demands in practice. Thus, for the welfare aides, the home territory of the immigrant women was in fact a threatening place, despite the fact that they used to enter it freely. They realised they were often despised and ridiculed there when they were not present, and were ignored when they were. The women's disregard of the welfare aides can also be demonstrated by the comments of Liora, a young immigrant woman, about her welfare aide: 'She does not do anything. She comes once a week, sits with me for a short time in the caravan and then goes away.' Little expertise was passed on; whatever the welfare aides' official role, the actual instruction of the women in how to do housework was apparently marginal or even nonexistent.

The officials in the Centre shared the belief that the welfare aides were 'doing nothing', expressing this attitude many times in my presence. An example is the task that Lussy, the Director, invented for the welfare aides. When the Centre received a limited number of jackets as a donation, Lussy demanded that the welfare aides visit all the caravans and find out the immigrants' dates of arrival to Israel, deciding to hand out the jackets to those who had arrived most recently. Yardena the Secretary commented, 'at least the welfare aides will be doing something'. It was therefore imperative for the welfare aides to be seen to be 'doing something' useful in order to validate their role in the eyes of the officials.

The need of the welfare aides to present themselves as experts on female issues influenced their rhetoric and actions concerning birth control devices and female sexuality. Discussions of women's sexuality played a significant role in everyday encounters between welfare aides and immigrant women. For instance, one immigrant woman, Ada, had difficulties in breastfeeding her premature baby. When Alice, her welfare aide, wanted to provide 'Materna' baby formula for her, the Matron told her that she must try to convince Ada to breastfeed the baby. Alice said she had tried it already, stating 'she does not want to hear about it'. The matron said: 'You have to tell her she must breastfeed the baby. She is so lazy. She is so apathetic. You give her Materna only if there is no choice. Tell her that if she does not breastfeed the baby, he will die.' Another, similar instance, this one involving birth control, also reveals the welfare aide's almost desperate need to seem involved in 'their' women's lives. A short time after Dorit's one-year-old baby, Avi, died, her welfare aide told me, 'I am going to take out Dorit's diaphragm, I have fixed her an appointment with the doctor for tomorrow.' Thus, the welfare-aide used the tragic situation of 'her' woman to emphasise her own position as a carer for the woman's well-being.

It seems, therefore, that in their encounters with the immigrant women the welfare aides were expected, and were even encouraged by their superiors, to exert control over them. These relationships between the woman and the welfare aide defined and symbolised, for those involved in the interactions, their respective duties and responsibilities. Both the welfare aides and the immigrant women were encouraged to comply with their belonging to 'their' niche as 'women', but there was a degree of vagueness in the welfare aides' position and authority. The relationship between the women and the welfare aides is best described in terms of mutual power dependence rather than anuthority, as the immigrant women had to endure regular intervention in their personal lives as a condition of the permission to stay in the caravans and the Centre, which was controlled from the outside by Jewish Agency representatives. This analysis follows Emerson (1962), who argues that social contact necessarily entails both mutual dependence and control. These relations imply that partners to social encounters desire objects that others own and can provide them with. In this case, the welfare aides needed the daily encounters with the immigrant women to substantiate their claims to the vital nature of their positions on the Centre's staff and, for their part, the immigrant women needed the continuous implicit permission to use the Centre's facilities and services granted by the officials.

One day I was invited by Lilian, one of the welfare aides, to accompany her when visiting one of 'her' women. I followed her into the woman's caravan, which she entered without knocking on the door. A woman was washing the floor, which was flooded with water. The radio was loud. With no hesitation Lilian stepped straight ahead to the bedroom and came back with a baby on her arms. She was excited and full of pride. Lilian said: 'I am crazy about this baby.' I asked her carefully whether the baby was not asleep. She answered, 'This is not what I care about.' She came closer to me and showed me how sweet the baby was, boasting of how much money she could get out from American visitors for taking pictures of this baby. She claimed: 'This is the prettiest baby in the Centre.' The mother continued to wash the floor. The radio went on playing, the welfare-aide beamed triumphantly over every smile of the baby, who was trying to close his eyes. Then Lilian loudly reproached the woman, 'All you need is that Rachamim should see you washing the floor like that!'. When I asked her what was wrong about the way she was washing the floor, Lilian explained: 'This is a PVC floor and flooding it with water spoils it. It must be washed only with the rag.'

Later on I asked her if she was instructing the woman. She replied, 'What for? She does not need to be taught any more. She knows everything, I come only to see how things are ... if everything is O.K.' Lilian felt free to enter the caravan without knocking on the door, and to behave freely, even reproaching the woman in front of me, as if she were a little girl. The immigrant woman seemed to behave in a passive, helpless way, as if it was not possible to reject the intrusion into her private life or to object to the domination of the welfare aide over her baby. All she seemed to be able to do was to ignore the offence, to keep doing what she was busy with.

As much as the weakness and passivity of the woman is highlighted in the above case, it is the welfare aide's dependence on 'her' woman that is of interest here. Lilian still visited the caravan and presented herself as having an interest in the woman, when it was obvious, even to herself, that her functions were over and she was not needed. In this encounter Lilian presented herself to me as the right person to evaluate the woman's functioning as a 'good housewife'. She struggled to be perceived as having professional skills, and seemed rather pathetic in her efforts to show herself as the mother's and baby's patron, while the baby was sleeping and the mother continued to be busy with her work. Moreover, Lilian revealed a weakness: specifically, that I represented a threat to her. Finding me walking among the caravans and visiting the immigrants, she became very active in demonstrating her control over the whole situation and over 'her' territory and everything in it.

I conclude that rather than actually functioning as a role model, the welfare-aide merely projected such an image to convince her colleagues of her professional authority and indispensability.

Concluding remarks

The literature on organisations emphasises the formal aspects of control which convey an impression of stability, essentiality and self-evident 'formalisation, codification, and enforcement of rules and regulations', as Kunda notes (1992: 220). At the same time, Arnold Tannenbaum argues: 'Organisation implies control ... it is the function of control to bring about conformance to organisational requirements and achievement of the ultimate purposes of the organisation' (1967: 3). In social frameworks which structure social distance and power gaps between social categories (an important example is Goffman 1961, and the Absorption Centre another), the basic impression that emerges is of dichotomised relations between dependent powerless immigrants and powerful dominating officials. Such an analysis is implied, for instance, in Bernstein's (1981) work about the transition camps for immigrants in the 1950s.

However, other writings stress the informal and dynamic aspects which are essentially embedded in organisations, and which render elasticity and vagueness to the concepts of organisational power and control. Strauss (1981) associates organisational control with ongoing negotiations between participants in the organisation. Burawoy (1979) suggests that consent to control is not automatic and must be worked out. Kunda elaborates on normative control under which behaviours and activities 'are driven by internal commitment, strong identification with company goals, intrinsic satisfaction from work'. It is 'the attempt to elicit and direct the required efforts of members by controlling the underlying experiences, thoughts, and feelings that guide the actions (1992: 11). Greenberg (1982) argues that there is no self-evident control that creates social categories of powerful versus powerless people, even in institutions that structure extreme power gaps, such as prisons.

My data indicate that in the Absorption Centre people used symbols or images of control in the absence of actual control. This may seem more like an illusion than a working reality; however, bureaucratic and professional control were inseparable from daily encounters as negotiable constructs of reference. Control was associated with theatrical performance by actors who presented their claims for control before an audience, trying to impress and convince others of their professional skills and formal authority. There was a vague authority, but only limited professionalism (or even none at all), behind the workers' activities. Furthermore, these were not even actually needed to achieve the Centre's formal goals. The Centre's residents, staff and visitors were all aware of the situation, but nevertheless all contributed to its continuation, due possibly to the Centre's perceived temporariness and impending exclusion, and the loss of needed resources. Being part of larger bureaucratic systems, the officials could rely on other state organisations (such as the police) to support their claim for control when consent was not assured. At the same time the immigrants' cooperation could be expected, as they were quite aware of the fact that the prices paid for living in the Centre were only temporary.

Nevertheless, whether control was perceived or real, power gaps between the two main categories, immigrants and officials (and their support staff) were constructed into everyday life. The term 'everyday resistance', suggested by some scholars, may contribute to the understanding of these uneven confrontations and to the immigrants' behaviour in particular. Scott (1992) compared the hidden transcript of the weak with that of the powerful, and of both hidden transcripts to the public transcript of power relations. He describes (1990) 'everyday resistance' as weapons held by relatively weak groups. Exploring the fugitive political conduct of subordinate groups contributes to the understanding of resistance to domination. The weak may use simple means, such as slowing down, faking, false consent, stealing, false ignorance, and even sabotage. In this class struggle, the weak refrain from direct symbolic confrontation with the authorities and with the norms of the dominating elite. Similarly, Abu-Lughod (1990) suggests that acts of resistance carried out by powerless groups disclose larger processes of power and social dominance. Feierman (1990) suggests that if everyday resisters want to be effective they cannot reveal their intentions openly, because the authorities are too powerful for a vulnerable group to confront directly.

In the Israeli context Motzafi-Haller (2002: 189) discusses Mizrachi ('Eastern') intellectuals' subversion practices and discourses, in the first half of the twentieth century, in resisting the Ashkenazi ('Western') hegemonic discourse. She distinguishes between two kinds of subversion. The one derives from open protest, which is the outcome of explicit and conscious act of resistance. The other is the unintended potential of subversion, which its carriers are not completely aware of. Describing the confrontation of immigrants from Ethiopia with the authorities in Israel, Kaplan (1997) considers 'everyday resistance' as the immigrants' most significant ongoing activity. Kaplan criticises scholars (e.g. Weill 1995 and S. Kaplan 1988) for considering only explicitly political or ethnic activities, such as demonstrations and protest marches that are formally and openly organised. He claims that this Western-based thinking produced mainly documentation of riotous outbreaks of discontent, but neglected the resentment and anger that were part of the immigrants' everyday life. However, it should be stressed that the weakness had nothing to do with the immigrants' cultural background, nor with their migrant position. The power relations and gaps were the outcome of the 'absorption policy' that concentrated the immigrants in the Centre and fostered their weakness and dependence on the officials and the 'absorbing' organisations.

Acknowledgement

I am grateful to Professor Emanuel Marx for his insightful comments.

Notes

1. I conducted my research, which was part of my Ph.D. thesis (Herzog 1990), between 1983 and 1985 at the time of Operation Moshe, the first of two waves of immigrants brought over from Ethiopia by the Israeli government. During that period I lived in a caravan, one of the tens that were inhabited by the immigrants, with my two-year-old son, Dan. Residing with the immigrants enabled us to socialise with them. Also, I volunteered to work as an assistant to the cultural coordinator. This activity facilitated my access to the 'office' daily life, thus enriching significantly my observations.
2. Absorption Centres were established in the 1960s to accommodate immigrants from Eastern Europe and Anglo-Saxon countries. In the 1980s and 1990s they were used mainly for immigrants from Ethiopia and a few immigrants from Russia. These immigrants were taken directly from the airport to the Absorption Centres.

    A 1970 document produced by the Jewish Agency defined the main aims of the Absorption Centres as follows:

    'A. To allow the heads of families to learn Hebrew. B. To prepare the immigrants for permanent settlement. C. To bring the immigrants close to Israeli society and the values of its people and the state.'

    Nevertheless, in relating to the 'absorption' of the immigrants from Ethiopia the aims were conspicuously enlarged, as the immigrants were collectively described and treated as needing extensive social help and cultural change in order to adapt themselves to the new context.

The following document of the Jewish Agency (1984) demonstrates the rhetorical transformation that the Agency went through with regards to the absorption of immigrants from Ethiopia in the Absorption Centres:

The tasks before us are: training the immigrants from Ethiopia for absorption into Israeli society, passing on to them knowledge, understanding and the tools that will allow them to cope with a new reality while preserving their traditional social and cultural frameworks. In order to ensure their absorption in Israel, the Ethiopian immigrants need to undergo the following stages of preparation: A. The acquisition of skills needed to care for their families and home according to Israeli standards. B. The knowledge and the ability to understand contact with, and the reception of services from, the establishment. C. The understanding of the family cell and the direct responsibility parents have for children and the functions of each member of the family. D. The learning of the language. E. The study and understanding of various aspects of life in Israel: cleanliness, health, dress, living quarters, work, salary, rights and obligations, payment of services rendered, etc. F. The study of religious customs as practiced in Israel, etc. These needs can be answered within the transitional framework of the absorption centre. This framework offers a basic project that aims at alleviating the shock of transition, arranging medical treatment, facilitating socialisation processes, offering study programs and vocational training, and imparting the first stages of language learning.

3. Much of the vast sociological and anthropological literature on the integration of immigrants in Israel assumes that they are divided into two main categories, namely 'Eastern' and 'Western' or 'traditional' and 'modern' immigrants. Most of them describe the 'absorption process' as a 'cultural' phenomenon, and deal mainly with the difficulties of the integration of 'Eastern' Jews (e.g. Eisenstadt 1954; Bar-Yosef 1959; Shokeid and Deshen 1977). They suggest openly or imply that the 'Eastern' immigrants need to go through extensive social and cultural changes in the process of becoming Israelis and in their adaptation to the 'modern', 'Western', way of life in Israel. All governments used this 'academic' analysis in their 'absorbing' policies and pursued practices that imposed on the immigrants' 'Israeli' values and norms. Nearly all studies on the 'absorption' of Ethiopian immigrants follow this ethnocentric rhetoric and focus on cultural gaps and differences between the immigrants and 'veterans' (e.g. Ben-Ezer 1985; Rosen 1985). Earlier studies on absorption centres emphasise the ideological aims of the 'absorbers', in terms of the social, psychological, and educational services offered to the immigrants, who are supposedly in need of help to overcome the trauma of immigration (see Horowitz and Frenkel 1975). However, a few studies like that of Marx (1976), Bernstein (1981) and mine (Herzog, 1990, 1999), have argued that the 'absorption of immigrants' is better understood in terms of bureaucratic control. These studies emphasised the central role played by state agencies. They suggested that the integration of immigrants is characterised by power dependence relations that develop in the bureaucratic settings in which specific groups of immigrants, namely of Asian and African origin, have been concentrated for long periods of time. A recently published anthology (Hever, Shenhav and Motzafi-Haller 2002) which discusses Mizrachi perspectives on society and culture in Israel, elaborates on the issues of 'absorption' of immigrants from Muslim countries and of 'Mizrachi' identity, in terms of postcolonial theory. This study criticises the cultural domination of the Ashkenazi hegemonic discourse and adapts the academic, ideological and political 'project' that challenges prevailing dominant concepts which produce 'Mizrachi' identity as a 'problem'.

Bibliography

Abu-Lughod, L. 1990. 'The Romance of Resistance: Tracing Transformations of Power through Bedouin Women', *American Ethnologist*, 17 (1): 41–55.

Bar-Yosef, R. 1959. 'The Moroccans: Background to the Problem', in S.N. Eisenstadt et al. (eds.), *Integration and Development in Israel*. Universities Press, pp. 419–28.

Ben-Ezer, G. 1985. 'Cross-Cultural Misunderstandings: The Case of Ethiopian Immigrant Jews in Isareli Society', *Israel Social Science Research*, 3: 1–2.

Bernstein, D. 1981. 'Immigrant Transit Camps: The Formation of Dependence Relations in Israeli Society', *ERS Ethnic and Social Studies*, 4 (1): 26–40.

Burawoy, M. 1979. *Manufacturing Consent, Changes in the Labor Process Under Monopoly Capitalism.* Chicago and London: University of Chicago Press.

Eisenstadt, N.S. 1954. *The Absorption of Immigrants*. London: Routledge and Kegan Paul.

Emerson, M.R. 1962. 'Power-Dependence Relations', *American Sociological Review*, 27: 31–41.

Etgar, T. 1977. *Chonchim Vesomchot, Services for Assisting and Advancing Families.* Jerusalem: Ministry for Welfare and Labour.

Feierman, S. 1990. *Peasant Intellectuals: Anthropology and History in Tanzania.* Madison: University of Wisconsin Press.

Goffman, E. 1961. *Asylums.* Garden City, NY: Anchor.

Greenberg, O. 1982. *Women in Israeli Prison.* Tel Aviv: Cherikover.

Herzog, E. 1990. *Closure and Power-Dependence Relations, in an Absorption Centre with Ethiopian Immigrants.* Ph.D. Thesis. The Hebrew University, Jerusalem.

————. 1999. *Immigrants and Bureaucrats: Ethiopians in an Israeli Absorption Centre.* Oxford: Berghahn Books.

Hever, H., Y. Shenhav, and P. Motzafi-Haller (eds.). 2002. *Mizrachim in Israel: A Critical Observation into Israel's Ethnicity.* Tel Aviv: Van Leer institute/Hakibbutz Hameuchad.

Horowitz, T. and C. Frenkel. 1975. *Immigrants in Absorption Centres: Organisational and Sociological Aspects.* Jerusalem: Jewish Agency.

————. 1984. *A Model for the Absorption of Ethiopian Immigrants in Transition Frameworks.* A Working Paper for the Planning Team, Directors of Absorption Centres for Ethiopians. Jerusalem: Jewish Agency.

Kaplan, S. 1988. 'The Beta Israel and the Rabbinate: Law, Politics and Ritual', *Social Science Information* 28 (3): 357–70.

————. 1997. 'Everyday Resistance among Ethiopian Jews: A View from the Research, and a View on Research', *Theory and Criticism* (Summer): 163–73.

Kunda, G. 1992. *Engineering Cutlure, Control and Commitment in a High-Tech Corporation.* Philadelphia: Temple University Press.

Marx, E. 1976. 'Appealing Violence', in E. Marx (ed.), *The Social Context of Violent Behaviour: A Social Anthropological Study in an Israeli Immigrant Town.* London: Routledge and Kegan Paul, pp. 63–74.

Motzafi-Haller, P. 2002. 'Mizrachi Intellectuals 1946–1951: The Ethnic Indentity and Its Borders', in H. Hever, Y. Shenhav, P. Motzafi-Haller (eds.), *Mizrachim in Israel: A Critical Observation into Israel's Ethnicity.* Tel Aviv: Van Leer institute/ Hakibbutz Hameuchad, 152–190.

Ouchi, W.G. and L.A. Wilkins. 1985. 'Organisational Culture', *Annual Review of Sociology* 11: 457–83.

Rosen, C. 1985. 'Core Symbols of Ethiopian Identity and Their Role in Understanding the Beta Israel Today', *Israel Social Science Research* (3) 1–2.

Scott, C.J. 1990. *Weapons of the Weak*. New Haven: Yale University Press.

———. 1992. *Domination and the Arts of Resistance: Hidden Transcripts*. New Haven: Yale University Press.

Shachak, O. 1985. *The Absence of Power and the Negative Stigmatisation as Central Components of project Renewal in Yerucham*. Beer-Sheva: Ben-Gurion University.

Shokeid, M. and S. Deshen. 1977. *The Generation of Transition*. Jerusalem: Yad Ben-Zvi.

Strauss, A. et. al. 1981. 'Negotiated Order and the Co-ordination of Work', in A. Strauss (ed.), *Psychiatric Ideologies and Institutions*. New Brunswick and London: Transaction Books, pp. 292–315.

Tannenbaum, A. 1967. *Control in Organizations*. New York: McGraw-Hill.

Weill, S. 1995. 'Representations of Leadership among Ethiopian Jews in Israel', in S. Kaplan, T. Parfitt and E. Trevisan Semi (eds.), *Between Africa and Zion*. Jerusalem: Ben Zvi Institute, pp. 230–39.

4

LOYALTY AND POLITICS:
THE DISCOURSES OF LIBERALISATION

Simone Abram

Introduction

In this chapter, I examine attempts to introduce a new governing system into a Norwegian municipality and trace the transformations of identities and relationships within the bureaucracy. In Norwegian law, the roles of politicians and bureaucrats are relatively clearly circumscribed, yet this fundamental relationship is a constant theme, particularly for council officers in local government. The division of labour between the political and the administrative is a central problematic in the management of the public sector. The significant differences between the management of public and private organisations congregate around this relationship as the crux of democratic practice.

Since the 1970s, major changes have been taking place in the practice of public sectors in many countries, particularly in response to the pressure from right-wing politicians to mimic market systems within state bureaucracies. One of the most dramatic processes was the set of transformations carried out in Britain known as 'Thatcherism', characterised by Jenkins (1995) as a ruthless savaging of the welfare state by an unaccountable ruling class. In the Scandinavian countries, the welfare state has encountered difficulties resulting from economic crises, but one of the most resilient democratic welfare states has persisted in Norway. Even here, however, after nearly half a century of domination by the Labour party, the Conservative and Christian Democrat coalitions have caught the 'liberalisation' bug, and local government is being transformed according to similar models to those found in other northern European countries.

The extraordinary pervasiveness of this mentality of governing requires many levels of analysis. On one level, international networks support what is called policy-learning from state to state and region to region (with specific financial support from the EU), with international academic debates helping to spread new paradigms, on another level there are microprocesses of change within each organisation. The interpretation of international models of government happens through both national and local government, and at the local level it encounters particular contexts where its implementation is transformed and transforms. The study of these localised processes indicates how a new way of thinking about bureaucracy has been so effective in taking hold in so many diverse situations.

Problems in the encounter between public management and markets have been a growing issue in both management studies and political science, where the introduction of market style structures and ideologies has been referred to as 'the New Public Management' (Farnham and Horton 1996; Ferlie 1996; Stoker 2000). A key notion in the New Public Management (NPM) is that it is a politically motivated transformation in bureaucratic practice which therefore threatens the Weberian insistence on the separation of the administrative from the political. By introducing pseudo-market-mechanisms into public administration, the roles of local government bureaucracies change, for example from service production to the management of tenders and contracts, implying a fundamental change in the structure of government organisations and the professions and skills required by their employees.

Such transformation of the public sector has also been recognised as an international phenomenon (Minogue, Polidano and Hulme, 1998) with early examples in the U.S.A., U.K., New Zealand and Australia promulgated heavily by the World Bank, for example (see Common 1998). Responses to this phenomenon have been emerging within Norway since the rules for the management of local government were significantly loosened during the 1990s (Baldersheim et al. 1997; Aarsæther and Vabo 2002). In contrast to many European states, local government in Norway has carried an extraordinarily high degree of public legitimacy, and has maintained responsibility for a much greater range of public service and state activity. Norwegian local government has long been the locus of delivery of the welfare state and has historically been a relatively autonomous power, although in recent years this status has weakened. The move towards so-called New Public Management has perhaps come later than in the U.K., but is rapidly gaining ground in Norwegian municipalities, particularly under the post-2002 liberal government. As private-sector management credos are introduced to municipalities, the role of the political is becoming more difficult to define, and a struggle is ensuing over the staking out of ground for legitimate political action.

In the lives of local government administrators, particularly among senior-level bureaucrats – as opposed to what Lipsky (Lipsky 1980) calls 'street level' bureaucrats, or service deliverers – attention to being nonpolitical is key. During fieldwork in a Norwegian local council (*kommune*) during 2000 (with repeat visits since) and in a set of interviews in another council in 2003, I found that the separation of political and administrative roles was often emphasised. More significantly, though, this issue fed into a series of reorganisations which had in common a move towards free-market liberalism in welfare services and the adoption of elements of the so-called New Public Management. During this period the national government shifted from a Labour-dominated to a right-wing dominated coalition, consisting in the 2002 government of an unstable three-way coalition between the Conservatives (H), the Christian Democrat Party (KFP) and the populist 'Forward' party (FRP). This coalition was dominated by a market liberalism ideology and pressure to cut public expenditure and privatise public services (with, of course, the implicit, although not proven, assumption that privatisation would lead to decreased costs).

The consequences of dogmatic privatisation were felt extremely sharply in early 2003, when a lengthy period of extremely cold weather coincided with the stock market flotation of electricity provision, leading to a quadrupling of the cost of electricity to the consumer. The liberalising ideology which marked even the Norwegian Labour party throughout the 1990s had freed the electricity-pricing mechanism from the moralised social principles on which Norway's hydro-electricity was built up during the twentieth century to a stock-market based free-market system. In this, it is possible to detect a gradual but enormous shift in the moral ideology of governance in the second half of the twentieth century from one of social responsibility to one of free-market liberalism, which I hope to demonstrate here in the context of local government.

I will argue in this paper that a discourse on the separation of administrative and political roles in local government was used in a number of municipalities to legitimise a move towards a market ideology and the creeping privatisation of welfare services. In the name of clarifying political roles, supposedly in the interests of re-engaging public interests in local politics and enhancing democracy, and through the construction of a disciplined 'public face', a number of local government bureaucracies introduced the most political of all changes, the move to free-market liberalism, with significant implications for the moral self-perceptions (identities) of both politicians and administrators. These roles, therefore, can be understood as intertwined with both personae and identities of participants.

The context of liberalisation

Why, in a country with what may be the strongest economy in Europe, should the welfare state be perceived as in crisis? Norway was the only country in the Western economic world which did not suffer from a recession in the late twentieth century, and despite an economic downturn during the first years of the twenty-first century, has invested heavily in the stock market through a so-called 'oil fund', from its North Sea oil revenues. Despite this extraordinary economic success – or, some would say, because of it – the Norwegian welfare state has expanded beyond all expectations. Whereas welfare was built up as an antidote to extreme poverty on a principle of egalitarianism amongst Norwegian citizens, the welfare budget has continued to expand even as the general 'standard of living' in Norway has grown. It is now generally accepted that welfare services follow a particular pattern of need and demand whereby rather than the *need* for welfare declining as standard of living rises, in fact *demand* for welfare increases as expectations rise and the scope of welfare continues to expand (Hanson 1999). Since the 1980s, Norwegian local government has begun to respond to the notion of scarcity, with both national and local welfare budgets being gradually reduced. The result has been an overwhelming focus on budgets as the dominant framework for local politics, and the use of euphemistic metaphors for budget cutting: efficiency, effectivisation, improvement, etc.

There has also been a discourse within the larger local government organisations (larger municipalities) that sector-based organisation has led to internal power struggles and the proliferation of government for its own sake. This discourse emerges from the paradigm of New Public Management itself, being one of the justifications for change through a notion that emphasis ought to shift towards the 'users' of services rather than the interests of the workings of the bureaucracy. In addition, the argument that welfare creates dependency has been widespread, not only within right-wing political parties but across the political spectrum, supporting moves to reduce public spending. As it is difficult to reduce welfare spending, this has become another of the key motivations for administrative change. Much of the reorganisation in municipalities has been intended to create a role for politicians which requires them to be aware of 'levels of service' and to be responsible for adjusting criteria for entry to welfare privileges. Thus, rather than considering the rights of citizens to certain standards of living, they are concerned with the distribution of services from a range of public and private organisations to differing demands from 'customers'.

It is not possible here to go into details of the Norwegian state government's response to global liberal political economics, other than to say that Norway has not been immune to global political processes and has followed a widespread right-wing shift in European politics. What is striking here is the pervasiveness of liberal discourses from central government through what is claimed to be a relatively politically autonomous local government sector, and it is my argument here that the traditional ethical and managerial concerns of a welfare-oriented local government are paradoxically providing the legitimisation for the introduction of liberal politics at the local level. The relationship between politicians and administrators is becoming the arena for the politicisation of local bureaucracy and the depoliticisation of local politics.

The discourse of distinction

Two particular discursive forms can be identified in this process, and both can be illustrated from my fieldwork in a Norwegian *kommune*, or local government municipality, which I refer to as 'Vestforstad'. Fieldwork[1] consisted not of residence, as the field in this case is not constituted by a cohabiting group, but a society defined by the workplace (Kunda 1992). Instead, the range of activities included presence in the town hall (where I was furnished with an office) and other municipal offices, 'shadowing' of various municipal employees, frequent attendance at council meetings, both formal and informal, and a wide range of related activities, including visiting informants' homes and accompanying them on residential 'seminars'. In addition, a series of interviews complemented the more informal fieldwork. Fieldwork was limited, however, to the council, and contact with residents not directly involved in municipal activities was less systematic (for a fuller argument, see Abram 2003). For the purposes of examining discourses through which political changes are progressing, however, focus on the internal practices within the council were more appropriate. Access offered by the council was extremely good, allowing me to trace arguments through a range of processes and to explore a range of different perspectives in different sectors and amongst different groups of actors. In order to tell the story of the reorganisation of the council, it is necessary to look at a range of sources, of course, including both the views of key senior individuals but also of the various actors around them. By building up a picture through the use of many different perspectives, it is possible to begin to fathom the extent of particular discourses and the range of interpretations adopted towards them.

Vestforstad can be characterised as a relatively highly populated *kommune* (in Norwegian terms, with a population of 50,000) some miles west of the capital, Oslo. The Conservatives form the largest of seven political parties represented in the *kommune*'s council, which is elected on a four-year cycle by a list system of proportional representation. Property prices are high, income levels are high, and the population has grown by a factor of ten within fifty years, being within convenient commuting distance of the capital and close to the former location of the country's principal airport.[2] In 1993 the *kommune* began a series of reorganisation projects with a variety of goals for various actors, but under a slogan of bringing 'service-users into focus', that is, of placing more emphasis on the views of residents than on the priorities of bureaucratic organisation. This process was a response partly to the Conservatives' aim of reducing welfare cost, partly to the gradual reduction of state-financing of local services, and also a response to the introduction of a Local Government Act in 1993 which opened up the possibility of greater variety in the structures in local government. However, the *kommune*'s chief executive, the *Rådmann*, was also influenced by the Bertelsmann Institute's international campaign for 'improvement' in the public sector. The key themes, therefore, were client focus and budget reduction. The latter arose from the *Rådmann*'s concern over a trend of increasing expenditure and decreasing income, about which he argued it would only be a matter of time before, as he put it, the graphs would cross and the council would go into economic deficit. One of his main aims during the reorganisation process was to make what he saw as an economic inevitability clear to politicians so that they would take what he called 'responsible' economic decisions.

In the *kommune*, the relationship between the administration, personified in the *Rådmann*, and the elected representative body, personified in the mayor (*Ordfører*) is a key to the workings of the council and the formal and legal separation of political and administrative activities. This relationship symbolises the fundamental principles of the Norwegian welfare state, not only in its formal characteristics, but in its uneasy lack of clarity between formal statement and enaction, and is the first of the discursive forms which I believe have been key to the current transformations. Although the creation of the legal separation was based on an ideology of public interest and a non-partisan state, the Mayor of Vestforstad, elected on the Conservative list, used a business metaphor to describe the roles of the two key symbolic figures in the Norwegian *kommune*:

> In very simple terms, you could say that the Rådmann is the administrative director in 'Vestforstad plc'. He is responsible for management and the delivery of service production that is decided by the politicians. He has complete responsibility for personnel. He has responsibility for the work that is done. The Mayor can be thought of as the CEO in the company and is responsible for ensuring that the decisions taken by the council are put into action.

The two people who occupy these roles are called by their positional titles (*Rådmann, Ordfører*) in all formal situations. If they are referred to by their personal names, this is done to indicate that they are being addressed as citizens rather than as the holders of these posts. In council meetings, for example, the Mayor, as chair, is always addressed by every speaker as the opening to their contribution to a debate. If the Mayor wishes to make a contribution, he will metaphorically step down from his position as non-party chair of the council, and address the chair himself, at which point he may be referred to by others by his personal name. Similarly, *Rådmann* is the formal personification of the administration of the council, and he was almost exclusively referred to as *Rådmann* in conversations, formal and informal, within the town hall. As the mayor commented by way of explanation: 'It is a way of trying to make explicit the Mayor's and the *Rådmann's* roles. I don't really understand what else we could use?'

In practice, the relationship between the two figures in Vestforstad was close, according to both individuals. Keeping the boundary between politics and administration presented a challenge, which the *Rådmann* described as follows:

> It's impossible really to draw a clear line. So we don't get too worked up about it. What is important is that there is a good dialogue between politicians and the administration. So we talk together all the time and correct each other. And I can say to the Mayor, 'that's my job', and the Mayor can say to me, 'now you're doing politics, that's my job'. That we can exchange views through a continual discussion, without starting to battle with each other.

Others in the *kommune* felt that it was too close, however, muddying the separation of bureaucracy from politics which was considered to be crucial for the proper functioning of a municipality. The creation of a distinct political arena was central to the reorganisation of the council, although the stated intention from the *Rådmann* and mayor was more in line with the NPM discourse of focusing on service users. The *Rådmann's* explanation was as follows:

The most important reason for reorganisation was to set a clearer focus on service-users. ... that's why we are here: they are our customers. They need to get more attention and that is why we are strengthening the service-units, giving them more authority, because our users know them. So users can get responses from service-units without things always being sent over to the bureaucracy and back again. We want to delegate more authority so that users can be dealt with more effectively.

While the *Rådmann* identified it as his intention to reorganise the council with a view to efficiency and user focus, the head of personnel framed the changes within contractual conditions:

It began with a council decision where we [administrators] were asked to look at the sector leaders' fixed-term posts, or rather at the sector structure ...

Sector leaders have been employed on six-year contracts ... which run out now ... So before we started with a new round of contracts, the council asked us to look at the way we organise ourselves in sectors, whether we ought to change them before we began with a new round of contracts. So then we began the [administrative reorganisation] project. When we began to think about it, we realised we couldn't just look at the structure, it is more complicated than that, we had to look at the whole system, planning systems, employment policy, etc.

So we brought in an external consultant for the start-phase and established a rather comprehensive project with many working groups which have worked on a number of proposals, one of which was to change the organisation's structure so that we wouldn't have sectors any more.

This account offers a number of what we might call post hoc rationalisations of a process with multiple motivations (Flyvbjerg 1998). It suggests that a routine examination of contract renewals expanded to take in more general issues. It begins with a declaration (of timing) phrased in the formal discourse of council practice: that the council received the suggestion to examine the fixed-term contracts as a proposal from the *Rådmann*. In formal terms, any case discussed by the council is a transaction between the mayor and the *Rådmann*, who is obliged, according to municipal law, to offer appropriate advice and information, and then to implement council decisions. However, a more historiographic account came from a legal expert in the executive's office, who had been secretary to the political committee considering change. According to him, the process of change derived from the revised Local Government Act of 1993, which allowed councils to choose their own structure, rather than following a national standard, an opportunity seized upon by the ruling Conservative Party. They began by setting up a political committee to examine making changes in the political structure of the council, but when this was voted down by the full council of the municipality, they focused instead on making administrative changes and came back to political reorganisation again later (changes were implemented in 2002).

It is also worth noting that the *kommune* used an external consultant (from the international management consultancy KPMG), bringing private-sector management principles into the public sector. Abrahamson characterises these consultancies as diffusing 'managerial fads and fashions' (Abrahamson 1991), and it would appear that within Vestforstad the KPMG consultant was influential in expanding the structural review of contracts into a comprehensive reorganisation. As one of the project-group leaders explained, officially the start of the process may have been that the *Rådmann* put forward a proposal to the council, before the end of the directors' contracts, that the appropriateness of having four sectors ought to be reviewed, but the process soon became much more all-encompassing, with a wide range of objectives taken on by nine administrative project groups over several months: '*so administrative reorganisation is about very, very many different things ...* 'as the project group leader remarked.

In a retrospective interview (2003), the *Rådmann* suggested that the whole reorganisation was inspired by Bertelsmann's criteria, although these were never mentioned during fieldwork in 2000. The *Rådmann's* use of Bertelsmann indicates the politicisation of administrative change, as Bertelsmann clearly promotes privatisation, competition and audit-style management. Although officially the council requested the administration to engage in a reorganisation, the *Rådmann's* retrospective account suggests that he was active in bringing reorganisation onto the agenda. Indeed, it seems likely that he was appointed in 1993 partly for this reason. Comparative research in another *kommune* that has undergone a very similar reorganisation indicates that the *Rådmann's* enthusiasm for New Public Management has been key to the transformations, although it is those councils led by the Conservative party which have been first into the fray for this type of reorganisation. According to Bertelsmann's principles, a key element of reorganisation lies in the delegation of decision making from a centralised management structure to the individual service providers, in what is referred to as a 'flattening ' of the organisational structure. This flattening is illustrated by a very simple visual metaphor, the organisational structure chart, as adopted in Vestforstad (see Figure 4.1a, b). In these diagrams, 'result units' are service delivery organisations with direct contact with council clients (e.g. social service providers, educational establishments, etc. Where these were formerly grouped into service sectors, each with support staff providing, say, accounting, personnel and managerial services, in the new system they operate independently and 'buy in' support from a central services division. Sector managers who form part of the *Rådmann's* team have strategic policy roles, rather than direct managerial duties over sectors as before. In practice, this structure was not really achieved, although it is partly my point that such managerial diagrams perform a communicative act rather than merely representing 'reality'. The diagram of the flattened structure, with its associated discourse of 'efficiency', was used as a persuasive tool to generate enthusiasm among staff for the reorganisation of their working practices.

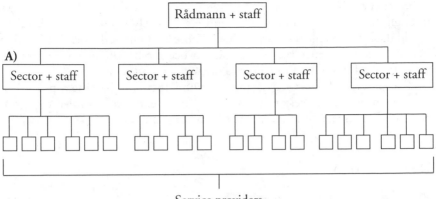

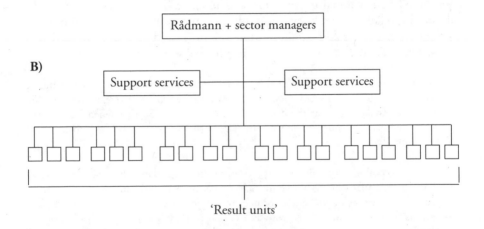

Figure 4.1 (a) 'Hierarchical' structure: each layer has its own support staff. (b) 'Flat' structure. All result-units use centralised support services (personnel, accounting, legal, etc.)

Another key element adopted is the introduction of a purchaser-provider model, or what can be called an 'internal market', opening up the possibility of competition with private companies to deliver council services (a form of privatisation).

The *Rådmann* believed (with advice from the consultant) that the best – if not the only – way to effect such a reorganisation was to address the *process* of reorganisation, rather than simply to impose the desired outcome. This process was to involve as many as possible of the *kommune*'s staff, in order that they may feel 'ownership' of the process, and therefore be more interested in implementing the outcomes. The process would therefore become a kind of 'rite of passage' through which administrators would 'reinvent' themselves and the administration would then also emerge transformed into a more 'customer-oriented' organisation (see Vike 2003). Hence the administration became heavily involved in group meetings, leadership meetings, process discussions, and so on.

The process of reviewing sector structures therefore became a process of change which affected very many of the council's employees and led to a great deal of instability and uncertainty within the organisation.

Depoliticising

As the reorganisation process began to take over the daily life of the council's employees (in terms of attendance at meetings or informal conversation), the meaning of the reorganisation began to come into question. At the same time, my questions about council organisation and practices began to elicit comments about the relationships between employees and politicians, and about the separation of politics and administration as entities and practices with different aims. The head of personnel explained in a formal way:

> The *Rådmann* has responsibility for the administration committee. ... the committee makes decisions. And therefore *Rådmann*, and I, as the professional responsible within personnel, make sure that the decisions are carried out. So that when I sit on the committee, or in meetings, I sit there by way of the *Rådmann*. So I have to act as if I were him, if you like.

> ... in these political committees, it is the committee and its members who discuss and proceed particular cases. My role in such a meeting is to offer support ... and to be present in case they require any information they might require. But I will never go in and discuss the case or proceed with a case; that is not my job. The discussion on the case will be present in the case documents. All the important sides to the argument will be drafted there, so that politicians can make their decision on the basis of the case papers they have received.

The rules laid out in the Local Government Act (*Kommuneloven*) set out the roles of the mayor, deputy mayor, executive committees, and the appropriate accounting procedures required of councils. The Act, for the first time, allowed councils to choose their own structure, and offered rules for setting up business wings of the council. Its comments on the administrative structure were limited to brief comments on the role of the chief executive (see Figure 4.2), delegation, control committees and the rights of employees representatives. A short paragraph also details which combinations of roles are excluded (employees may also hold political posts but only outside the most powerful executive positions).

§ 23. The functions and powers of the chief executive

1. The chief executive is the highest administrative officer for the overall management of the municipality or of the county municipality, with the exceptions that follow from statute and within the framework laid down by the municipal council or the county council.

2. The chief executive shall ensure that those items of business that are placed before popularly elected bodies have been properly elucidated, and that resolutions are implemented.

3. The chief executive has the right to be present and speak, in person or represented by one of his or her subordinates, at meetings of all popularly elected municipal or county municipal bodies with the exception of the control committee.

4. Popularly elected municipal and county municipal bodies may empower the chief executive to make decisions in individual matters or in types of business which do not involve questions of principle, unless otherwise resolved by the municipal council or the county council.

Figure 4.2. Local Government Act 1993, chapter 4, paragraph 23.

These bare bones are filled with a discourse on the correct behaviour of the administration and the proper activities and interests of politicians. The head of personnel acknowledged as much, in her comments:

> Well, the Local Government Act gives guidance on the political system. And then, so to speak, relationships of co-operation, bargaining develop, if not written, that is just 'the way it is'. Unwritten rules.

These unwritten rules rely to some extent on a framework of relationships of trust and loyalty which people in the council described to me. Formally, as proposed by the Act, the *Rådmann* puts forward cases for political consideration and decision. Before the reorganisation, cases came forward from sectors, and were prepared by case officers, approved by their boss and passed up the system to the *Rådmann*. An economist from the social sector explained:

> It is the *Rådmann* who puts forwards proposals to the executive committee [of the council] so it is important that we don't change our opinions in the administration along the way, right? So in cases that will go up to the executive committee and the council, the *Rådmann* wants us to explain beforehand what the administration thinks. That's the system. So if I write a case for the council, the *Rådmann* will see it first. *Rådmann* reads all cases and if he doesn't agree, it has to be changed.

Interviewer: Is that what you meant about being loyal to him?

Yes, that's it. Because he may have a different opinion because he sees a whole which the Head of Health and Social hasn't seen, for example. And that seems fine to me. *Rådmann* has never questioned our professional opinions, because he has confidence in the sector leader. If he loses confidence in the sector leader, he could begin to ask about all sorts of things. But in practice he doesn't do that, and he says himself that it is because he has confidence in the evaluations of the sector leader. As long as we do our job, bring forward proposals to make up the deficit and to keep to our budget, then he has confidence in us. But as soon as things start to go out of control, he comes in and manages more.

This question of loyalty holds together a strained relationship which tries to distinguish between the political and the administrative, despite the knowledge that administration can have political effects (Forester 1989). Loyalty as a concept plays a role in *disciplining* the relationships between administrators and politicians. The *Rådmann*, as observed, must implement council decisions, a duty he interprets as being 'loyal' to decisions voted for by the council. Within the organisation, administrators must be loyal to the Rådmann, but individual administrators do not have relationships of loyalty to politicians. Their loyalty is channelled upwards through the organisation to be embodied in the relationship of loyalty between the *Rådmann* and the Mayor (as personification of the council). Again, this relationship is key, although it can be enacted by others with delegated powers, such as chairs and secretaries to political committees.

At the very least, however, party politics should be kept apart from administrative decisions, but in a system where council employees can also hold roles as politicians, a further element must be kept distinct. A politician who works with the Health and Social sector, for example, may find themselves on a committee which is deciding on the budget, and by implication working conditions, of employees. The identity of the politician in this instance embodies both employer and employee. Individuals make great efforts to hold these roles separate, partly by declaring when they have an interest, but also in trying to keep a distinction between their knowledge of a service as an employee, their personal experiences as a citizen and their political role as a representative and a party member, as one such individual explained:

I sit there as my own employer, and at the same time I don't get any economic advantage from it. But I have to be a bit careful so that it doesn't seem like I am talking about things that I am concerned about from my job point of view. I have to try to think holistically and put forward what my party is concerned about.

The concept of keeping separate politics from administration is under constant supervision, not only for the reasons above, but because of the perception of a crisis of political legitimacy. Parties reported that it is becoming increasingly difficult to recruit people to be politicians at the local government level, and voter turnout is decreasing. In a state that was built up from very high levels of citizen participation in politics, at least through party membership, the question of regeneration of political activism weaves through the process of reorganisation as one of the main leitmotifs. The *Rådmann* interprets this as the need to define more openly the responsibilities of politicians: politicians choose the overall policy directions, and the administration puts these into practice. The form in which he puts this distinction into operation, however, is where the move towards liberalism appears, as he operates through a discourse of budgets and accounts. The economist, above, interpreted the *Rådmann*'s strategy as follows:

> *Rådmann* will have the most responsible policy and budget possible. It is not up to him to lobby parliament. That is for the politicians. Similarly it is not the Head of Health and Social who lobbies for the Health and Social sector. We use the money we have in the most effective way.

> But if there is a waiting list, or if we have too many clients, we have to ensure that the politicians are informed about what we can do with the money we have, and we can inform them that now we need to change the criteria so we have fewer clients, or we will have to lower the quality if we are to offer services to everybody. But if the politicians say it is all right that people wait, then it is all right for us too. But we are responsible for giving them the basis for decisions, for letting them know.

Keeping administration separate in this sense implies not adopting a view as to whether political decisions are 'sensible' or not. Whatever the politicians decide is to be put into practice: this is the key tenet of public administration. Generally speaking, most senior administrators commented that if they are unable to act on decisions they personally find disagreeable, they ought to find another job. Distancing is therefore a crucial skill for administrators, and one which shaped not only their interactions with politicians, but, I would argue, their use of voice and body.

This became particularly apparent in seemingly informal settings. For example, the executive board of the council held an annual meeting to summarise the previous year's activities and set the guidelines for the next year's plan. Meetings were held over two days – and therefore overnight – at a conference hotel some two hours' drive away from the municipality. Although instigated by the politicians on the executive board, the *Rådmann* was requested to invite senior council officers, as appropriate. At these meetings, the senior officers of the council were invited to sit round the table and join in discussions of key issues. However, typically for meetings where politicians and administrators were present, not only did they sit on opposite sides of a long conference table, but their behaviour was what one might call guarded.

An example was a long discussion about nursery (kindergarten) provision within the municipality. The politicians spent nearly fifteen minutes arguing over the detailed specifications for nurseries until one turned to the *Rådmann* and asked whether the head of nurseries, who was present, could perhaps offer the relevant information, which he did. This form of only speaking when spoken to led to uninformed debate which could be interpreted as a waste of time: had the head of nurseries offered the information at the beginning of the discussion, the discussion might have been more usefully directed to other points. However, while taking an evening swim in the hotel's luxurious pool,[3] some of the administrators tried to explain their withholding from discussion as a reluctance to slip into political debate. 'I always check myself, once, twice, three times, before I make a comment, to make quite sure I am not making political points', one insisted. Indeed, two politicians who also worked in the council explained that they go to great lengths to try to discipline their political and administrative roles to avoid contamination of one to the other. Mixing of roles would be 'unprofessional', not only for the administrator but for the politician in them. The discourse on keeping the administration nonpolitical was thus embodied through the reticence or speech acts of individuals in different roles, both when those roles were fulfilled by separate individuals, and when they were demanded of the same person.

A further dimension of the speech control demanded by this loyalty relationship concerned what one might call the public face of the corporate body of the bureaucracy. Part of the loyalty expected of administrators to politicians was not to criticise them in public. In the *Rådmann*'s terms, public statements about council decisions were reined into his duty to implement political decisions, which he interpreted as loyalty to the council:

> [my loyalty to decisions] is quite unshakeable if the press then ring the next day and say, 'They decided this and that, do you have any comment?' … Then I say that it is a clear and good decision that I shall immediately act upon. They won't get me to say anything negative about it. And they have given up trying. Because they know that is how it is.

He also expected that all other employees would adopt the same interpretation of loyalty. In one instance, a service leader was called by the press to ask about the consequences of a political budget cut decided at a committee meeting the previous evening. Her professional answer was that it would undoubtedly lead to the demise of one area of the service, a response which was turned into a full-page spread in the local newspaper. During the meeting, none of the politicians had asked this question, and her superior had removed the presentation of consequences from the committee papers before they were presented. As the service leader was not secretary to the committee, she was not able to interject her views into the debate, as this was a political forum, not an administrative one. The secretary had the delegated powers of the *Rådmann*, but chose not to make explicit the consequences of budget decisions (some of his other employees suggested that he was keen to make highly political decisions easier for the chair of the committee– in order to be able to present 'good results' to the *Rådmann*, an argument there is no room to elaborate upon here). The service leader was dismayed, not least because none of the politicians had asked the question during the committee meeting, but also because she had 'foolishly' given the press an open answer to a technical question. However, her comments were interpreted as a betrayal of her obligations of loyalty, and when her post came up for renewal, she was not reappointed (and nor was the committee secretary). This case can be used to illustrate the significance of loyalty relationships within the municipality, since the service had achieved outstanding 'results' according to the usual reporting mechanisms of budgeting, outputs, etc. There was no doubt over her loyalty to implementing decisions made by politicians. The service leader's tendency to debate policy matters and to ask critical questions at internal policy meetings had gained her the reputation of being critical of the executive, which was interpreted as being disloyal and appeared to override other functions or qualities.

Repoliticising

Having established the currency of an (embodied) discourse of depoliticisation of the administration through the concept of 'loyalty', it is possible to examine how this discourse contributed to the politicisation of the positioning of the political council as a bureaucratic actor. There is a fairly nuanced trick of the tongue involved, as it were, which transforms the rational into the political and back again before it is generally noticed. There is no doubt, in the context described here, that the administration ought not to behave in political ways. Consequently their personal political views are repressed, through the transformation of moral dilemmas into economic and other audits. Should the health sector offer sufficient services, such that people can receive treatment as soon as they need it, with the consequence that the nursery budget is decreased and the shortage of nursery provision continues; or should people wait in a queue for a place at a nursing home in order that investment be sustained in after-school care for children? For the administrator, this is a nonquestion, as it is essentially political. The relevant question for the administrator is: what level of service can be maintained within this budget, and when do we notify politicians that people are unhappy with the level of service provided? As one economist in the health and social sector explained:

> We have a lot of elderly people in Vestforstad and we have waiting lists. People don't get the home help they need from the service and the waiting lists get longer and longer. ... And the administration sees that. So it is our responsibility to maybe write a paper on new criteria for the service. We come along with a proposal that we have only so much money and that we must change the criteria, but the Health and Social committee say 'no, no, we must have more money'. But we cannot recommend that. We can only recommend how to use what we have.

In this scenario, the role of the politician is to decide how the budget of the *kommune* should be divided up between the many forms of service: is health care more important than maintaining the museum? If so, how much more important? How many *kroner* should be moved from one budget to another? In this version of politics, the politician is a kind of moral accountant. But many politicians are concerned about individual moral problems in terms of the difficulties faced by individuals in receiving the care or service they need. Many Norwegian politicians, as Vike has also observed (Vike et al. 2002), are concerned about experiences of constituents in their encounters with the council. How should the council care for people with health problems? How to satisfy the demand for a new swimming pool since the old one was closed? How to make the council give swift and clear responses to people's applications for building-regulation approvals? What kind of management ought to run the council museum? Of course, politicians have always had overall responsibility for distributing limited resources. However, in the *Rådmann*'s terms a 'real' political discussion was one which he characterised as value-based prioritising: 'Shall we go for institutional care for elderly people or home-carers? What about the school situation versus care of the elderly?'

The more important sleight of hand is in the way that individual committees are being asked to make choices. No longer are politicians to be concerned about the way services are managed or run, as production of services is being transformed into an exchangeable commodity by the introduction of a market system of distinction between management and production. Under this system, services are transformed, discursively, from transactions between humans to criteria-based evaluations. We are familiar with the distribution of services according to criteria: does individual A have need x, y, z? Then they are eligible for services M and N. In the new management model, services are also evaluated according to criteria: does service M provide functions d, e, f? And does it do so at cost Q? Politicians, in this new system, are required to balance the functions d, e, f, with the cost, Q. If Q is proving to be too high and exceeding the budgetary allowance, they must choose between restricting functions d, e, or f, in order to meet the budget, or restricting the functions provided by services M or N. And it is the fact that services M and N, and functions d, e and f are not comparable which makes the problem a political, rather than an administrative one. However, by transforming the activities of the council from the production of services to the provision of services, the council was transformed into a market regulator. That is, rather than managing production, the council concentrated on developing the knowledge required to prepare tendering processes by documenting the details of services according to sets of criteria. The council, in other words, would retain its role in evaluating cases of need and distributing resources but would be prepared to relinquish its role in delivering services to people. In this, their activities altered from the professional management and production of services to the *describing* of council activities, for the purpose of auditing and tendering. This, in theory, would make political choices appear equivalent through budget redistribution questions, rather than intense, personalised and complex case debates based on the moralisation of the reported experiences of constituents.

The problem, in this system, is that the people, with their complex needs, demands and experiences, disappear from the realm of the politician, whose role is now determined by the demands of budgetary accounting. Local politics is transformed from a moral duty for the individual, to care for others in society, to the regulation of technologies of government: criteria for service provision and the comparison of service providers in competition with one another. In the Mayor's business metaphor, the (political) council has become the executive board of a company, and the ethical fervour required for the maintenance of comprehensive welfare and the notion of 'fellowship' among equals, which has been the backbone of the Norwegian welfare state, is quietly subsumed as an irritating detail. This process is made possible by the introduction of particular discursive technologies of governance: a new form of distinction between political and administrative; the separation of 'management' and 'service provision' or demand and supply; and the demand for loyalty from administrative staff.

This may be easier to explain in a more contextualised way. The *Rådmann* wishes to use the budget as a guide for when to involve politicians in decision making. Within the health and social sector, for example, politicians were unwilling to reduce services. Politicians on other committees, however, were also unwilling to cut services in other areas to such an extent that the money would be transferred to the health and social sector. In consequence, the health and social sector carried forward a deficit. In the *Rådmann's* view (echoed by many other administrators), politicians ought to see the whole picture and their role is to give clear overall priorities, rather than getting involved in detailed decisions about the day-to-day running of services. Keeping these issues distinct relied on the maintenance of a split between the administrative and the political which shifted towards a boundary between management and production. In order to maintain this, the *Rådmann* required complete loyalty from administrators. If politicians voted for a budget which was insufficient to run a service, the service provider ought not to complain and demand more money from the economists at the town hall, but should prepare a case for politicians, outlining their options for prioritising services so that the budget should be met. If the budget was not sufficient, then politicians would be required to make a choice between outputs, in a kind of feedback effect:

1. Politicians choose the budget.

2. The administrator outlines service options within the budget chosen.

3. Politicians choose between cuts available.

4. Residents complain to politicians that service is inadequate, thus:

    a) politicians realise the budget must increase or

    b) politicians make choices in the full knowledge of their consequences.

Achieving this distancing effect requires that administrators – service providers – put into action service cuts, even if they know that they may cripple the service, or they must be particularly clever in manipulating the politicians, bringing them 'on side' and ensuring that the budgets are maintained. Given the lack of general contact between administrators and politicians, this is only really possible for secretaries to committees. In a political environment dominated by the right-wing parties who have declared that their priorities are education and health, this can be particularly demoralising for service providers in culture and leisure, for example. Few public-sector administrators join municipal government in order to run down a service which they are professionally trained to value. At some point they must confront the competing pressures of professional pride or values and loyalty to the decisions of politicians, which they receive via the *Rådmann*. Having used loyalty as a governing principle to achieve the perfect division of politics and administration that makes the above process appear feasible, the *Rådmann* appeared to extend the principle to cover employees' freedom to criticise and question the management of the *kommune*, and to require a style of loyal behaviour from his immediate colleagues as a condition of work.

This might be illustrated by the following example. During the reorganisation, the changes to the structure of the *kommune* resulted in an increase in the most senior staff directly answerable to the *Rådmann* from four heads of sector to six council directors. The change of name was meant to signify the shift from sectors with their own staffs to directors who assisted the *Rådmann* as a team, although they would retain sectoral interests. However, as mentioned, the whole reorganisation was performed around the end of the contracts of the existing heads of sectors, and the new director posts were advertised as new positions. Of the existing heads, two applied for the new posts and were successful, one was approaching retirement and decided not to apply, and another was told that he could apply for the new posts, but that he would not receive an offer of a post. He told the leaders of services under his authority at one of their regular group meetings that the *Rådmann* had told him that he had not been as supportive to him as he expected, that in fact he had worked against him, so the *Rådmann* said that he thought he could no longer work with him in the leadership. His deputy, however, was one of the thirty-three internal candidates who had applied for a position. There was a silence in the room which did not disperse when the deputy explained that she had already been through psychological tests and had had a half hour's discussion on her 'profile'. Leaders within the group had commented on the troubled relationship between the two before: chiefly, that their boss tended to express his disagreement with the *Rådmann* quite openly even while putting his decisions into practice to the letter, even by stifling the complaints of his staff. They had also said to me, on other occasions, that the *Rådmann* shouted at his immediate subordinates; one even argued that he was psychopathic in his demand for total loyalty.

We should not be surprised that members of the *kommune* gossiped and speculated on the *Rådmann*'s motives for his behaviour since his position meant that strategies that might be hard to account for outside his immediate circle could, however, have consequences for all employees. During any process of reorganisation one may expect destabilisation of the kind that leads to an increase in gossip as people try to rationalise the uncertainty and instability they are thrown into. Stapley (1996) argues that although institutions or organisations have no actual substance, their members act towards them as though they have a kind of personality or identity. At times of radical change, therefore, the instability of the organisation can have extreme emotional consequences for its members and those who have a relationship with it.

One of the indications of this is rumours and stories circulating within the organisation, and in particular about the motivations for the reorganisation. Talk about the *Rådmann's* ulterior motives was one example, perhaps encouraged by the *Rådmann's* attempts to keep himself personally distant, and retain a calm exterior. Rather than becoming preoccupied with the individual leadership style and personality of the *Rådmann* in this particular context, therefore, it is important to retain a perspective on the form of the speculations about him and the reasons for their significance. The argument put forward here is that the Rådmann was responsible for a programme of change not simply in the structure of the bureaucracy, but in the distribution of political action, and in the very definition of what the political was, and that that was coded through a governing principle of 'loyalty'. Although this emerged in the language of the Local Government Act – that the administration in the person of the *Rådmann* must support and enact policies voted for by politicians – in its implementation it signalled a shift from social democratic welfare principles to a market model. In order to effect this change, it relied on a discipline (in the Foucauldian sense) based on internal loyalty within the administration and between the administration and the council, and on a corporate image of discipline and cohesiveness. The restrictiveness of the form of loyalty required to bring about such transformations of the practice of local government was then translated into the requirement for a 'certain type of person' to be able to work in the council.

Closing comments

Although trends in management structure might appear to bring superficial changes to organisational relations, a close observation indicates that these may have a profound bearing on the daily experience of life in public sector bureaucracy. Pressures brought to bear on individuals within situations where the resolution of conflicting demands is not possible are translated into demands for particular personality traits, which I interpret as a form of disciplining of the individual into the chosen technologies of government. In a broader perspective, however, these organisational-level managerial changes effect a categorical shift in the nature of politics and administration, such that politicians become alienated from the subjects of their politics, and citizens become alienated from public services. Given that this managerial shift has been introduced in the interests of 'reinvigorating local politics', the result is deeply ironic and not a little disturbing.

According to Mouffe (2000), this may be interpreted as a case of duplicitous propaganda being used to usher in elitist centralisation, as neoliberal capitalism undermines the public service ethos of welfare states. For actors within the town hall there was dissension. While some of the opposition politicians and service providers may have sided with Mouffe, others expressed a belief in the energising qualities of 'constant change' in the organisation. Their capture by inspirational belief systems appears to lend weight to the suggestions by, for example, Tourish and Pinnington that management changes are 'cultish' (2002), or Salamon that management has taken a 'spiritualist' turn (2005). However we characterise it, it is hard to deny that a new mentality of governing has emerged in the public sector, and that its implications for the definitions of self of those working both within and with the public sector are profound.

Notes

1. A key factor in access to the fieldwork was the help offered by 'key informants' – friends – particularly fellow anthropologists to whom I am extremely grateful. Funding was provided by a visiting fellowship at the University of Oslo, and ESRC Future Governance research grant number L216252051.
2. The airport was re-sited 50km the other side of Oslo in 1998. See Ording (2000).
3. Ethnographic methods demand the utmost commitment from the practitioner.

Bibliography

Aarsæther, N. and S.I. Vabo. 2002. *Fristilt og Velstyrt? Fokus på kommune Norge.* Oslo: Samlaget.
Abrahamson, E. 1991. 'Managerial Fads and Fashions: The Diffusion and Rejection of Innovations' *Academy of Management Review* 16: 586–612.
Baldersheim, H.J., et al. 1997. *Kommunalt Selvstyre i Velferdstaten.* Otta: Tano-Aschehoug.
Common, E. 1998. 'The New Public Management and Policy Transfer: The Role of International Organisations', in M. Minogue, C. Polidano and D. Hulme, (eds.), *Beyond the New Public Management.* Cheltenham: Edward Elgar, pp. 59–75.
Farnham, D. and S. Horton. 1996. *Managing the New Public Services.* Basingstoke: Macmillan.
Ferlie, E. 1996. *The New Public Management in Action.* Oxford: Oxford University Press.
Flyvbjerg, B. 1998. *Rationality and Power: Democracy in Practice.* London: University of Chicago Press.
Forester, J. 1989. *Planning in the Face of Power.* London: University of California Press.
Hanson, T. 1999. *Municipal Self-Government in the Service of the Welfare State.* Oslo: Odin.
Jenkins, S. 1995. *Accountable to None: The Tory Nationalisation of Britain.* London: Hamish Hamilton.
Kunda, G. 1992. *Engineering Culture: Control and Commitment in a High-Tech Corporation.* Philadelphia: Temple University Press.
Lipsky, M. 1980. *Street-Level Bureaucracy: Dilemmas of the Individual in Public Services. Publications of the Russell Sage Foundation.* New York: Russell Sage Foundation.
Miller, P. 1990. 'On the Interrelations between Accounting and the State', *Accounting Organisations and Society* 15 (4): 315–38.

Minogue, M., C. Polidano and D. Hulme. 1998. *Beyond the New Public Management: Changing Ideas and Practices in Governance.* New Horizons in Public Policy. Cheltenham: Edward Elgar.

Mouffe, C. 2000. *The Democratic Paradox.* London: Verso.

Salamon, K.L.G. 2005. 'Possessed by Enterprise: Values and Value-Creation in Mandrake Management', In O. Löfgren and R. Willim (eds.), *Magic, Culture and the New Economy.* Oxford and New York: Berg, pp. 47–55.

Stapley, L. 1996. *The Personality of the Organisation: A Psycho-Dynamic Explanation of Culture and Change.* London: Free Association Books.

Stoker, G. 2000. *The New Politics of British Local Governance.* Basingstoke: Macmillan Press in association with the ESRC Local Governance Programme.

Tourish, D. and A. Pinnington. 2002. 'Transformational Leadership, Corporate Cultism and the Spirituality Paradigm: An Unholy Trinity in the Workplace?' *Human Relations* 55 (2): 147–172.

Vike, H., R. Bakken, A. Brinchmann, H. Haukelien and R. Kroken. 2002. *Maktens Samvittighet: Om Politikk, Styring og Dilemmaer i Velferdsstaten.* Oslo: Gyldendal Akademisk.

5

IDENTITIES UNDER CONSTRUCTION:
THE CASE OF INTERNATIONAL
EDUCATION

Hilary Callan

Introduction: contexts of the chapter

This chapter has a number of contexts. Descriptively, it relates to international higher education viewed as an emergent field of professional practice; and to those engaged in it. The discussion has affinities with other debates surrounding the 'anthropology of organisations', of which Wright (1994) provides an excellent review. It also resonates with studies of 'transnational communities', although there are differences. Transnational communities are normally taken to be those displaced by choice or compulsion, at least temporarily, from a 'home location', whereas my subjects here are linked by a commitment to transnational educational aims and a set of practices following that commitment.[1] Lastly, situating myself as author within the material and in relation to it has presented some special conundrums about the nature of the ethnographic base, which is not of a conventional kind. To explain this I must be briefly autobiographical.

In previous work (e.g. Callan 1984) I have addressed some of the special conditions of studying the situation one is intimately 'in'. Part of what can make this possible is the cultivation of a double vision, in which ethnographic detachment can, at least part of the time, coexist with 'living inside' the world one is striving to describe. This double vision in turn can require facilitating devices such as a certain scepticism or provisionality in adopting the identity under study; a kind of divided self.

The ethnographic setting described here has been, for me, comparable but importantly different. For some ten years until 2000 I was employed in the field now known as international higher education. For the greater part of this period I was Director of the Amsterdam-based European Association for International Education, and in what follows I shall refer to this as the Association. My position naturally involved taking responsibility for real issues and problems, and sometimes being a public figurehead for the Association and the aims and actions it stands for; it required a total commitment. I spoke, wrote and published in that character, and still do so on occasion. No room here for ethnographic detachment or a split self. All of me had to be there. If I made ethnographic observations, I could not do so from the standpoint of an observer contemplating the 'other', because I was not standing on that ground. I have written elsewhere about the epistemology of interrogating one's own experience. Here, I could not have done this at the time, nor could I have applied fieldwork methods in any systematic way, because such would have been incompatible with the self required to do the job I then held. My unconventional mode of occupying this particular ethnographic space is, perhaps, an extreme instance of reflexive subversion of the subject/object relationship in ethnography. Not only was I an actor in the processes in question; I held a significant degree of formal responsibility in respect of them.

The association

The European Association for International Education (EAIE), of which I was Director from 1993–2000, is an international non-governmental organisation in the field of higher education. It was founded in 1989 and now has a membership of some 1,900 individuals, the majority of whom hold junior to mid-level university posts in the administration and management of international educational programmes. Membership is not confined to Europe, however defined; members are based in over fifty countries including Eastern and Western Europe, North and South America, Australia and the Pacific region. Activities, however, are focused on European issues, so practitioners outside Europe tend to become members because of a need to engage professionally with European educational concerns. The Association's most visible public activity is a large (by European standards) annual Conference, held in a different European city each year, which attracts around 1,500 participants from throughout the world. It is also active in publications (for which I was the general editor and occasional contributor) and in professional training in international education. As we shall see, this notion of 'professionalism', like that of 'international education', is both central and problematic.

The principal spur to the formal creation of the Association was the rapid expansion and investment by the then European Community, beginning in the mid- to late 1980s, in programmes of exchange and mobility in post-secondary education and professional training. Behind this expansion lay a political and economic agenda: the creation of a European consciousness, citizenship and economic sphere. This agenda itself became successively more confident and articulate over the same period. At the same time I would argue that structural uncertainties remain at the heart of the 'official' European concept and, further, that these uncertainties are preserved and disguised in tactical obscurities of language written into key policy documents of the Commission and its agents. This notwithstanding, the Maastricht Treaty of 1993 and subsequent instruments gave the European Union, for the first time, formal competence in education and further stimulated European-level activity in the field.

An effect of these developments at ground level, by which I mean that of universities and the conditions of those working in them, was that, from the mid-1980s, offices were set up to manage participation in the new programmes and staff were recruited in significant numbers to work in them. This happened, however, differently and unevenly across the university sectors in the member states eligible to participate in the programmes. In general, and with exceptions, it was the traditions of University governance and management in Northern and Western Europe – Scandinavia, the Benelux countries, Germany and the U.K. – that best lent themselves to the establishment of specialist, professionally staffed units for European cooperation, sometimes run together with International Offices whose mandate was more global. The U.K. was to some extent a special case since for some years, for national political reasons which are not our concern here, the financial pressure had been on Universities to market their wares competitively to non-EU (i.e. fee-paying) students. Consequently, international activity had become more or less synonymous with recruitment of fee-paying overseas students, and was (and is), to that extent, finance-driven.

In most of the member states of Southern Europe, by contrast, the prevailing tradition was for a university's international and European activities to be entrusted to Vice-Rectors elected for limited terms, whose credentials were academic and who would return to their academic departments after their term of office. This tradition was clearly far less conducive than that of Northern Europe to the formation of any lasting professional constituency. The predictable result was that the constituency that emerged under these conditions of expansion in European-level programmes, and which found concrete form in the Association, did so pre-endowed with practices and discourses seen then and now as dominated by the 'North'. This imbalance, as we shall see, continues to be a line of fracture cutting across attempts at identity construction built around 'professionalism' and 'Europeanness' in the field.

The public history of the Association (see e.g. Richardson 1999) is a narrative in which, more or less simultaneously across Western Europe in around 1988, awareness crystallised of a need for a professional organisation to represent the interests of the large numbers of people newly entering this emergent field from all manner of occupational backgrounds, academic and clerical. An early Statement of Purpose, circulated to interested persons throughout Europe during 1988 to invite support for what became the Association, captures the tone:

> European universities have been international in character from the foundation of the first institutions in the Middle Ages. As European countries are moving together in the last few decades there is a growing need to professionalise and organise those on the university staffs who are involved in international affairs. European action programmes like ERASMUS and similar schemes being developed make the foundation of a professional organisation mandatory. (quoted in Richardson 1999)

Because of the historical conjunction of these developments in European education with the wider, seismic events of 1989, the public narrative also encompasses what happened in that year. The story is indeed dramatic, and as it happens I was myself witness to parts of it. At the beginning of the year, planning had begun for an inaugural Conference in Amsterdam in early December which was to launch the new Association, then provisionally named the Association of European Educational Administrators. The Berlin Wall fell a matter of weeks before the Conference date. In the ensuing days, with the successive collapse of former Eastern bloc regimes, the Cold War was seen to be ending and Europe itself suddenly seemed new-made. At the conference itself, at which I was present as a participant, twice the expected number turned up and the atmosphere was electric. The cry went up in the corridors that 'from today, Europe stretches to the Great Wall of China'. A keynote speaker from Russia made an impassioned appeal for the support of Western educators in the institutional transformations of post-Soviet education that could now be foreseen and openly desired, but were also feared. Another, from the West, cautioned against triumphalism: 'We must never forget that "we" [meaning the West] did not win– "they" lost.' In a debate of great emotion, the working title was dropped and the name 'European Association for International Education' was adopted for the newly created organisation, which was at that moment legally constituted as a nonprofit association under Dutch law.

In this public narrative, the inclusion of the words 'European' and 'International' in the Association's name is highly significant. 'Europe', as we have seen, was suddenly laden with all manner of new meaning and promise. 'International' made possible a resonance with preexisting symbols and images which had and continue to have a powerful binding effect in face of the otherwise highly diverse backgrounds and interests of the Association's members. In fact the Association has had, from its earliest period, a Mission Statement which states that its goal is 'to stimulate and facilitate the internationalisation of education, in particular higher education, in Europe; and to meet the professional needs of individuals active in international education'. Despite many rewritings of the Statement, this wording has remained unchanged.

Binding values: 'internationalism', 'professionalism' and 'culture'

To understand why such constructs have the binding potency they have, we need to look beyond and behind the Association's public history as I have recounted it. In particular we need to examine the 'prehistory' of its most important constitutive values: those of 'internationalism' and 'internationalisation', 'professional' and 'professionalisation'. In relation to both of these, we also need to consider the role of ideas of 'culture' and of 'cultural competence' in relation to education.

The 'wandering scholar of the Middle Ages' is much in evidence as an ancestor-figure in accounts of the origins of 'internationalism' in education. The image is sometimes a rather romantic one of a borderless world of the past in

which communities of scholars established themselves at will, and through which the individual moved freely in search of intellectual nourishment and inspiration. On occasion Erasmus himself is cited as exemplar of this world, based on his impressive network of scholarly correspondence across Europe. Hamlet, too, has been creatively invoked as a figure from literature who, having travelled from Elsinore to do his degree at Wittenberg, foreshadows the international student of today (Rinehart 2000). While those writing in this vein are certainly not naïve enough to claim that such a world could be literally restored, the feeling is present that it represented one kind of intellectual ideal. The author of an essay published by the Association in 1995 as part of a comparative study of international education in different regions of the world, cites an earlier writer as follows:

> The universities of the world are today aspiring to return to one of the basic concepts of their origin – the universality of knowledge. Many are also seeking to discover and adopt procedures that will restore the desirable aspects of the itinerant character of scholars that was an accepted part of university education until growing nationalism created the barriers of language. (de Wit 1995)

The point at issue here is not the historical accuracy of the image presented in accounts of this kind, nor its appropriateness to a discussion of contemporary constructions of 'internationalism' and 'internationalisation' in education. There are in fact other accounts (for example, Scott 1999) which stress the conceptual dependence of the 'international education' idea on the contemporary nation state and its geopolitical boundaries: a world very different from that of mediaeval Europe. It is also true that recent policy developments in Europe invoke a vision of a Europe-wide 'educational space' to which the mediaeval image may indeed offer a precursor. What is pertinent here, however, is the potency this image has for a disparate assembly of individuals with jobs in the field, who (I shall argue) are striving to construct a common identity across their diversity, using whatever imageries and handles to legitimacy come to hand.

Overlaid on this evoked imagery of primal borderless scholarship is a series of recent usages. There is now a considerable literature on the 'internationalisation' of higher education, which shows that for many years since the Second World War the concept has been understood and applied in a highly variable fashion. Interpretations have shifted according to changing perceptions of the rationales and incentives for internationalisation; different activities included under the label; and differing political and economic circumstances in which the activities are situated. Clear regional differences are apparent; 'internationalisation' carries different historical associations, and hence different contemporary resonances, in Europe, North America and other parts of the world; and within Europe from one region to another. For example, in the U.K., as already noted, it means little other than the marketing of universities and courses to fee-paying foreign students; job advertisements for posts in International Offices of British universities invariably stress overseas student recruitment as the primary responsibility of the post. This diversity notwithstanding, commitment to 'internationalisation' as a core value is powerful and general.

The concept of 'internationalisation' is problematic in other ways, although it is not generally seen as such. It does not sit easily in many European languages including English; in fact it is a literal translation of a Dutch homologue which in turn makes allusion to a specific framework of national policy that, until recently, gave support to the development of international activities in Dutch universities. Comparable policy initiatives took place in a number of other European countries, and the term 'internationalisation' has come to refer to this loose clustering of policies and processes. It is best construed as a portmanteau construct of a kind fairly familiar to anthropologists, which functions simultaneously in several distinct domains with their accompanying discourses. The terminology has remained constant despite its multiple and shifting references, and it is this verbal constancy which has proved important as a rhetorical banner making possible the articulation of perceived common identities and interests among those working in the field. Its preservation in the Association's Mission Statement is thus no surprise.

Concepts of 'professionalism' and 'professionalisation' as pillars of identity provide an elegant parallel. From the Association's beginnings, the nurturance of a professional 'constituency' of expert practitioners in international education has been an explicit and primary aim. 'Professionalisation' has been seen as a means both of setting internationally respected 'quality standards' in the field, and of organising practice around those standards. Part of the agenda, also, has been the furtherance of material interests. In this field as in others, claims to a distinct professional identity are seen as instrumental to respect and advancement in the workplace. At the same time, ambiguities surround the idea of 'professionalism' in its regulatory aspect. The Association is certainly seen as a means through which the claim to a professional identity can be made good; as stated earlier, a professional training programme is in place which aims to articulate 'professionalism' and to instil it by imparting both knowledge and competences. However, what might ostensibly seem the logical next steps – those of certification and regulation of access to the profession, on the model of other professional associations – are fiercely resisted. This may change in the future, and there is recurrent discussion of the point, but the prevailing sentiment at the time of writing is in favour of an associative or collegial professionalism which stops short of any suggestion of gatekeeping.

Further illustration of the ambivalence which lies behind the apparently consensual commitment to 'professionalisation', and the assertion of a professional identity, can be seen in attitudes to cross-cultural competence and training. The latter is enormously popular, and no wonder, since those working in international education see themselves as, by definition, specialist operators in a quintessentially cross-cultural field. Issues of cultural contrast are brought home to them on a daily basis, and they tend to be made painfully aware of what can go wrong when cross-cultural understanding fails in an educational setting (horror stories abound). From this it is a short step to seeing cross-cultural awareness and skill as a specific and distinctive professional competence for the practitioner in international education. In common with other bodies, members and sub-groups of the Association frequently organise seminars and workshops bringing in outside specialists of various kinds, aimed at the development of cross-cultural awareness and sensitivity. These are always very well subscribed, and highly praised. Participants regularly say in their evaluations that the training event has fundamentally changed for the better their level of professionalism in their job, by inspiring them with the importance of culture and of cultural differences.

What is interesting about the content of these events is that they operate within a rather simple, essentialist conception of culture, and one which moreover derives from models originally developed under the influence of a management discourse. 'Cultures' are represented as static and bounded, often conflated with national groupings, and credited with fixed attributes according to various taxonomies, the most popular of which is that of Hofstede and his school (see, e.g., Hofstede 1984). The task of the international education professional as cultural translator is presented as one of detecting and diagnosing difference as if with a dictionary or checklist of these attributes, and so overcoming barriers to understanding.

Throughout the developed world, of course, a major industry has sprung up in recent years whose commercial product is 'cross-cultural training' for various work environments, and whose claims to 'expertise' in this area are sometimes problematic. Whatever reservations one may have regarding particular examples, the principle is hard to reject out of hand. It is presumably better on the whole for people working in culturally sensitive areas, such as international education, to be encouraged to reflect on cultural differences, than not to be. However, the understanding of culture being sold to them is a very domesticated, disarmed one, in which there is no room for notions of culture as subversive, divisive or contested. (For a more extended critique of essentialist notions of culture imported wholesale into practices and policies, see Wright 1994 and 1998.) In international education, despite the alternative explanations, I believe that there are specific reasons why the ideas are kept simple and the essentialist, 'checklist' construction of culture is accepted as readily and enthusiastically as it is. For practitioners confronted daily by issues in which cultural factors are self-evidently implicated, and striving simultaneously to articulate a sense of what is common and distinctive in their work, this construction offers something apparently learnable and knowable, which in turn can be seen as a building block for a shared, 'professionalised' identity. A simplified representation of 'culture', in other words, proffers 'capturable' knowledge which can in turn be claimed as 'professional' knowledge.

The practitioners and their conditions of practice

So far, I have spoken of the binding power of a few core constructs and their ready appropriation, along with their referential fields, as banners in the construction of self and identity by people working in international education. I now turn to those people themselves, as exemplified by the members of the Association, and consider the circumstances in which identity-construction is important to them.

As noted earlier, this is a highly diverse population grossly differentiated by occupational history, nationality and first language, national and institutional environment in which they work, and the nature of their work in international education. There are eight self-governing 'Professional Sections' within the Association and several Special Interest Groups, each representing a specialist subfield of international education such as international admissions and credential evaluation, student advising and welfare, or management of the EU exchange and mobility programmes. One of the few things these practitioners have in common is allegiance to a broad understanding of the field under the 'banner constructs' I have described. The English language, which is the second language of most European practitioners, has become for convenience the principal working language of the Association and offers some common frame; but, as may be expected, this is disputed and there are recurrent complaints from native speakers of some other languages about the 'dominance' of English.

An important source of diversity is the relation of the individual's work to its policy environment, whether at institutional or national level. As stated earlier, some national governments and education systems have highly explicit, articulated policies for international relations, and have encouraged investment by universities in dedicated international offices. In others, policy is tacit or nonexistent. Individuals working in these different settings may have superficially identical job titles, descriptions and task lists; but their experiences are very different. A practitioner in an environment where policy commitments to international activity are tacit or indirect will not have the same conversations and transactions, available resources and means of accessing them, as someone exercising an equivalent role in an environment where the governing policy is explicit, visibly accountable in managerial and political terms, and clearly connected to a broader frame of strategic objectives. One of the imbalancing factors resulting from the 'Northern bias' in the early design of the Association, to which I referred earlier, is that constructions of 'internationalisation', locked hegemonically (and unconsciously) to structures of the 'explicit' type, have tended to mute the perspective of those whose experience is not of this kind. It is, now, no easy task for an association seeking to be genuinely representative of all its members to find ways of giving all voices a means of expression; and attempts to achieve this have not, on the whole, been successful.

Whatever institutional backing individuals may have, they are often structurally very isolated in their posts. While some large European universities have European or international offices with four- or five-person staffs, it is more typical to find one- or two-person offices, with clerical support which may be part-time or shared with other units. The connectedness of an international office with the central governing structures of the institution varies greatly, but people have commonly told me that opportunities for solidarity within the institution are restricted. In some systems, the structural isolation is compounded by pressures placing institutions themselves in competition with one another, thus discouraging 'disloyal' cooperation with one's counterpart in the university down the road. It then becomes critically important to find this solidarity outside the institution, in horizontal alliances with others who can be seen as professional colleagues and equals. Clearly, one of the most important functions of the Association, like any other professional body, is to provide the conditions for this solidarity. And because of the parallel commitment to internationalism, it is important that the solidarity should also be international. Internationalism is therefore protective: it is often only in the setting of an international conference, such as those of the Association, that near neighbours in different institutions can make friends and exchange experiences.

This, I believe, lies behind the passionate resistance of the membership to two proposals which regularly come up and are (so far) regularly thrown out: that the Association should change its membership structure to an institutional, rather than the present strictly individual, basis; and that it should set up national or regional chapters. There are efficiency arguments in favour of both of these. Nonetheless members have so far rejected them vigorously because (although they may not express it in these terms) such changes would be seen as fatally compromising both the commitment to internationality, and the struggle for professional solidarity in structural opposition to the isolation of their individual institutional positions.[2]

Cutting across these elements of diversity and relative structural isolation, to which the Association is seen as an answer, there is, I believe, a commonality of experience which takes a negative form: namely the absence of an established history or tradition in which to locate professional community and practice. While international education has a rich conceptual ancestry, as noted above, as a set of organised practices linked to an occupational community in the modern sense it is very new. Consequently, there has not been an opportunity for the governing metaphors, the classifications of reality and the symbolic systems that are characteristic of mature organisations and communities of practice (Douglas 1987; Young 1991) to come into being and achieve solidity. Already separated by the diversity and isolation described above, the international education practitioners looking for solidarity as a basis for occupational community must do so in the absence of an elaborated symbolic equipment. In a form of *bricolage*, they must fashion and legitimise a discourse from whatever component elements come to hand. The eagerness of recourse to 'internationalisation' and other unifying notions is thus scarcely surprising. Once again a small number of core constructs, kept verbally constant despite shifts in their actual reference, are made to bear a heavy rhetorical load.[3]

Negating 'bureaucracy'

The question of 'bureaucracy' becomes important here; a rejection of perceived bureaucracy is an important, if implicit, unifying force within the Association. 'Bureaucracy' is of course classically associated with Weber's ideal-type of systems based on impersonality, functional specialisation, hierarchy of authority, and the impartial application of rules. I am emphatically not referring here to bureaucracy in this technical social science sense. Rather, I refer to a folk construct of 'bureaucracies' in which people see themselves as enmeshed, and in opposition to which they wish to find an alternative construction of self. The sense of frustration and suppression of individuality and of the possibility of personal initiative, for which 'bureaucracy' provides a convenient negative label, is of course common to many people working in complex organisations in contemporary society. To use the language of Mary Douglas (see, e.g., Douglas 1987) this experience is characteristic of those working in high-grid, low-group occupational environments. The experience of international education administrators and managers in European universities is not at all unusual.

For those whose work requires dealings with external bodies such as the European Commission, which holds power and resources but is seen as impenetrable, the problem of perceived bureaucracy is compounded. Typically, the practitioner in such a position is required to put together (for example) a funding application to the Commission for support under one of the programmes. This entails piloting the submission through what are seen as multiple layers of institutional 'bureaucracy', while simultaneously ensuring compliance with the equally intricate 'bureaucracy' of the Commission's own reporting and accounting requirements. From the perspective of those whose jobs require them to mediate between the 'bureaucracies' of the institution and the Commission, the latter can appear monolithic, impenetrable, rigid and powerful.

It is therefore scarcely surprising that the members of the Association deeply want it to be a force against perceived 'bureaucracy'. They want it to be a vehicle for the construction of self and identity on an anti-bureaucratic ticket; and at the same time a stick with which to beat the multiple 'bureaucracies' in which many of them feel trapped. To borrow again from Mary Douglas, they want, by means of the Association, less grid and more group in their working existence.

This comes to the surface in interesting ways. Sociability, for example, is highly valued, and the tradition was established early in the Association's life that the meetings of various governing boards and committees, which take place several times a year in different European venues, are accompanied by much conviviality. There is a pride in friendliness, informality and hospitality, and a conviction that these make the Association 'special' and different from other structures of working life in which members are involved.

An ironic consequence of the above is that members tend to be hypersensitive to any sign of the Association itself becoming, in their eyes, 'bureaucratic'. Throughout the years in which it has expanded greatly both in numbers and in the complexity of its operations, the desire has persisted for it to be managed in a hands-on, spontaneous style characteristic of organisations in their pioneer phase. The complaint of 'bureaucracy' readily goes up at any hint of departure from this style. And at the same time, of course, the members also want good governance, consultative decision making and a balanced budget. Reconciling these sometimes conflicting demands, in an environment of multiple traditions and languages, was and is a formidable governance task.

Identity and boundary

I now want to look briefly at ways in which, for members of the Association, identity construction is done by asserting boundaries between the constructed self and a range of not-selves or alternative selves. Some of this ground I have already covered by pointing to self-definitions by opposition. 'We' in our Association capacity are not bureaucrats, although in our offices that is precisely what we may have to be. 'We' in our internationalism stand opposed to narrow national interests, although in other contexts these will naturally come to the fore– and so on. Boundary-marking in a more political sense is also important for the work of identity construction that is going on here. At present, the most salient oppositional 'other' is, once again, the European Commission, although there are others and the balance could conceivably change in the future.

Constitutionally, the Association is fully independent of the Commission or any other governmental or intergovernmental body. It is governed and financed by its members, although, since the members' subscriptions and other contributions such as conference fees are normally paid by their employing institutions, independence from institutions can be somewhat fictive. In relation to the Commission, however, independence is important both substantively and rhetorically. Members, especially those whose work involves implementation of the EU programmes within their institutions, see the Association as a vehicle for solidary criticism of what is seen as 'bureaucratic' or plain wrong-headed in the programmes; and the Association has been as successful as it has largely by providing a platform for collective, independent comment and criticism of the programmes as they have developed. The assertion of 'professionalism' is readily harnessed to an argument that the Association represents the 'voice of the professionals' in opposition to the 'Eurocrats' responsible for the design and (under)funding of the programmes. Indeed, the second of a series of Occasional Papers produced by the Association in 1992 (shortly before I became Director) is subtitled 'A Professional Response to the Educational Programmes of the European Community'.

Time and again, as Director, I found myself in an interesting position of mediation, both structural and political. Through cultivating personal contacts in the Commission, I was well aware of the directional uncertainty, the lack of internal transparency, the burden of management accountability and the chronic pressure of unreasonable deadlines and resource constraints which dominate the working lives of the Commission staff. On the other side, it was my responsibility to coordinate the reactions of Association members to successive phases in the development of the programmes, and to articulate these in the form of 'official' comments to be presented to the Commission on behalf of 'the professionals'.

Invariably, there were strong pressures from militants among the membership for the Association to take a line of automatic suspicion and disaffection against the Commission and its policies. Such pressures were amplified, I believe, by the attractiveness of a construction of self and identity in opposition to an equally constructed and exaggerated oppositional 'other'.

The Commission, of course, plays its own game. For the Directorate-General which now has responsibility for education, the Association's independence of any political control is a helpful means of access to 'independent professional opinion'. This provides essential feedback information on the reception of the programmes and policies in what the Commission sees as 'the field'. Further, the independent provenance of this feedback gives it a legitimacy which can be, and is, used internally by Commission staff genuinely concerned to improve the programmes and policies; and to fight for better budget allocations for the educational programmes vis-à-vis their own oppositional 'others' elsewhere in the system. It gives them a means of bypassing the 'silencing constraints' imposed by their own structures of management accountability. They are able to 'borrow' the Association's perceived independence and professionalism to carry internal arguments of their own, without being seen to do so. It is my experience that these arguments often coincide rather closely with the wishes of the 'professionals'. Paradoxically, there is a hidden coincidence of aim which overarches the construction of identities through opposition to the 'other'.

Concluding observations

In this chapter, using the Association and its members as my ethnographic field, I have sought to document the effort that goes into the construction of identities, the allegiances and values pressed into service for the purpose, and the reasons why this effort is necessary to practitioners who, after all, have alternative (including occupational) identities available to them. The identities are 'under construction' in a temporal sense: international education is a fluid, developing field of activities, and the institutions created to sustain it, such as the Association, are similarly fluid and relatively unfixed. The consciousness of common identity is also fragile, subject as it is to limiting constraints. The 'North/South' division, as it is perceived and named (although the disjunction is of course far more complex) is felt as a severe obstacle to the Association's aspiration to be truly 'representative' of a European constituency in international education. The relative structural muting of the workplace experience of those whose policy environment is unspecific or unstated is less openly recognised, but is still detectable. The perceived dominance of English is a recurring point of sensitivity within the Association. Ironically, however, the disaffection does not tend to come from native speakers of less used European languages such as Dutch and Danish, who are well accustomed to the need for a *lingua franca* for international dealings and do not find it divisive; nor on the whole from those of less-spoken

Southern European languages such as Portuguese and Greek, for whom competence in English seen as a necessary professional qualification for work in international education. It is not English in any simple way that is seen as a barrier to internationalism, but rather the perceived dominance of 'Anglo-Saxon' modes of organisation and action.

To the above, I would add a new source of internal discontinuity which has become apparent in the recent past. The Association, as stated earlier, was founded in a spirit of pioneering solidarity and there is great sentimental attachment to this principle. More recently, the conception of a voluntary association which is owned and governed by its members and in a sense is its members, has come under challenge from a competing conception of the Association as a service provider to paying customers, with accompanying notions of value-for-money and consumer (as distinct from democratic) accountability. There are many global and local reasons for the rise of this alternative, consumer-led conception, which is certainly not confined to the Association. At present, the two conceptions coexist uneasily, and consciousness fluctuates somewhat unhappily between them. Their co-presence certainly makes the construction of self and identity by means of membership in the Association more problematic than it was in the 'early days' of collective memory.

Finally, I would like briefly to raise the general question of self-awareness; how conscious is it possible for people to be of the work they are doing in the construction of self and identity? To this, needless to say, I have no definitive answer; but in the case of the Association and its members my judgement is that it is just beginning to be possible for a dimension of critical self-awareness to emerge. Until very recently, the discourse of international education has been dominated by unquestioning acceptance of its intrinsic value and virtue, and by a solidarity founded on the core constructs of internationalism, internationalisation, professionalism and professionalisation as analysed above. Only now is it becoming possible for some practitioners to turn a questioning gaze on the conceptual foundations of their commitment, and to subject them to open debate. For many, the identity construction made possible by international education (and concretely in Europe by the Association) will remain for some time to come too new and fragile to be subjected to the 'threat' (as some will see it) of critical examination. In what form and on what ground a shared consciousness will come to rest, the future will show.[4]

Notes

1. Much more could be said about this relationship than I have space for. For example, the working conditions of university-based international educators typically require constant travel, giving them a shared transnationality often jokingly termed the 'APEX culture'. Further, many of them have jobs relating closely to international students, who often do approximate to transnational communities in the more conventional sense.

2. Some years ago, at a time when educational cooperation and convergence between Western Europe and the former Eastern Bloc countries was particularly urgent and topical, a group of Western European colleagues formally proposed the establishment within the Association of a special interest group on Central and Eastern Europe (CEE). In their eyes the intention behind this was innocuous: to encourage East/West interchange and to provide a base for cooperation and development within CEE. Colleagues from the region, however, were implacably opposed; they sensed a ghettoising tendency and insisted that they wanted to be recognised as international educators in their own right, without a regional label. The proposal was thrown out.

3. In this connection a word on age and gender is in order. The mean age of Association members, when last surveyed, was 35–45, and there is a majority of about three to two in favour of women. Women also tend to be overrepresented among the elected officers and senior committee members, despite efforts to encourage a gender balance. This suggests that there is a connection between age, gender and 'professionalism': i.e. that a newly emergent field such as international education, represented as 'professional' but without the historical accretions of entrenched structures and glass ceilings common to some older professions, provides an unusually open route for women to enter in mid-career and to find advancement. Such advancement may have its limits; in most university governance systems, service departments (such as those in which the Association members mainly work) are not in the track for promotion to the very top posts. This notwithstanding, and in marked contrast to other international bodies representing historically more entrenched sectors of higher education, the Association is a very gender-open environment.

4. This paper was written during 2000, and thus presents a snapshot view of events, perceptions and processes at a particular, relatively narrow, historical moment. There is. of course, a wider context of debate on the rationales of internationalisation before, during, and after this period which is not addressed here. The Bologna process, in particular, was in its early stages in the period covered. The transformations it has brought about since then, both in institutional structures and in the identity and consciousness of practitioners, merit a study in their own right but are beyond the present scope.

Bibliography

Callan, H. 1984. 'Introduction', in H. Callan and S. Ardener (eds.), *The Incorporated Wife*. London: Croom Helm, pp. 1–26.

Douglas, M. 1987. *How Institutions Think*. London: Routledge.

European Association for International Education. 1992. *International Education in Europe: A Professional View on the Memorandum on Higher Education in the European Community*. Occasional Paper 2.

Hofstede, G. 1984. *Culture's Consequences: International Differences in Work and Related Values* (abridged edn). Beverley Hills: Sage.

Richardson, D. 1999. 'Before the Beginning', in P. Timmann et al. (eds.), *Europe in Association: The First Ten Years of the European Association for International Education, 1989–1999*. Amsterdam: European Association for International Education.

Rinehart, N. 2000. 'Study Abroad – Traditions and Current Challenges', in H. Callan (ed.), *International Education: Towards a Critical Perspective*. Amsterdam: European Association for International Education Occasional Paper 12 pp. 13–17.

Scott, P. 1999. 'Globalisation and the University'. Keynote address presented at the 52nd biannual conference of CRE Association of European Universities. Valencia, 28–29 October 1999 (cited with author's permission).

de Wit, H. 1995. 'Strategies for Internationalisation of Higher Education: Historical and Conceptual Perspectives', in J. Knight and H. de Wit (eds.), *Strategies for Internationalisation of Higher Education: A Comparative Study of Australia, Canada, Europe and the USA*. Amsterdam: European Association for International Education, pp.1–18.

Wright, S. 1994. '"Culture" in Anthropology and Organisational Studies', in S. Wright (ed.), *Anthropology of Organisations*. London, Routledge, pp. 1–31.

———. 1998. 'The Politicisation of "Culture"', *Anthropology Today*, 14 (1): 7–12.

Young, M. 1991. *An Inside Job: Policing and Police Culture in Britain*. Oxford: Clarendon Press.

6

PORTRAIT OF AN AID DONOR: A PROFILE OF DFID

Anne Coles

Introduction

This paper presents a profile of the Department for International Development (DFID)[1] as one among other bilateral donor agencies. DFID was, and is, a remarkably complex organisation and, in the second part of the 1990s (this paper covers the period from roughly 1993–2000), it experienced an extraordinary dynamic for change.

This is a personal interpretation that reflects a particular period in ODA/DFID's history. It may be too ambitious to call it a 'portrait'; perhaps it is best to call it instead a 'snapshot', and, moreover, one which is already dated. I was a staff member of DFID for five years in the mid-1990s and, following that, undertook a series of short-term consultancies for a few years, particularly in India and Bangladesh. I moved, therefore, from being an insider to being a regular consultant, and then to a more distant situation where reflection became possible. My perspective is that of a Social Development Adviser (see following sections). From late 1995, as part of my portfolio, I was responsible for the gender equality brief, so my comments on policy are often based on my experiences in this area, which almost all donor agencies have found difficult to operationalise. My understanding of other agencies comes largely from contact with colleagues as a member of the OECD[2] Development Assistance Committee's Working Party for Gender Equality and the Poverty Network. Subsequently I was involved in the evaluation of how member states had taken forward the OECD's High Level Statement on the place of gender in their aid programmes in the five years following the Beijing Conference on Women.

There were major developments in the conceptualisation of aid on the part of the global donor community in the second half of the 1990s. DFID has both contributed to and been part of the development of that thinking. The Anglo-Saxon and Northern donors have been prominent in contributing to this new global policy development. The World Bank had and has tremendous prestige, funds and therefore power, but was slow to become socially aware, while the Mediterranean countries initially retained much of their individuality in their approach to aid.

What were these new dominant discourses?

There has been an increasingly strong focus on and explicit commitment to poverty reduction as the overarching goal of development assistance. This has been accompanied by the recognition of the multidimensional nature of poverty: that poverty is not simply about inadequate economic growth but also about lack of access, social exclusion and vulnerability. There has been recognition that active participation of the poor themselves in their own development is important, both in terms of understanding the nature of poverty and because their 'empowerment' is part of the solution. DFID became a particularly strong advocate of 'pro-poor' policies and, later, of the associated Millennium Development Goals.

The concept of partnership has come to the fore: commitment by both recipient governments and donors to working together, on an increasing basis of equality,[3] to achieve jointly agreed development targets. With this has come emphasis on good governance, with the concept of support for democratic political environments and accountable institutions responsive to the needs of the poor and issues of gender and ethnic discrimination. There has also been more emphasis on the processes by which aid is provided in order to promote local ownership and foster true 'people-centred sustainable development'.

These precepts were promoted, adapted and reinforced at high-level meetings between donors and recipient governments – at Consultative Group events, at discussions over Poverty Reduction Strategies and so on (see Whitfield, this volume). However, such policy objectives have not always been visible on the ground. In bilateral donor organisations, and even more so in the multilaterals, there has often been a huge gap and long time-lag between rhetoric and reality, between policy and practice: the failure of trickle-down to trickle, let alone cascade downwards in a timely fashion. In the words of Robert Burns, 'The best laid plans of mice and men gang aft agley.' Moreover, the culture of managerialism and neoliberalism, which increasingly affected many donor organisations during this period, seemed at times to conflict with the conceptual vision. The concepts themselves, words such as 'participation' and 'partnership', were seldom defined. Thus, field officers could give the words their own unspoken meanings as they presented projects encapsulated within this policy framework, and host country governments were able to interpret them according to their own lights.

The evolving identity and role of social development advisers

Most social development advisers, unlike myself, began life as anthropologists. When I joined the Overseas Development Administration (ODA) in 1993 there were thirteen of us social development advisers (SDAs). By 1999 there were over fifty and the social development cadre had escaped from under the wing of economics, a position it had found fraught with professional tensions, to become a fully fledged independent social development department (SDD), headed by a chief adviser. Numbers had increased as a result of demand. Almost none were on the civil service permanent payroll: most were on relatively short contracts of two to five years, recruited for and paid for by the geographical departments. Since mid-2000 most have achieved permanent positions, essentially reflecting a change in British employment law, but also appearing to endorse the fact that the discipline had truly 'arrived'. DFID was in fact unique among bilateral donors at this period in having a fully fledged social development department.[4]

SDAs' role, status and identity have changed radically over the years.[5] Originally they were largely troubleshooters. They were called in when technical projects got into difficulties for human reasons. They then assumed a preventative role, becoming increasingly involved in project design, albeit initially sometimes rather late in the process. By the early 1990s most SDAs were assigned to work for geographical departments, whether overseas or in headquarters; a few were seconded to multilateral organisations; and the most senior also engaged in organisational policy making. When teamworking was encouraged from about 1995, they became full members of almost all project teams and key contributors to country strategy papers. SDAs had basic skills in social analysis and were increasingly recognised as the professional champions of policy issues related to the nonfinancial aspects of poverty, gender equality, vulnerable groups and participation, as well as contributing to the new work on human rights and civil society. They began to obtain finance for social development initiatives and their influence correspondingly increased.

This change in status was not achieved without problems. Individual SDAs were frequently overworked since, inevitably, as the cadre grew, demand often temporarily outstripped supply; ability to prioritise was a key attribute. It was important to focus on larger and strategically more important overseas projects, on the fundamentals of the design and, during implementation, on substantive project reviews rather than routine monitoring. As social scientists, SDAs inevitably had a 'softie' image in comparison with engineers or economists, and other staff often perceived social assessments as unduly time-consuming, however necessary they might recognise them to be. During this transitional period SDAs saw themselves as strategists and a fair amount of their time was spent negotiating within the bureaucracy as to the most effective way of influencing the broader development agenda. This was particularly true for gender equality, a subject which, as in all development agencies, tended to be marginalised and the promotion of which would prove to be a long-term struggle (Coles 2001). Thus, for SDAs, an understanding of the anthropology of the organisation was important for the job.

The national context in which the organisation's identity was formed

The identity of an organisation depends in part on the culture, traditions and history of the country in which it is established. ODA/DFID was no exception; its roots lay in Britain's overseas past. Thus, to this day, the direction of aid flows has been strongly towards the former imperial territories, historical and language links coinciding for the most part reasonably well with political and poverty reduction objectives. The colonial heritage has also contributed to DFID's internal culture, as we shall see.

The political, regulatory and institutional framework within which an organisation exists also contributes to its identity. In the case of ODA/DFID, being a department of the Foreign Office when the Conservatives were in power and an independent ministerial department under the Labour government produced a yo-yo effect unhelpful to the development of a coherent identity and image. Either way, its profile was inevitably modest, given that overseas aid was unlikely ever to be a British government priority.

Under the Conservative governments prior to 1997, the Overseas Development Administration (ODA), as it then was, came under the Foreign and Commonwealth Office (FCO). The broad distribution of aid, the budget and the range of activities pursued were inevitably shaped by FCO policies, although this was seldom acknowledged internally because to do so would detract from the purity of the aid motive, one of the organisation's most fundamental assumptions. After the Labour victory of 1997, ODA became the Department for International Development (DFID), a separate government department with its own cabinet minister.[6] This represented a hike in status and, given the new minister's forceful personality, led to a much stronger public profile both at home and internationally. A government White Paper (DFID 1997),[7] the first on aid for twenty years, marked the change and the department's power grew with increased allocations of funds.

As an independent ministry, DFID was, in fact, rather unusual among aid donors. The commonest arrangement for the delivery of development assistance was that of an agency under a Ministry of Foreign Affairs (MFA). But the range was wide. Occasionally development cooperation functions were carried out by a department of a Ministry of Foreign Affairs and sometimes there were several different agencies involved in different aspects of aid – as in the case of Germany or Japan – and these agencies had considerable independence. Most though not all agencies had staff in the offices of their main country partners, either in separate field offices or housed in their embassies. Some donors, like the Dutch, restricted their assistance to certain 'priority' countries; others, like France, Spain, Portugal and the U.K., favoured their former colonial possessions.

The department's relations with the Foreign Office were interesting. There was an FCO perception and concern that, as an organisation, ODA/DFID's activities could obscure the aims of foreign policy and even obstruct them. Foreign policy was, and is, guided by a fairly hard-headed concept of British interests, but the aid department usually seemed to be guided by 'something else': a concern for the

Third World, do-gooding or whatever. The FCO, with its role of coordinating Britain's overseas policy and representing the nation as a whole, found that, particularly after 1997, DFID developed its own policies leading sometimes to uncoordinated activities overseas, which it found irritating. In contrast to this, many NGOs (non-governmental organisations), both international and national, admired ODA/DFID precisely because it seemed comparatively little influenced by short-term, national, political agendas. It was seen as more independent and thus more objective and reliable than many other donor agencies, such as USAID.

The bureaucracy

As a government department, DFID was, and is, part of the civil service. It is a bureaucracy like other British bureaucracies; its heavy volumes of Office Procedures testified to this. As we shall see, its systems were an important influence shaping the identity, attitudes and behaviours of staff both internally within the organisation and in external negotiations. Like other parts of Whitehall, DFID was accountable to Parliament, notably to the Public Accounts Committee, for its expenditures. This accountability to the British government existed, not always comfortably, alongside the moral accountability that many staff felt to their stakeholders, particularly the poor in the developing world. Loyalties might be strained and, particularly overseas, it led to a Janus-like profile.

During this period, government by objectives became an important mantra and a serious influence on the bureaucracy. Business management techniques were introduced. All civil service departments were required to have clear, short-term objectives and, at least in ODA/DFID, the achievement of these was systematically translated down through the system into individual annual work plans. In some ways DFID was already well prepared for this approach. Staff members were familiar with the way in which each project had its hierarchy of objectives, the list of activities required to achieve this and the statement of hoped-for results. They were accustomed, too, to tight time frames, for projects typically lasted for only two, three or perhaps five years at most.

There was an extreme emphasis on written skills[8] and paper as a means of taking forward the organisation's work. Carefully worded minutes, concise, critical but ultimately constructive, provided a paper trail against which progress could be measured and a record against which individual staff could be held accountable. During this period the use of email came to provide a faster means of communication and the mail messenger service in headquarters gradually declined; however, this did nothing to reduce the length of formal documents or to detract from their purpose. A project memorandum (PM),[9] complete with its many professional annexes, submitted to the Projects Evaluation Committee in London, was one of the main ways in which an overseas office or geographical section showed its competence. Much effort went into its perfection, to make it an elegant, crisply worded PM of precisely the correct length.

Behaviour was 'neutral', to use one of the terms used by Fons Trompenaars (1993):[10] in other words emotionalism was avoided within the office. Disagreements were largely couched in terms of procedures or professional judgement. Moreover there was a clear distinction between the world of the office and the world outside. Often other staff knew little about the interests or family circumstances of those they worked with until there was a chance to chat one evening on a field trip or if presents had to be bought for children before the return home. Only junior administrative staff shared rooms, and the dispersal of homes far into London's outer suburbs doubtless contributed to this separation. Compared with the FCO at this time, much less official attention was given to ensuring that families of staff in overseas offices were well settled, although informally the process might go smoothly enough.

The culture was predominantly male-centred, the discourse masculine ('levelling the playing field' and 'going for goal' were common expressions). In terms of gender policies, DFID compared badly with most civil service departments in the U.K. In 1999, only ten out of almost sixty people in the senior grade were women, a proportion that was well below that in most other civil service departments. And although several women had been heads of profession or geographical divisions during the period, in early 2001 there were again none. Throughout the 1990s, however, the numbers of women reaching the middle grades in all parts of the organisation greatly increased. SDD itself was unique in that at this time it always had more or less equal numbers of men and women.

Internal identities and their negotiation

DFID had a matrix structure: advisers were responsible to their professional departments for the quality of their work but were commonly 'task managed' by administrators in the geographic departments. This created considerable potential for both tension and co-operation (see Moore, this volume). Group and individual identities were forged, fine-tuned, renegotiated and in the medium-term reassessed and altered in the daily processes by which projects were designed, implemented and monitored. The administrative cadre, permanent civil servants, had the formal power. They had responsibility for spending the aid budget. And the senior management board consisted largely of administrators, including those who headed the geographical divisions of the bilateral aid programme. Then there were the professional departments: economics, rural livelihoods and environment, health and population, education, infrastructure and rural development, and governance. These had an advisory function, and thus a critically important role in developing new initiatives and in determining the quality of the aid programme. There were two kinds of advisers: the cross-cutting advisers, the SDAs, the economists and often the institutional and environment advisers, who were concerned in the development of all new initiatives, and the sectoral advisers whose work was mainly confined to initiatives in their own professional disciplines.

Advisers showed an interesting age distribution. They were recruited at different times according to the demands of the aid programme; thus, many engineering and natural resource advisers were middle-aged, and dated from the time when there was a focus on initiatives in these sectors. There were a very large number of economists, reflecting the emphasis given to macroeconomic solutions. The older advisers, mainly men, came from a variety of backgrounds and had often acquired extensive experience before joining ODA/DFID. The younger ones were the products of the proliferation of university masters courses in applied subjects such as social policy or development studies but their prior practical exposure to the field was often very limited.

The groups perceived themselves to be very different – and, indeed they were. The administrators emphasised their membership of the civil service. In this they were followed by the economists, all of whom had satisfied the examination for government economists. The other advisers, some of whom were on short-term contracts, retained their own professional identities; identities that were regularly honed and reinforced as each contributed its own critique to the design of new initiatives. Whether they were writing sharp, cutting 'minutes' in the early part of this period or participating in project teams in the latter part, each contribution reflected their professional perspective and their identities were thus continually renegotiated.

Bearing in mind the apparently uncontrollable heat of much of the London headquarters, staff often seemed dressed, appropriately enough, for subtropical climes. But while administrators favoured white shirts and ties, advisers might allow themselves a touch of ethnicity or even a hint of eccentricity in their dress as a mark of their professions.

The roles and backgrounds of the two groups of staff were very different and, inevitably, stereotypes developed. There were conflicts between advisers, who were seen as professional perfectionists, and administrators keen to keep the throughput of projects going. Administrative staff felt that advisers placed too much emphasis on academic achievement and that operational realities were neglected, while advisers saw administrators as demanding and insufficiently concerned with quality. This might be reflected in further tensions between 'junior' staff, some of whom controlled quite large aid budgets, and advisers, who were felt to be using professional mystique and hierarchy to exclude them from the discourse. At the same time, the individual adviser often felt conflicting loyalties, both to a geographical department and to a professional cadre. While his or her work was based around country-specific projects, chances of promotions depended largely on satisfying their head of profession.

The internal complexity of DFID in the U.K. was reinforced by its being divided across two sites. The central London headquarters, in bustling Victoria Street, was where the most senior managers and chief advisers were located and where policy was made. Here, too, were some of the geographical departments, for example those for China, West Africa and the former Soviet Union. Far off in Scotland in East Kilbride, an overspill new town for Glasgow, were departments administrating pensions, procurement and appointments of staff and consultants (whom they seldom if ever met), with more substantive sections dealing with aid statistics, NGOs (less than ten per cent of U.K. aid went directly to NGOs) and, from 2001, evaluation. The emphasis was inevitably on procedures, on throughput and on clerical and financial efficiency. The differences in the staffs' nationality, background, roles and status compared to those of the London staff, together with its remoteness from much of the global development debate, resulted in a very different organisational identity, perspective and culture in the Scottish office. Yet it was this office which traditionally supplied many of the junior administrators posted overseas, thus strikingly replicating DFID's internal diversity in its field offices.

There were long-established regional offices, some dating back several decades, based in Bangkok, Nairobi, Harare, Southern Africa, the Caribbean and, declining in importance, the Pacific. There were also an increasing number of newer single-country aid management offices initially set up in India, Bangladesh and Nepal. Each developed its own identity, an identity that partly, but only partly, reflected the characteristics and culture of the host country. Each was also strongly influenced by the management styles of both the first and current office heads and his or her senior advisers. There have been some charismatic leaders, some standard civil servants and the occasional eccentric. Some heads ran field offices that responded to and related very closely to London; others seemed at times to be protecting their staff from the exigencies of headquarters and, fostered a distinctive office personality, although they were by no means able to escape the bureaucratic tentacles of the centre.

Many stakeholders in recipient countries, however, related most closely, not to the main DFID country office but to a further organisational layer composed of non-DFID personnel. A confusing series of individual consultants and consulting firms undertook much of the background work of project and programme development. Implementation was undertaken by field management offices and by technical cooperation officers (TCOs) contracted by DFID or by consulting firms appointed after a competitive tendering process. Often largely ignorant of DFID's policy debates, skilled as technical experts and sometimes as managers, usually slow to accept the need for social analysis, they were, however incorrect the perception was, the 'face' of DFID that most people overseas saw. ODA/DFID had long used commercial organisations, particularly for engineering projects, but as the 1990s progressed, a broader range of firms entered the development arena, reflecting an increasing role for the private sector.

ODA/DFID's perception of itself

We have seen how the structure of ODA/DFID resulted in groups of staff having very different identities. However, staff tended to have a rather vague feel for the identity of the organisation as a whole. Given the lack of emphasis on induction (except, of course, in procedures), and the fact that advisers might be recruited in mid-career from academic or NGO backgrounds, this was hardly surprising. Nevertheless there were clearly discernible underlying values and assumptions. There was a strong commitment to helping developing countries. There was a touch of lingering colonial values and a hint of missionary zeal, for, in the early 1990s, there were still a few staff members who had begun their overseas careers in the immediate postcolonial period when large numbers of expatriate technical officers had been sent overseas to assist the newly independent countries. Then there was the idealism of the younger staff, who also recognised that, in this postimperial era, DFID provided one of the most satisfactory ways of seeing life and 'serving' overseas as, compared with international NGOs, the civil service salaries were higher and conditions of employment were more secure.

ODA/DFID had a high regard for its own professionalism as a donor organisation. Other donors agreed: they were often envious of DFID's professional cadres and the way in which DFID had an advisory team in each field office. However, although in many ways at the 'cutting edge' of the development debate, over-work and the rigidity of DFID's procedures often delayed the application of new concepts. Many staff members became workaholics. Advisers admitted in private that though they might be at the sharp end of their disciplines when they joined the organisation, lack of time to read or discuss meant that they soon felt out of date.

How ODA/DFID was perceived by other players

As one observer of the British aid community put it, 'What you think of DFID depends on where you encounter it. It is a hugely complex organisation.' This section focuses on how ODA/DFID was seen by some of its partners in the development process, particularly at the country level.[11]

Field offices and the local context: images of 'apartness'

Despite the establishment of field offices, ODA/DFID was, for most of the period, surprisingly little concerned with the culture of the country in question. Briefing for postings was erratic and induction was usually strictly task-related. There was little information on cultural awareness and, although lessons could be paid for out of public funds, there was no encouragement to learn the local language. The fact that most postings were only for two to three years did not help. This continuing and partly-conscious 'Britishness' was encapsulated by a visual cue. In contrast to some other aid offices, DFID staff normally wore European clothes, except for visits to the field, when women might adopt local dress in the interests of modesty. Within field offices local staff could only fill junior posts[12] and their knowledge of the local context, their contacts and their continuity in terms of long-term memory often went unappreciated. For a long-time even SDD maintained that it did not matter what countries its advisers covered: analytical skills not geographical or cultural familiarity were what mattered. Yet comments from local partners showed that knowledge of their country, its language and its ways was much appreciated. And greater understanding might have ameliorated the fairly frequent clashes of bureaucratic culture with bilateral partners.

The distance between partners and potential partners was sometimes reinforced by a further aspect: the need for security. Several field offices were co-located in British embassies or High Commissions for this reason. Inevitably this meant that partners had to run the gauntlet of the guards before being admitted, an experience that many found uncomfortably off-putting and one which DFID staff much regretted. They, too, found it distasteful.

Relations with government

Relations with government officials tended to be formal and quite distant, being largely confined to work. Only towards the end of the period did DFID place emphasis on interpersonal skills, on the ability to network and influence as well as negotiate. Yet socialising was critical in countries where personal relationships with colleagues were highly valued and trust a prerequisite for conducting effective business. Efforts by individual staff to spend time getting to know local professionals or partners were not always recognised or appreciated, let alone commended. DFID's communications, moreover, were largely with senior officials, who themselves might be ignorant of the realities of their departments. Practical aspects, critical for the success of an aid initiative, might require more contact between middle-level officials and middle-level DFID staff.

This formality of the relationship might be understood by government partners but it could nonetheless be a disadvantage in societies where relationships were important and where trust needed to be developed over time to achieve effective working together. The PALS (Participatory Approaches Learning Study) report on India voiced Indian criticism that DFID did not capitalise on the goodwill of its many professionals who were Anglophiles. Moreover, while DFID staff were quick to criticise local bureaucracies for lack of continuity, resulting from frequent staff moves and slowness in decision making, these were precisely the characteristics which Indian bureaucrats found most annoying in DFID. It was a case of mirror images, of pots calling kettles black. Both bureaucratic cultures also placed great emphasis on accountability of funds, a factor that often detracted from discussion on more substantial developmental issues when projects were routinely monitored.

Relations with governments took place within the framework of the project cycle and this had implications for how the partners perceived each other. The project or programme management process was central to the aid delivery system. Critics regard it as too 'front-loaded', with too much attention given to design and insufficient attention to implementation and constructive (as distinct from financial) monitoring. Much senior management time on both sides went into fulfilling its submission requirements; the final details were often made at the last minute. Then, once agreed, there would inevitably be a delay, sometimes quite a long one, while the arrangements for implementation were made. Usually at this stage different sets of actors took on the task of carrying out the 'grand design', with only sporadic inputs from DFID staff.

The core of the project proposal was the 'logical framework', a table which set out objectives, activities and outcomes. Originally it was designed for use with 'blueprint' technical projects. It was then reinterpreted to record the milestones and achievements of process projects. Later, the log-frame was promoted as a tool for developing partnerships, with DFID and the host government working together on it to develop a joint vision of what the project would consist of. However, although log-frames were increasingly used by the whole development community, donors such as DFID were often more at home with the technique than were local partners, whether government or NGOs, and thus the process of log-frame development reinforced the very hierarchy that it was supposed to diminish.[13] Moreover, implementers, whether host government personnel, TCOs or commercial firms, who had seldom been involved in the design, sometimes found parts of the log-frame, with its inevitably abbreviated and coded language, hard to conceptualise in practice. Nevertheless, at best, it was a flexible monitoring tool and a useful guide for assessing progress and any need for project realignment.

The international donor community

Weak overseas governments were sometimes overwhelmed by the multiplicity of donors, each with their individual projects, different agendas and diverse accounting systems. But cooperative donor action was more readily advocated than achieved. Competition was and is often more instinctive than collaboration. For example, in Bangladesh after Beijing a few bilateral donors rapidly signed up to supporting the 'best bits' of the post-Beijing agenda. Only after almost nothing had happened two years later did the UNDP-led WID Group adopt a more constructive collaborative approach.

Primary stakeholders

As a bilateral aid donor, DFID tended not to deal directly with beneficiaries. Its relationships in the countries in which it worked were rather with secondary stakeholders – civil servants and NGO staff – and with its implementing agents. Yet DFID also needed and wanted to relate to primary stakeholders, to ensure their participation and empowerment. Working at second hand could be a frustrating business, particularly to advisers who had come into the organisation from a background in field research or the more 'hands on' NGO sector. Sadly for these staff members, it was, and is, undoubtedly true to say that most primary stakeholders involved in DFID-funded projects were not aware of the organisation's existence.

Relations with local NGOs overseas: mutual perceptions

DFID perceived NGOs as better able to reach poor people 'at the grassroots' than it could as a bilateral donor, and also came to see supporting NGOs as a means of strengthening local civil society (in fact, NGOs were typically equated with civil society in the minds of Northern donors during this period). For their part, NGOs saw donors such as DFID primarily as a source of funds. Some NGOs were founded by local professionals more or less specifically to access development resources: others were prepared to adjust their organisations' agendas to better fit donor requirements. In countries where governments had ambivalent feelings towards NGOs, the latter often came to see donors as a source of potential political support.

However, DFID's relations with overseas NGOs were often coloured by the sheer difficulty of disbursing grants on a small scale to local organisations better at community mobilisation or service delivery than management. NGOs perceived DFID's internal procedures as being overwhelmingly complicated. They were frustrated by the amount of 'training' and 'capacity building' needed before acceptable applications for projects could be made. They felt particularly disadvantaged if further drafts of a project document were required in a situation when their finances were already in a precarious condition. DFID staff, in turn, were frustrated by the amount of their time required to disburse relatively tiny sums of money. One solution was to set up 'umbrella' organisations as intermediaries to speed up the flow of reporting and funds.

Advisers and consultants: defining images

DFID made and makes extensive use of consultants, and, during this period, the social development group, faced with a growing demand for advice, made full use of individual consultants. This section examines the ambiguities in the adviser-consultant relationship and how these affected both the generally united face that they presented to the rest of the office and the tensions between them that contributed to how each group distinguished themselves.

At this time, social development advisers and social development consultants tended to come from roughly the same backgrounds. Their academic training was typically in anthropology or a related social science; they had at least a masters' degree; had done field research; and had worked overseas for at a minimum of several years. Assuming all went well with a commissioned piece of work, adviser and consultant presented a coherent professional stance to the rest of the office, the adviser supporting the consultant's findings and the bulk of their recommendations. Personality and familiarity came into it. Understandably, advisers preferred to work with consultants they related to as colleagues and comrades, with whom debriefing might include a pleasant evening of general professional discussion. Experience in consultancy and with DFID's 'ways' was important too, particularly when time was pressing.[14]

Despite these elements of 'togetherness', advisers and consultants were in very different structural positions. The adviser was responsible for commissioning work and for the ultimate quality of the product (officially payment would not be made until a satisfactory report was produced). But while the adviser outwardly had the power, the consultant knew that he or she was needed and therefore had a fair degree of bargaining clout. Facing each other across the table in the adviser's office, consultants might perceive advisers as demanding, abrupt and preoccupied with hidden internal political agendas. On the other hand, the adviser would worry that the consultant, particularly if an academic rather than a full-time freelancer, might go off on a tangent or fail to deliver on time. There was another underlying source of tension. Many SD advisers had strong field research backgrounds and, at times, fretted in their office-based environment. This applied whether they were located in the U.K. or in an overseas post. They felt that the consultant was having all the fun: the chance to concentrate on a single issue, to be at the cutting edge, to sharpen his or her understanding and to develop new concepts. The adviser-consultant relationship was thus complex and this complexity influenced their stereotypes of each other.

Trends in performance, outreach and impact: evolving identity

During the 1990s, the characteristics of DFID's aid programme and its identity altered. Conscious that in money terms it was not a big player, DFID placed less emphasis on infrastructure projects, particularly large-scale ones: these became seen as more appropriate to the mega-funding agencies, such as the World Bank and the EU. Instead, in accordance with the new discourse, there was an increase in initiatives fostering institutional development (it was realised that lack of management capacity in host governments reduced the effectiveness of many aid efforts)[15]. There was a new interest in human rights and in supporting 'good' civil society, although in this DFID was behind several other agencies, notably some of the Scandinavians.

There were changes in the balance of aid: an increasing proportion of DFID's budget went to multilateral institutions so that eventually only about half was disbursed bilaterally (directly from government to government). DFID, with its strong professional views, spent increasing time influencing the World Bank and attempting to improve the European Commission's performance. Secondments of professional staff, had, in fact, taken place regularly over the last decade or so. To take SDD as an example, during the 1990s it sent several staff in succession both to the World Bank and to DGVIII in the Commission. In 2000 SDD had advisers in the ILO (International Labour Association), the InterAmerican Development Bank and working with UN agencies in New York.

As far as the method of aid delivery was concerned, projects were becoming less important. General support for a broad-sector programme such as education, water or health was becoming more common. There was recognition that most development activities required a longer time span than the typical three years of a project cycle. (The stop-go process whereby one project ended before the next project began was scarcely efficient.) But DFID was often reluctant to make the ten- or fifteen-year commitments that some donors were trying out. And it was cautious in moving to full sector support both because of concerns about accountability and because it meant relinquishing some of the 'hands on' influence which it considered important for capacity building. Moreover, sector support involved working with other donors, typically under the aegis of the World Bank, and, while this could theoretically be very effective, it could also involve arguing the toss with a range of partners.

With growing recognition that projects were often 'implants in a hostile institutional environment', DFID involved a wide range of its staff in the process of changing that environment. For example, SD advisers were expected to be able to engage in policy dialogue and promote 'pro-poor' social policies across a wide range of government activities. In these circumstances, understanding the local players and their personalities, as well as political and economic trends, assumed a new importance, as did good social networks.

DFID, in theory at least, had a results-based culture, more so than many other donors. So what was the effect of all this assistance? It was hard to assess. At the macrolevel, bilateral aid agencies recognised, though sometimes forgot, that their contribution to the development of a particular country was usually modest and that trade and political agendas had far greater influence. At the micro-level, DFID's routine monitoring forms were preoccupied with money and basic activities. The aggregation of monitoring reports provided measurable indicators of the department's progress but was of little use for lesson-learning. Project completion reports were brief, along the lines of 'good in parts' and vaguely optimistic. Independent, commissioned evaluations tended to report too long after the event to be really useful and, in any case, covered only a small range of projects. Reviews were perhaps the most satisfactory means of assessing progress in substantial programmes. Usually carried out at mid-term, they typically enabled staff to engage with stakeholders in the field, and provided an opportunity to revise the work as necessary.

As more aid was disbursed through sectoral programmes with multiple donors, attribution was becoming increasingly difficult, though such programmes offered greater possibility of beneficiary involvement in monitoring. Measuring the impact of influencing policy in the recipient country presented and presents a challenge to the most imaginative evaluator. Besides, possibly the most interesting results were unexpected and not easily captured by routine processes – the indirect dissemination of new ideas outside the project zone, the emergence of female role models following support to women's teacher training, or the effects of a scholarship thirty years on. Despite these constraints, reflections on the value that its programmes added influenced how DFID saw its role and the ways in which it worked.

To sum up, ODA/DFID's identity and image have been shaped by its position in Britain's national government structure and political scene, as well as by Britain's imperial past. It has been strongly influenced by the nature of the civil service of which it is part, in particular in terms of its working practices and accountability to parliament. Within the organisation, the matrix structure resulted in strong constantly reinforced identities, particularly between advisers and administrators. However, images of DFID were complicated, blurred and fragmented by the decentralisation of offices both in the U.K. and overseas and by the use of non-DFID personnel for many project design and implementation tasks. Stakeholders' perceptions of the organisation varied according to the group concerned, its status and how it interacted with DFID over time. In turn, DFID's approach was affected by its evolving working relationships with partners and as its own values and systems adapted to the changing landscape of the global aid environment of which it formed a part. DFID's identity thus develops out of complex, dynamic interactions and discourses between host country and overseas operations, donors and recipients, and different staff members within the organisation.[16]

Acknowledgements

I would like to thank Pat Holden for reading the manuscript and Pat and Rosalind Eyben for providing material for the period after 2000.

Notes

1. Until 1997 DFID was called the Overseas Development Administration or ODA.
2. OECD = Organisation for Economic Co-operation and Development. DAC = Development Assistance Committee.
3. This ignores the reality of the relationship. The donor has the final power because it has the funds. However, in many cases the recipient is conscious of the local representative's need to spend his or her budget and their need to have new programmes of assistance in the pipeline.

    The World Bank towards the end of this period recruited some sixty social scientists and some donor organisations, notably SIDA, showed interest in developing a social development cadre.

5. For a description of social development in an earlier period ODA, see Conlin (1985) and also Rew (1997).
6. Clare Short also negotiated that DFID rather than the treasury should represent the U.K. at the World Bank.
7. The White Paper
    *   emphasised the eradication of poverty
    *   introduced human rights as a development issue
    *   was holistic in that it emphasised policy consistency throughout Whitehall and the involvement of the private sector (business and unions) as well as NGOs
    *   emphasised partnerships– partnership with recipient governments and with the multilaterals (the World Bank, UN systems and above all the EU) in both cases with the aim of improving aid effectiveness.
8. This excluded many able practitioners from its permanent ranks.
9. A project memorandum was the official project proposal submitted for agreement to senior management in DFID and to the relevant parts of the host government for approval.
10. I have looked at DFID's cultural characteristics across some of Fons Trompenaars' seven cultural dimensions. He carried out megaquestionnaire studies of global businesses, looking at the effects of national culture on business culture and particularly at how overseas subsidiaries differed in their behaviour norms and values compared with their Western head offices (in the U.S.A., Canada, U.K., Germany etc.).
11. I am grateful to those development professionals, consultants, academics and members of international NGOs who worked closely with DFID overseas offices during this period and who contributed their views for this section. I am also indebted to the PALS reports which looked at participation with secondary stakeholders in 1996–1998 (INTRAC 1998, 1999).
12. Grades and salaries were related to those in the FCO, where the roles for local staff were limited by the need for confidentiality and security in political matters.
13. On one occasion an SDA remarked complacently that a particular NGO consortium had 'come a long way' as, at their fifth attempt, their log-frame was 'almost acceptable'.
14. Office-wide, experienced consultants, whether individuals or firms, were preferred to inexperienced, since they would provide a report that did not require rewriting. This could make made entry into the consultancy pool difficult, particularly for non-British professionals, even though all major work was subject to competitive tendering. SDD, keen to be 'inclusive' and also desperately short of consultants, emphasised training in consultancy skills (both occasionally running courses itself and encouraging other institutions to do so.)
15. Just as SDD had expanded rapidly during the 1990s, Governance Department now began recruiting fast to meet the demand.
16. Much has changed since 1993–2000, the period covered in this chapter. There have been major internal organisational changes that outsiders have found confusing. Advisory departments now have virtually no resources and only residual powers. (There are still many staff with social development skills but they may be heading up small overseas offices or have different job titles such as 'poverty adviser'). The professional identity so dear to traditional advisers has been diluted. There are no longer multi-disciplinary team field visits, which older staff remember with nostalgia, for the emphasis away from projects has continued. The focus instead is on donor coordination and budgetary support, so that

more time is spent with ministries of finance in capital cities. Funds for development have continued to increase substantially and DFID has become a stronger Whitehall player. The role of commercial firms in global development has continued to grow.

Bibliography

Considerable use was made of ODA/DFID grey literature. Only a selection of the more readily available documents are cited here. DFID's Annual Departmental Report provides a valuable overview of its aid programme.

Coles, A. and P. Evans with C. Heath. 1998. 'Impact Assessment, Process Projects and Output-To-Purpose Reviews: Work In Progress in the Department for International Development (DFID)', in D. Mosse, J. Farrington, and A. Rew (eds.), *Development as Process: Concepts And Methods For Working With Complexity*. London and New York: Routledge, pp. 84–96.

Coles, A. 2001. 'Men, Women and Organisational Culture: Perspectives from Donors', in C. Sweetman (ed.), *Men's Involvement in Gender and Development Policy and Practice*. Oxfam Working Papers, Oxford: Oxfam, pp. 4–10.

Conlin, S. 1985. 'Anthropological Advice in a Government Context', in R. Grollo and A. Rew (eds.), *Social Anthropology and Development Policy*. London and New York: Tavistock Publications, pp. 73–87.

Department for International Development (DFID) 1997. *Eliminating World Poverty: A Challenge for the 21st Century*. White Paper on International Development. November 1997, cm 3789. Norwich, U.K.: HMSO.

Development Assistance Committee (DAC). 2000. *Progress towards Gender Equality in the Perspective of Beijing +5: Beijing and the DAC Statement on Gender Equality*. Paris: OECD/DAC.

———. 1996. *Shaping the 21st Century: The Contribution of Development Co-operation*. Paris: OECD/DAC.

Eyben, R. 2003 'Mainstreaming the Social Dimension into the Overseas Development Administration: A Partial History'. *Journal of International Development*, 15: 879–92.

Herzfeld, M. 1992. *The Social Production of Indifference*. Chicago and London: University of Chicago Press.

INTRAC. 1998. *Overview Country Reports for PALS Study on Ghana, Egypt, Nigeria, India*. Oxford: INTRAC.

———. 1999. *The Participatory Approaches Learning Study (PALS) Overview Report*. London: Social Development Publications.

Overseas Development Administration (ODA). 1995. *A Guide to Social Analysis for Projects in Developing Countries*. London: HMSO.

Preston, R. 2003. 'Partnership for Human Development: Consultancy and Communication in Complex Projects.' Unpublished book manuscript.

Rew, A. 1997. 'The Donors' Discourse: Official Social Development Knowledge in the 1980s', in R. Grillo and R. Stirrat (eds.), *Discourses of Development: Anthropological Perspectives*. Oxford and New York: Berg, pp. 81–106.

Trompenaars, F. 1992. *Riding the Waves of Culture*. London: Nicholas Brealey.

Wright, S. (ed.) 1994. *Anthropology of Organisations*. London and New York: Routledge.

7

IDENTITY CONSTRUCTION IN DEVELOPMENT PRACTICES: THE GOVERNMENT OF GHANA, CIVIL SOCIETY, PRIVATE SECTOR AND DEVELOPMENT PARTNERS

Lindsay Whitfield

Introduction

Since the 1990s, the literature produced by donor agencies and 'development practitioners' has tended to schematise governance in aid recipient countries in terms of a partnership between government, the private sector and civil society. Notably, this model conceals the significant influence donors wield in aid recipient countries, especially their influence on other actors and in shaping the domestic political landscape. Development practices employing this model have generated new identities. This chapter looks at the creation and functions of these identities, providing another example of the construction and destruction of boundaries between the public and private sectors. A key theme is the blurring of boundaries and blending of identities, in contrast to the simplified and codified identity categories implied in the model. Using the case of Ghana, I will show how these identities do shape people's actions, but also how they can distort our understanding of the societal landscape in which such actions take place.

With the return to multiparty representative government in Ghana under the Fourth Republic, an impetus to modify the political system emerged from a combination of political will among elites and expanded opportunities for political expression resulting partly from donor interventions, and partly from pressure exerted by citizens. Political liberalisation produced a shift in the relationships among donors, government and citizens. In the mid-1980s, with the introduction of Structural Adjustment, donors developed a relationship with the government largely through policy-based lending and separate relationships with Ghanaian social organisations through NGO-isation. By the mid-1990s, citizens and their organisations began to join the 'policy dialogue' previously exclusive to the government and donors. This shift in the relationships among actors occurred alongside discursive shifts linked to the concepts of good governance and civil society. However, efforts to create more democratic forms of government by opening up the policy-making processes to greater participation eventually confront the International Monetary Fund (IMF) and World Bank, who still act as the trustees of development despite shifts in their discourse at the turn of the century. This confrontation and its reverberations within the framework of modern representative democracy and the ad hoc mechanisms for civil society and private sector engagement have produced debates over the definition of identities, of participation and of the roles that different actors in Ghanaian society and in the donor aid system should play. These debates take place within, and are influenced by, the collective identities of government of Ghana, civil society, private sector and development partners.

These identities are produced and sustained by the model of governance propagated in donor agencies' policies and much of the mainstream literature on development, which shares an understanding of governance systems as the result of interaction between the state (hierarchical order), the market (self-organising driven by competition) and civil society (cooperation driven by voluntary association) (Castro, forthcoming). This understanding of governance is often idealistically portrayed as a balanced interaction among partners. Donors employ this governance model as an *analytical tool* for understanding the processes of development and as a *practical tool* for intervening in them. The application of the model in donor operations involves a rigid categorisation of social identities. It assumes cohesive and coherent group identities and then assigns them a role – a role reinforced through repetition in discourse and through donor funding according to these identities. Donors are conspicuously absent from this model, envisioning themselves as exogenous to it.

The structure of this chapter is as follows. It first addresses the relationship between the government of Ghana and donors by examining their relative positions within the policy-making field. It then focuses on donors, highlighting the shift in their identity from donors to 'development partners'. The chapter next examines the construction of civil society and the shift from NGOs (non-governmental organisations) to CSOs (civil society organisations). It also looks at the relations among civil society, government and donors. While the private sector is not dealt with as extensively as the other identities (due to the nature of the research), we point out the blurred boundaries between the private sector and civil society as a result of the multiple roles that NGOs can play and of the ideological impetus to separate non-state actors from the state. Throughout the chapter, we indicate implications of the construction and deconstruction of these identities for development processes.[1]

Government and donors in the policy-making field

The debt relief regime, together with the foreign aid regime, constitutes the broad parameters of the policy terrain within which Ghana's constitutionally determined policy-making process is situated. The paths of policy-making in Ghana weave in and out of externally driven donor/creditor and domestic political/administrative institutions, procedures and arenas. Institutions encompass the IMF, the World Bank and other donors as well as government (the executive) and Parliament. Processes include donor assistance strategies and operational procedures as well as government-introduced legislation based on policy positions and parliamentary approval of the budget and of the legal framework for policy reforms. Arenas are forums for policy discussion among donors and between donors and government. Here we focus on government-donor policy dialogue arenas and domestic governance processes.

Donors exhibit powerful influence over policy not only through conditionality, but also through policy dialogue arenas. Donors have created a plethora of arenas for what they call 'policy dialogue' with government, as well as for coordinating their operations, sharing information and experience, discussing policies, and identifying opportunities to engage government on policy reforms. Consultative group meetings held every second year constitute the most institutionalised arena in which the government and donors interact. Mini consultative group meetings provide a more regular arena in which donors and the government meet to review the country's economic situation. These quarterly meetings serve as the forum where donor pledges of aid are received or confirmed and where draft sector policies may be presented for broader donor input or the need for sector policies proposed. There are also sectoral-level arenas for government-donor discussions on, for example, health, education and decentralisation, as well as monthly donor meetings where the heads of donor agencies discuss issues that 'advance the development agenda'. The latest innovation in such arenas is the Multi-Donor Budgetary Support mechanism, which pools participating donors' resources together to provide financial support directly to Ghana's budget (rather than through individual donor projects or collaborative sector programmes). Dispersal of this money is linked to the completion of negotiated policy reforms and action. With nine donors participating, led by the World Bank, it is seen by many donors as an arena of 'high-level dialogue'.

In contrast, Parliament as an institution in the policy-making field is constrained by structural, historical and situational factors. Structurally, Parliament's law-making and oversight functions are weak, making it mostly a deliberative body. The Constitution mandates the President to appoint the majority of ministers from Parliament and permits the appointments of Members of Parliament to the boards of state institutions. The effect is to blur the boundaries between the legislative and executive branches of government and to limit the ability of parliamentary oversight of the executive. Parliament's law-making function is further weakened by a constitutional provision which prohibits MPs from introducing bills that impose taxes, charges or withdrawals from public funds. This article severely reduces the scope of private member bills and has led to the belief among a majority of MPs that legislation must originate from the executive. The Constitution also gives the executive branch the responsibility for drafting all supporting legislation that defines how policies will be implemented. A parliamentary committee has some oversight of this process, but the scope of its review is limited to accepting or rejecting legislation. Without the ability to allocate itself resources, Parliament is dependent on the executive for what it receives.

These constitutional constraints are buttressed by the historical marginalisation of Parliament. There is a legacy of the centralisation of power within the executive since independence throughout constitutional history. The current constitution follows its predecessors by placing most authority in the executive. More debilitating than the selection of the majority of ministers from Parliament is the effect of this legacy which results in Parliament ceding its role in policy-making through its inaction.

In terms of situational constraints, Parliament is largely bypassed in the process of donor-government policy dialogue. This situation results from the structural limitations discussed above and from tendencies inherent in the donor aid system to marginalise Parliament as an institution. The arenas for donor-government policy dialogue are not accessible to Parliament as an institution. While Parliament is constitutionally delegated the power to approve loan agreements, both domestic and international, entered into by government, Parliament's role is largely relegated to approving the legislative framework for policy reforms; it does not engage in their formulation. Minority members use the tactics of boycotts on voting or walkouts as public expressions of disagreement with government policy, but these strategies do not leverage Parliament's participation in policy discussions. Parliament is, however, increasingly providing an arena for policy discussions between MPs and the executive, and between MPs and citizens.

Based on the idea of good governance, several donors have governance programmes which, among other goals, strive to enhance the capacity of Parliament in terms of making inputs into laws and policies and of engaging with segments of society.[2] As a result, some MPs look to donors to provide resources for Parliament. MPs and citizens capitalise on such programmes to put pressure on the executive to pursue certain reforms or to leverage resources that the government does not have or is unwilling to provide. The power dynamic is obvious where it is donors trying to raise the status of Parliament in the policy-making process. The reality of this unequal relationship may underline the assumptions on which donors construct their good governance policies and may contribute to their tendency towards micromanagement of governance in recipient countries. Donors often realise, even if they only admit it within their organisations, the fine line they walk between 'partnership' and 'patron'.

From donors to development partners

At some point in the mid-1990s, donors began to be identified as 'development partners'. This new identity is indicative of changes taking place in the discourse and practices of donors. The World Bank in particular adopted a new discourse emphasising a 'partnership' between donors and governments, invoking a contrast to the previous relationship characterised by conditionality and financial coercion. 'Development partner' connotes an equal responsibility in the development process, in terms of both financial assistance and policy content. As I shall demonstrate, its appearance paralleled an increase in donors' presence in recipient countries and their representation in recipient governments' policy-making processes.

The realisation that conditionality was not working as intended occurred alongside a shift in the economic reform agenda from first-generation reforms (concerned with reducing the scope of the state) to second-generation reforms (concerned additionally with the nature of state action) and a realisation that institutional reforms could not be affected solely through conditionality (Kapur and Webb 2000; Harrison 2004: 18–22). The response of donors to this new situation has taken two forms, which are inherently linked. First, donors adopted more persuasive, noncoercive mechanisms in order to convince recipient governments of the need for reform. Second, donors moved closer to the workings of the State apparatus and thus de facto became part of government. Even though the World Bank admits that economic reform must come 'from within', in practice this has meant working more closely within the state and with societal actors.[3]

Through the proliferation of donor-government dialogue arenas, donors have routinised and semi-institutionalised the ways in which they interact with a myriad of state institutions, and in which they participate in the design, implementation and monitoring of government programmes and policies. To some extent, donors operate intimately with the government, and are themselves either governing, or governing the government. Again, donors often perceive the tension between the reality of their influence in policy-making and their lack of accountability to Ghanaian citizens, or beneficiaries, as well as the contradiction of this position vis-à-vis their efforts to promote democratic participation, or less ambitiously, good governance. Donor staff in country offices may prioritise loyalty to beneficiaries or 'the poor' in recipient countries over loyalty to the head office, but they are accountable to their home governments, not to beneficiaries or recipient governments.

This expanded donor intervention is the result of several colliding factors. First, it is the product of aid dependency. Foreign aid since the start of Structural Adjustment has led to a massive increase in Ghana's external debt. Even though Ghana suffered from debt since the 1960s, it was during the Structural Adjustment process that its arrears increased substantially and became unsustainable (Tetteh 2003). The majority of Ghana's obligations are owed to multilateral creditors. Continuous debt servicing restricts government spending on investment and on social sectors (Osei and Quartey 2001). The economic reforms implemented since 1983 have had a positive impact on the macroeconomic position of the country, but they have not generated enough foreign exchange to shore up its chronic balance of payments deficit, leading Ghana back to donors again and again.

The experience of two decades of Structural Adjustment has left government institutions with extensive knowledge of the bargaining process of adjustment and of the economic paradigm pushed by the Bretton Woods institutions.[4] Many government officials and civil servants have internalised this paradigm, partly out of ideological symmetries in dominant ministries such as the Ministry of Finance, and partly out of self-interest, or just to make the job easier. Government representatives regurgitate World Bank terminology, such as 'enabling environment' and 'private-sector-led development'. Decades of economic reform led by lending arrangements with the Bank and Fund have ingrained certain ideas and norms and created incentives for the maintenance of the status quo. The new discourse of participation, partnership and ownership has seen donors suggesting what government should do, rather than imposing it explicitly. Conditionality is still negotiated. Officials and civil servants know that certain things have to be said to access donor money, and sometimes it may be easier to say what donors want to hear first, rather than go through the process of negotiating. Offering more money for donor-preferred reform options, and offering generous financial flows to new governments in power, are other noncoercive mechanisms used by donors.

Donors also decentralised their operations by opening offices in recipient countries, thus increasing their ability to attend government meetings as 'observers' and to hold donor-government meetings more frequently. Yet although donors have country offices, important decisions on aid programmes and loans are still taken at their headquarters. The expansion of donor agendas into all areas of development, and thus their interest in all imaginable policy issues (e.g. chieftaincy relations), has increased the scope of donor involvement in Ghana and concomitantly the scope of conditionality. Moves towards greater coordination among donors through sector-wide approaches and budget support (which pool resources and create agreed lists of conditions) further intensify the intimacy of donor involvement and the pressure of conditionality. The IMF and World Bank employ a multitude of assessment tools that keep the government under constant surveillance. They also use their analytical work to influence the policies of recipient countries or other donors working in these countries. IMF and World Bank analytical work was always important, but it has expanded from macroeconomic policy to include a wide range of policy issues. The Bank continues to be the dominant purveyor of development ideas and claims the status of 'expert' on all that is development.

In addition to working closely with policy-making processes, donors leverage additional control over governance processes by funding special structures, technical assistants and consultants in ministries, agencies and departments, and by providing a larger percentage of funding to some ministries than does the government budget. Donor-funded technical assistance introduces new methodologies of governance based on corporate plans and budgeting/ monitoring techniques. Expatriate personnel on donor-funded contracts reinforce the international orthodoxy of reform and these new methodologies (Harrison 2004). Donors capitalise upon those they identify as 'like-minded' people in government to push their agenda, especially consultants and donor-funded technical assistance positions.

Expanded donor intervention also entails greater interaction with Ghanaian society and with domestic political processes. Donors participate in non-state arenas which were once considered purely domestic affairs, such as public forums organised by non-governmental actors, public hearings organised by the government, submitting memoranda to Parliament and attending parliamentary committee meetings. The World Bank in particular has resorted to 'communication strategies' to convince the Ghanaian public of the merit of its prescribed reforms, as in the case of private sector participation in urban water provision. Some bilateral donors also fund government bodies to carry out such public relations campaigns.

This extensive level of donor involvement has led some Ghanaians to feel increasingly ruled by two governments: one formed by an elected president and the other consisting of unelected donors. Some respond by seeking to alter this situation, using the contemporary global euphoria around spreading representative democracy to legitimise their argument that donors are not accountable to Ghanaian citizens. Others try to use the influence donors wield with their elected government to make it more accountable to them or to achieve other goals. An individual may pursue both avenues without the inherent tension between the two becoming obvious or inhibiting.

In sum, the notion of 'partnership' embodied in the identity of development partners idealises relations among donors, government and citizens, and fails to acknowledge the power imbalances at play in their interactions. Donors can equally appear as partners or as competitors, competing for influence in the policy-making field and competing for who represents the interests of the poor. Some donors only want to be *seen* as representing the interests of the poor, while others actually push the current Kufuor government to adopt stronger 'pro-poor' policies and thus *believe* themselves to actually represent the poor vis-à-vis a government that is more concerned with wealth creation.

From NGOs to civil society

Political liberalisation in the 1990s led, first, to greater input by non-governmental actors into the policy-making process; second, to a greater responsiveness from government regarding public opinion; and third, to a gradual shift away from the dominance of technocrats towards the influence of elected representatives. It redefined the political and policy environment 'by giving social and economic interests enhanced political space in which to articulate interests, negotiate with government, and organise opposition' (Hutchful 2002: 218). This period of political liberalisation differs from previous periods of multiparty constitutional rule, largely in the extensive donor funding of NGOs and in the influence of the idea of civil society.

Donor interventions through NGOs at the national, regional and district levels have repercussions for power relations, political influence and social mobility (Hutchful 2002: 182–86). Firstly, donors, recipient governments, international and domestic NGOs are inserted into a hierarchy of dependencies in a variety of ways and with very unequal power relations. During the 1980s, the major donor governments channelled an increasing proportion of their development aid through NGOs from their own countries to fund activities of NGOs in recipient countries. Donors and foreign NGOs funding local NGOs have tended to retain tight control over the process, determining local agendas and demanding adherence to administrative procedures (Mohan 2002). Secondly, a new vocabulary emerged within development discourse in relation to NGOs – 'empowerment', 'accountability', 'participatory development' – but these intrinsically political terms were presented in a depoliticised way. By emphasising the participation of affected groups in specialised, micro-level action, NGO activities initially encouraged particularistic and fragmented levels of action rather than broad political processes and alliances (Mohan and Stokke 2000). Thirdly, existing community and social organisations are transformed into NGOs as a result of bureaucratisation (establishing administrative structures), encadrement (professional interlocutors with administrative skills and knowledge of grant applications), grantsmanship (cultivation of access to donor funding opportunities), dollarisation and officialisation (recognition by the state). NGOs should not be seen as contiguous with commoner organisations and town associations of the colonial and post-colonial periods. The adoption of a preexisting organisation by a foreign NGO or donor can undermine its self-reliance and confidence and create the temptation of corruption, even if improving its technical capacity. Rural self-help groups seeking resources from government, NGOs or donors are identified as Community-Based Organisations (CBOs) and often aspire to upgrade their status to NGO, so they may gain access to greater resources with which to help their communities and themselves.

NGO-isation in the 1980s and early 1990s was followed by further identity construction and deconstruction in the mid-1990s, with the permeation of the idea of civil society from academic literature to the development profession and then to Ghanaian society. Emerging NGOs as well as occupational and social organisations that have existed since independence are now identified as 'civil society organisations' (CSOs), and universities, the media and churches are 'civil society institutions'. We look briefly at the causes and effects of this new identity

In pursuit of understanding political processes in Africa, academics have sought to explain how 'civil society' works to shape the rules of the political game, particularly the role of civil society in transitions from authoritarian regimes to more democratic ones.[5] While academics disagree on what civil society is, donors essentially adopted the 'conventional view of civil society', limiting the definition to specific kinds of non-state organisations in public life engaged in organisational activity according to particular criteria (Kasfir 1998: 1). The discourse of good governance, in both its apolitical, technocratic garb and its political instrumentalism in building a constituency for economic reform, led to the linking of NGOs and other organisations with the idea of civil society (Williams and Young 1994; Gary 1996). Donors perceive civil society as an instrument to make states more democratic, transparent and accountable. They channel aid through the frameworks of 'civil society' and 'good governance' to effect desired changes in the structure of society, in economic policies and in forms of government. In support of 'civil society', donors fund programmes that provide material and organisational resources to NGOs and research institutions. A significant impact of the application of the idea of civil society by donors, to a lesser extent by international NGOs, is the production of a 'hierarchy and differentiation of civil society' by privileging some sections of Ghanaian society over others through the provision of resources (Hutchful 2002).

Links among academics, donor agencies, international NGOs and their Ghanaian counterparts led to the infiltration of the idea of civil society into the social consciousness of Ghanaians. People realised that past actions could be described under a new identity and recognised the advantages that followed from using this identity. Activists and NGO workers wished to benefit from the international and national momentum behind 'civil society' and the resources available to civil society organisations. Some people made conscious efforts to repackage previous ideological beliefs into the acceptable discourse of civil society. Finally, by identifying themselves as part of civil society, individuals and organisations were able to further their existing objectives and to proclaim their actions legitimate.

Coming into Ghana during a period of political change, the idea of civil society became a new idiom in Ghanaian politics through which actors articulated and understood political processes, replacing or supplementing previous ideological discourses. In effect, the civil society identity is constructed through a process in which donor agencies, international NGOs, government and Ghanaian NGOs and social organisations engage in the discourse of civil society and use the idea to legitimise their actions. For government, civil society is a way to respond to and control increasingly articulate demands from sections of society for greater representation in policy-making. For donors, civil society is a means of influencing the government without falling prey to criticisms of conditionalities, and it is an end insofar as it is perceived as the new solution for democratic governance and a vibrant economy. For international NGOs, civil society is the key to linking citizens around in the world in common struggles. For Ghanaian organisations and activists, it is a tool for mobilisation and legitimation. Through consciousness of themselves as part of civil society, they create a common frame of reference, independent of the state and political parties, around which they can coalesce.

While the identity of civil society is defined loosely by those who use it or talk about it in the abstract, it tends to refer mostly to NGOs when put into practice. While they were initially assigned the role of champions of democracy, it is clear that NGOs cannot be assumed to be advocates for democratic reforms.[6] Leaders of NGOs and their objectives (employment and accumulation, status mobility, political aspirations, progressive political activism) determine the nature of its engagement with the political sphere. Organisational histories are also crucial in determining their objectives, actions and outlook. But what are NGOs, behind their masks of civil society and intermediary for development projects? Two answers include NGOs as patronage networks and as alternative sites for political activism.

NGOs are alternative employment opportunities for the public sector and sites of access to resources (e.g. computers, vehicles, foreign travel), partly because of Structural Adjustment Programmes, which have led to a reduction of the public sector, and partly because of the civil society paradigm, which has channelled lucrative amounts of funding to 'civil society organisations'. These employment opportunities generate patronage networks linking rural to urban, private sector to public sector, and donors to new elites. Such patronage networks and the new class of elites are not dependent on the State, unlike most other patronage networks, providing them with the space to critique government and its policies. However, their dependence on donors has sometimes mitigated their criticism of the government's financial and technical dependence on donors and the extent of donor influence over domestic policies. Similar patterns occur in assistance provided by foreign NGOs at the village level through intermediary Ghanaian NGOs (see Mohan 2002).

Nevertheless, NGOs can also serve as alternative sites for political activism. Once in power, opposition parties face the same aid dependency and conditionalities as the ruling party before them, implementing policies they may even have criticised while in opposition. NGOs provide an alternative platform from which to challenge government policies. They can garner external resources, especially transnational leverage and financial support. They also provide a new vehicle through which political activists can channel their energies following the delegitimisation of the Left and its ideologies after the adoption of Structural Adjustment Programmes. Students and intellectuals who were members of the 'progressive' or revolutionary organisations of the 1970s can now be found working in outspoken advocacy NGOs. Linkages to global social movements and advocacy campaigns have been critical to the rise of advocacy NGOs and the new brand of political activism they are leading. The inability of social organisations to construct a lobby group that parallels the leverage of the World Bank and IMF in shaping their government's policies, combined with cultural and historical legacies of centralised decisionmaking, has led Ghanaian activists to seek alliances with Western NGOs.

The government, civil society and private sector model

Society in general, and government leaders in particular, still hold that decision-making is the prerogative of the government and state apparatus, and that people who criticise government policy are against the ruling party. This political environment has led some citizens to use the identities of civil society and private sector to legitimate their demand to join the 'policy dialogue' between donors and government. A series of novel public policy forums took place between 1996 and 1998 (Akwetey 1998). Donor intentions to create a broader consensus on policy by enlarging the influence of businesses, political opposition and general interest groups played a large role in the materialisation of these forums. This political opening occurred in an environment marked by confrontational relations between political factions and by distrust between the Rawlings government (1993–2000) and many business enterprises.[7] The initiation of dialogue on economic policy occurred through the Tripartite Committee (with representation from the government, Ghana Employers' Association and the Trades Union Congress) in May 1996 in the form of the National Forum on the State of the Economy. A Forum for Policy Dialogue was then organised by the Private Enterprise Foundation in March 1997 for leaders of political parties, Members of Parliament and 'policy-makers'. The Foundation is comprised of the six major business associations in Ghana and was formed in response to the opportunity to engage in economic policy-making.[8] It aims to present a unified position on government policies which reflects a mutually beneficial position among individual enterprises with potentially disparate interests. The Rawlings government embraced the Foundation as the representative of the private sector in consultations on its economic policies.

In June 1997, another forum was organised by the Private Enterprise Foundation in the United States, financed by the United States Agency for International Development (USAID). At that time, USAID was supporting activities of the Foundation under its Trade and Investment Program. This forum brought together representatives from government, opposition parties, private sector, unions and the universities on neutral ground under the theme 'Ghana – Reaching the Next Level through Global Competitiveness: a Public/Private Partnership'. The Foundation, USAID and Sigma One Corp (a U.S. corporation) then organised a similar forum in Ghana, broadening its participant base and calling it a National Economic Forum. The string of forums ended here until the idea was picked up by the Kufuor government (2001–2004) and transformed into the annual National Economic Dialogue.[9] The Private Enterprise Foundation remains the main representative of the private sector.

The government and donors also organised several forums on good governance in the late 1990s. Since the initiation of these public forums, arenas for discussing policy are constantly created for the government and donors to 'consult' civil society and the private sector on various policy proposals. The national forums of the 1990s can be seen as a chain of events, building on each other and pushing the boundaries of inclusion further. The parameters of inclusion and the nature of engagement (who, when, on what terms, to what effect) remain the substance of political contestations.

The public had intentionally been kept out of economic discussions in the early years of Structural Adjustment. Even within the new environment amenable to greater input from non-state actors, the opportunity to participate in policy discussions did not directly translate into participation. Many NGOs and other social organisations lacked information and policy analysis skills necessary to engage effectively and productively in these discussions, and the monopoly on information held by government in the past continued, although to a lesser extent. These deficiencies gave rise to donor-funded programmes to 'build the capacity' of selected organisations, which can simply mean access to better technology and material resources. Some NGOs, mostly in Accra, are producing their own research and policy analysis and have developed strong advocacy skills and a publicity network with which they attempt to contribute to policy formulation. Such advocacy NGOs pursue individual avenues of lobbying as well as joining issue-based coalitions, which are formed and reformed according to the current issue and interested organisations.

Articulation of the role of civil society as unified, and as a third sector in relation to the government and the private sector, is common in Ghanaian media and political discourse. Besides indicating the extent to which the donors' governance model has permeated Ghanaian society, it also indicates the extent to which actors and organisations see themselves as having an equal right to participate in the development process. This claim has roots at the global level, as global 'civil society' exerts its right as an equal player alongside governments, multilateral institutions and transnational corporations. Foreign NGOs pressure the World Bank, and at the same time use donors to pressure the government of Ghana, to involve Ghanaian civil society in policy-making.

Donors serve as a source of information for citizens about government policies and as a mechanism through which citizens exert pressure on government to be more transparent. Donors also use their programmes and leverage to bring 'civil society' into the policy dialogue. On the other hand, citizens and their organisations may be found vying with donors to influence government policy just as often as they are seen collaborating them.

From NGOs to private sector

In the competitive realm of the development aid market, NGOs compete for contracts and for funding and often shift their focus in response to demand (i.e. donor and international NGO funding). The line between NGOs and private enterprises is becoming increasingly blurred. NGOs often act as, and are perceived as part of, the private sector. While NGOs do not operate strictly according to profit-maximising principles, they do reinvest in their organisation by expanding the reach of their activities, the range of their activities and their number of personnel. The main difference between NGOs and small or medium businesses may only be the adherence of NGOs to the principle of social responsibility, the goal of contributing to the social or physical welfare of society. Working in an NGO means that one can make money as well as help people.

This blurring of the private sector and NGO sector can be illustrated with the example of the national strategy for water provision in rural areas and small towns. This strategy emphasises community management, where communities are involved in the mobilisation, planning and implementation of water supply as well as the operation and maintenance of the water facility. Implementation of the National Community Water and Sanitation strategy depended largely on donor projects, particularly World Bank Community Water and Sanitation Project loans, and the activities of international and local NGOs. The Community Water and Sanitation Projects came with implementation manuals which outlined specific roles that different actors are to play, and all organisations engaged in non-urban water provision are supposed to adhere to these roles. District Assemblies (local government structures) were required to establish District Water and Sanitation Teams of two to three people whose role is to manage water supply and sanitation activities in the districts. Communities have to apply to the Assembly for a water facility of their choice. After communities' applications are accepted, a local government team oversees community mobilisation, planning and implementation processes. Assemblies and communities each contribute five per cent of the cost of the facility. Partner Organisations are contracted to mobilise the community, to establish bodies for community management and train them, to facilitate community needs assessment, and to support community hygiene and environmental education. At a higher level, Small Business Development Units (NGOs and commercial organisations with relevant expertise) are contracted by the Community Water and Sanitation Agency (central government structure) to provide training and support services for Partner Organisations and local artisans building pit latrines.

In the revised 2000 manual, the creation of names for each role was dropped; it indicated that private sector consultants, contractors, suppliers, and NGOs with the relevant skills and experience are to be contracted by District Assemblies and the Community Water and Sanitation Agency to provide goods and services required by the projects. Villages and small towns applying for water facilities must select members to voluntary committees, WATSAN Committees and Water and Sanitation Development Boards respectively, which are responsible for the future operation and maintenance of the facilities. The Community Water and Sanitation Agency is to facilitate the provision of services by private sector organisations rather than actually providing services.

The national strategy promotes private sector provision of water services and the World Bank's Community Water and Sanitation Project promotes competitive tendering for contracts among organisations available to provide these services. In northern Ghana, where commercial firms are scarce, Ghanaian NGOs are playing the role of Partner Organisation. The permeable boundary between civil society and private sector is acknowledged by their interchangeable use by some members of donor agencies and NGOs, emphasising that both identities refer to a non-state identity vis-à-vis the State and thus public provision of services. For many individuals, NGOs may always have been a business, a first job for some and a second job for others, supplementing income, if not with a salary then with material benefits. Under the national community water and sanitation strategy, NGOs appear to have become more explicitly businesslike in their orientation due to project guidelines and encouragement to develop corporate plans in anticipation of increasing competition. There is a lot of money to be made by NGOs in non-urban water provision because donors and international NGOs are providing funds for non-state actors to facilitate community management and to provide water services.

The policy of engaging the private sector to provide goods and services in non-urban water provision is not associated with much controversy, as is the case with private sector participation in urban water supply. The former is probably accepted because the private sector consists of Ghanaian contractors, consultants and NGOs, whereas in urban water supply the private sector means transnational water corporations. Donors promoting private sector provision of urban water created the same dichotomy between private and public provision and used this division to shift attention away from the fact that private sector meant foreign companies. They tried to focus the debate around an ideological argument that private provision is efficient and public provision is inefficient.[10]

NGOs are socially responsive private enterprises. The important question is whether they are substituting for a nascent or nonexistent private sector of traditional small and medium businesses at the community and district level. NGOs mostly provide services and rarely engage in the production of goods, thus they cannot substitute for a private sector in the production and manufacture of goods. Funding to Ghanaian NGOs from donors and international NGOs increases the supply of essential services, such as the provision of water and healthcare, in a context of receding government expenditure in service provision. Donors are often supporting both NGOs and the government budget, effectively pitting one against the other in the search for scarce resources. Notably, the exodus of government personnel to NGOs, where they carry out similar tasks for better pay, is a major cause of the 'weak capacity' of the Ghanaian state. Businesses are accountable to those who hold the capital. In the case of NGOs, the shareholders are donors and international NGOs. Thus, Ghanaian NGOs are mainly accountable to external funding agencies and continue to exist as long as their funding does. In sum, the NGO sector is growing in tandem with the shrinking role of the state, but it cannot substitute for a productive private sector.

Identity construction is linked to ideologies present among the majority of donors, i.e. assumptions about how development must unfold. The development paradigm propagated by donors, and supported by the Kufuor government, envisions the private sector as the engine of growth, and everywhere the private sector should take over as many functions of the state as possible. However, who the private sector is remains ambiguous, dependent on the context. Constructing an identity of the private sector as autonomous from the government ignores existing patronage relations between politicians and entrepreneurs as well as historically symbiotic relations between businesses and the state in countries that have undergone industrialisation. The promotion of the private sector as a single entity also conceals whether it is the *domestic* or *foreign* private sector that is being promoted.

Conclusion

How are these identities of government, civil society, private sector and development partners created and recreated? They are produced through a two-way process, through the interaction of top-down and bottom-up forces. Multilateral and bilateral donors reshape and transmit ideas through their institutional workings, neoliberal policies and development discourses (see Boas and McNeill 2004). In a top-down fashion, donors introduced and reinforced the governance model, assigning certain roles to the identities of government of Ghana, civil society and private sector. However, Ghanaians do not passively receive these identities, but rather remake them to fit their own objectives. Through this bottom-up process, identities are somewhat reconstructed.

People also move between these identities when it suits their purpose, both in terms of identifying their organisation or themselves with the public or private sector. We have already given the example of NGOs shifting between identification with the public or private sector. Another example is the way Ghanaians employed in donor country offices may be seconded to work in government agencies and describe this act as 'switching hats' from donor to civil servant. It is also common for civil servants in district administrative offices to hold a second job with local NGOs. To take another example, expatriates may work for Ghanaian NGOs or research institutions and then later be employed by donors. Despite this fluidity in identities, there is a rigid boundary between donor headquarters and Ghana, which reinforces the power relations between aid giver and aid recipient.

The identities constructed through the application of the donors' governance model are real in their effects on people's actions, but, as this chapter has shown, these identities fail to capture processes in society which are much more chaotic and fluid. This chapter also illustrates that the line between public and private sector is very permeable. Therefore, the governance model is limited in its usefulness as an analytical tool. As a practical tool, we have endeavoured to highlight its intended and unintended consequences of donors trying to mould societies in developing countries to fit this model. Lastly, donors must be included in any schema which tries to understand governance processes in aid-dependent developing countries. This model positions donors outside these societies, rather than capturing their position within recipient countries and their relationship with different social actors. Turning their model on its head, we ask: where would donors lie on the dividing line between public and private sector?

Notes

1. The paper is based on research undertaken for the author's doctoral thesis (Whitfield 2005).
2. For a critique of the good governance agenda in its early days, see Baylies (1995).
3. For more on this notion of economic reform from within, see World Bank (2001), which is similar to its notion of ownership embodied in its new lending framework, see http://www.worldbank.org/poverty/ strategies/overview.htm.
4. In short, Structural Adjustment aimed to reorient development policies from state-led growth towards the neoclassical economic model in which the state's main function is to provide the conditions for market and private enterprise-led growth (Engberg-Pedersen et al. 1996: 4). Despite changing the names of its lending policy and instruments, this remains the development paradigm of the Bretton Woods institutions.
5. This discussion of the idea of civil society and its implications is drawn from the author's previous work on this topic (Whitfield 2002, 2003).
6. Several authors make this point (Fowler 1993; Ndegwa 1996; Dicklitch 1998; Dorman 2001).
7. It has been argued that on the one hand most rich private entrepreneurs suffered under the PNDC revolutionary moment and resented Rawlings, and, on the other, the government feared that the growth of independent sources of economic power would become rival sources for political power (Sowa 1996).
8. These six associations include the Federation of Associations of Ghanaian Exporters, Ghana National Chamber of Commerce and Industry, Association of Ghana Industries, Ghana Association of Bankers, Ghana Employers' Association, and Ghana Chamber of Mines. Other smaller business associations work in relation to the Foundation but are not full members because they are unable to pay membership dues.
9. USAID contracts Sigma One Corp to organise the National Economic Forum/Dialogue in collaboration with the Ghanaian government, thus channelling its funding through a U.S. corporation. Contracting to donor country companies is standard fare among bilateral donors. Sigma One specialises in private enterprise development for global trade and investment, offering consultancy services to developing country governments as well as working directly with entrepreneurs to provide skills training.
10. For more on private sector participation in urban water supply, see Whitfield (2005, chapter 5).

Bibliography

Akwetey, E. 1998. 'Violence, Deliberative Democracy and State Reconstruction in Ghana (1987–98)', in G. Williams (comp.), *Essays Presented to Bjorn Beckman*. Oxford: unpublished manuscript.

Baylies, C. 1995. '"Political Conditionality" and Democratisation', *Review of African Political Economy* 65: 321–37.

Boas, M. and D. McNeill (eds.) 2004. *Global Institutions and Development: Framing the World?* London: Routledge.

Castro, J.E. Forthcoming. 'Private Sector Participation in Water and Sanitation Services, Water Governance, and the Water Poor: Some Lessons from Latin America and Europe', *Geoforum*.

Dicklitch, S. 1998. *Elusive Promise of NGOs in Africa: Lessons from Uganda.* New York: St. Martin's Press.

Dorman, S.R. 2001. 'Inclusion and Exclusion: NGOs and Politics in Zimbabwe.' D.Phil. thesis, Department of Politics and International Relations, University of Oxford, Oxford.

Engberg-Pedersen, P., et al. 1996. 'Structural Adjustment in Africa: A Survey of the Experience', in P. Engberg-Pedersen et al. (eds.), *Limits of Adjustment in Africa.* Oxford: James Currey, pp. 3–77.

Fowler, A. 1993. 'Non-Governmental Organisations as Agents of Democratisation: An African Perspective', *Journal of International Development* 5 (3): 325–39.

Gary, I. 1996. 'Confrontation, Co-operation or Co-optation: NGOs and the Ghanaian State during Structural Adjustment', *Review of African Political Economy* 68: 149–68.

Harrison, G. 2004. *The World Bank and Africa: The Construction of Governance States.* London: Routledge.

Hulme, D. and M. Edwards (eds.) 1997. *NGOs, States and Donors: Too Close for Comfort?* London: Macmillan.

Hutchful, E. 2002. *Ghana's Adjustment Experience: The Paradox of Reform.* Oxford: James Currey.

Kapur, D. and R. Webb. 2000. *Governance-related Conditionalities of the International Financial Institutions. G-24 Discussion Paper Series* (No. 6). New York & Geneva: United Nations.

Kasfir, N. 1998. 'The Conventional Notion of Civil Society: A Critique', in N. Kasfir (ed.), *Civil Society and Democracy in Africa: Critical Perspectives.* London: Frank Cass, pp. 1–20.

Mohan, G. 2002. 'The Disappointments of Civil Society: The Politics of NGO Intervention in Northern Ghana'. *Political Geography,* 21 (1): 125–54.

Mohan, G. and K. Stokke. 2000. 'Participatory Development and Empowerment: The Dangers of Localism', *Third World Quarterly* 21 (2): 247–68.

Ndegwa, S. 1996. *The Two Faces of Civil Society: NGOs and Politics in Africa.* West Hartford: Kumarian Press.

Osei, R. and P. Quartey. 2001. *The HIPC Initiative and Poverty Reduction in Ghana: An Assessment.* Paper prepared for the WIDER Conference on Debt Relief, Helsinki 17–18 August 2001.

Sowa, Nii. 1996. 'Adjustment in Africa: Lessons from Ghana.' Centre for Economic Policy Analysis (CEPA) *Discussion Paper* No. 8.

Tetteh, B. 2003. 'Ghana's Indebtedness and the HIPC Initiative.' M.A. in Economic Policy Management. Legon: Economics Department, University of Ghana.

Whitfield, L. 2002. 'Civil Society as Idea and Civil Society as Process: The Case of Ghana.' M.Phil. in Development Studies. Oxford: Queen Elisabeth House, University of Oxford.

———. 2003. 'Civil Society as Idea and Civil Society as Process: The Case of Ghana'. *Oxford Development Studies,* 31: 3, 379–400.

———. 2005. *Democracy as Idea and Democracy as Process: The Politics of Democracy and Development in Ghana.* Doctoral thesis. Oxford: Department of Politics and International Relations, University of Oxford.

Williams, D. and T. Young. 1994. 'Governance, the World Bank and Liberal Theory', *Political Studies* 62: 84–100.

World Bank. 2001. *Adjustment from Within: Lessons from the Structural Adjustment Participatory Review Initiative.* A Contribution from the World Bank to the Second Global SAPRI Forum, 30–31 July 2001, Washington, D.C., USA.

NOTES ON CONTRIBUTORS

Simone Abram has a doctorate in social anthropology from the University of Oxford. She has done fieldwork in France, England and Norway. In Spring 2000, she was a visiting fellow at the University of Oslo. Since then, she has been at the University of Sheffield.

Shirley Ardener, a social anthropologist, has done much fieldwork in Cameroon. She is a member of the IGS (formerly CCCRW), of which she was the Founding Director, and is a Senior Associate of the Department of international Development at Queen Elizabeth House, Oxford University. She has many publications on microcredit, gender studies and Cameroon studies.

Hilary Callan has been Director of the Royal Anthropological Institute of Great Britain and Ireland since 2000. Previous to this she was Director of the European Association for International Education for seven years, with headquarters in Amsterdam. An anthropologist by training, she has held academic appointments in the U.K., Canada and the Middle East, and is the author of a number of publications in anthropology and international education.

Anne Coles is a research associate at the International Gender Studies Centre in the Department of International Development, Oxford University. She was previously a senior social development adviser in the U.K. Department for International Development. Her career has combined university teaching (in geography and later development studies) with research and development practice. She has a particular interest in environmental aspects of arid lands and most recently published *Gender, Water and Development*, a book edited with Tina Wallace (Berg 2005).

Margaret Groeneveld received her doctorate in anthropology in 2004 from the University of Oxford for a thesis which considered personhood and property in the player transfer market of English Rugby League. She received her BA in anthropology and MBA in international business from the University of British Columbia in Vancouver, Canada. She held a JRF at the International Centre for Sport History and Culture at De Montfort University from 2002–2004. In 2005, she was a Departmental Associate in Social Anthropology at Cambridge

University and the recipient of FIFA's Joao Havelange Research Scholarship for ethnographic research on football academies in England. Since January 2006, she has been the leader of an interdisciplinary research team at Bocconi University in Milan, funded by a Marie Curie Excellence Grant from the European Commission, studying the relationship between sport and social capital in European sport governing bodies.

Esther Hertzog is a social anthropologist, and has been a senior lecturer in Beit Berl Academic College in Israel since 1991. Between 2000–2006 she headed the Social Studies department in the College, and has headed the department of Anthropology since 2003. Her book *Bureaucrats and Immigrants, Ethiopians in an Israeli Absorption Centre*, which was based on her Ph.D. thesis, was published in 1999 by Berghahn. She is a co-editor of an Israeli anthology on Israeli society (*Israel: Local Anthropology*) in Hebrew; the book will be published in English in the U.S. in 2007 by Wayne-State University Press. Her edited volume *Women and Family in the Holocaust* was published recently in Hebrew. She has a bi-monthly opinion column in Ma'ariv (an Israeli daily) since 1992. A collection of her columns was published in 2004 (*Op-Ed, Feminist Social Justice in Israel*) by Cherikover.

Fiona Moore received her doctorate from the University of Oxford, and is currently Lecturer in International Human Resource Management at Royal Holloway. She has conducted research with German business people in the City of London and Frankfurt, the managers and workers of a German automobile manufacturer's British and Bavarian plants, and Korean expatriates in Surrey. Her publications include the monograph *Transnational Business Cultures: Life and Work in a Multinational Corporation* (Ashgate, 2005) and papers in the *Journal of International Human Resource Management, Management International Review* and *Global Networks.*

Lindsay Whitfield is currently a Junior Research Fellow with the Global Economic Governance Programme at University College, Oxford University. She completed her Doctorate in Politics at Oxford in 2005, and earlier a Masters in Development Studies. Her work focuses on how practices of global economic governance interact with domestic politics in Sub-Saharan Africa and the implications of this interaction for both democratic governance and economic development in African countries. Her work is multi-disciplinary and touches upon the fields of development studies, democratic theory and practice, and African history and politics. To date she has focused on Ghana and the politics of aid dependency, publishing several articles in *Journal of Modern African Studies, Review of African Political Economy* and *Oxford Development Studies.*

INDEX